28

W9-AHY-882

# FRAMING MUSLIMS

# FRAMING MUSLIMS

Stereotyping and Representation after 9/11

PETER MOREY

AND

AMINA YAQIN

Harvard University Press
Cambridge, Massachusetts
London, England
2011

*Library of Congress Cataloging-in-Publication Data*

Morey, Peter.
Framing Muslims : stereotyping and representation after 9/11 /
Peter Morey and Amina Yaqin.
p. cm.
Includes bibliographical references and index.
ISBN 978-0-674-04852-2 (alk. paper)
1. Stereotypes (Social psychology)—United States.    2. Muslims in popular
culture—United States.    I. Yaqin, Amina, 1972–    II. Title.
HM1096.M67 2011
305.6'97091821—dc22     2011002757

*For Maleeha and Laila*

# Contents

# FRAMING MUSLIMS

# Introduction

"Islam and Freedom: Are They Destined to Clash?" *(Newsweek).* "Muhammad Cartoon Row Intensifies" (BBC). "Burka Makes Women Prisoners, Says President Sarkozy" (*Times* [London]). "Universities Urged to Spy on Muslims" *(Guardian).* The headlines that scream out at us every day from front pages and television screens seem unanimous in the picture they paint of Muslims: unenlightened outsiders who, while they may live and work in the West, still have an allegiance to values different from those recognized in Europe and North America. Whether the controversy is over veiling, cartoons of the Prophet Mohammed, conflicts in Afghanistan, Iraq, and Israel-Palestine, or protests about the knighthood given to Salman Rushdie, Muslims appear always as a problematic presence, troubling those values of individualism and freedom said to define Western nations.

Such images are distorted abstractions. Extrapolating from context-specific controversies, they paint Muslims as a homogeneous, zombie-like body, incapable of independent thought and liable to be whipped into a frenzy at the least disturbance to their unchanging backward worldview. Yet, just as such controversies are, to an extent, artificially manufactured in the post-9/11 atmosphere, where a "clash of civilizations" is supposed to mark the impassable divide between "Islam" and "the West" and stories are sought to prove the thesis, so too Muslims themselves are a far more varied set of communities and individuals than this picture allows. To an extent, this book is about the gap that exists between representation and reality when it comes to Muslims. Our focus tends to be on representation, both since there are many works in a variety of disciplines charting the social circumstances in which Muslims now find themselves across large swathes of the world, and because the stereotyping of Muslims takes place in repeated acts of representation by politicians, the press and media, and even those claiming to speak on their behalf.

For our purposes, then, one might almost say that this book is not actually about Muslims at all, in the sense of real people with lives, loves, and workaday concerns. Instead it is about the origin, circulation, and utility of an epithet and the way the term has come to signify a political problem to be solved. The subject of this book is, properly speaking, those images of Muslims that are repeatedly circulated in the cultures of Western countries, in particular at the present time. It seeks to trace the restricted, limited ways that Muslims are stereotyped and "framed" within the political, cultural, and media discourses of the West.

Far from being accurate or neutral, contemporary images of Muslims presented by politicians and in mainstream media and cultural forms are almost always tied to an agenda that simultaneously announces its desire to "engage" with them while at the same time forcing debate into such contorted and tenuous channels as to make a meaningful flow of crosscultural discussion almost impossible. "National security," "strategic interests," "multiculturalism," "integration," "preventing terrorism"— in fact, all the buzzwords of contemporary political life do little more than obscure a chronically one-sided dialogue that Muslims are invited to join but not change, or forever remain outside the boundaries of civil debate, doomed to be spoken for and represented, but never to speak themselves. Such a situation does a gross disservice to the variety and vitality of Muslim life, beliefs, and cultural forms of expression, as well as being a bad idea for those who are genuinely concerned about addressing pressing social problems.

The sheer ubiquity of images of Muslims and the insistent repetition of certain reductive tropes convinced us of the importance of looking more closely at what we term here "structures of representation." The bearded Muslim fanatic, the oppressed, veiled woman, the duplicitous terrorist who lives among "us" the better to bring about our destruction: all these stereotypes have emerged with renewed force since 9/11.

To be sure, they existed before. Yet the scale and spectacle of the Twin Towers and Pentagon attacks, and the reaction to them, has thrust a certain type of Orientalist stereotype firmly back onto our cinema and television screens, into our news media, and into the mouths of politicians who either lack the historical sense to understand where they come from, or whose agendas are best served by ignoring their provenance. What we see, and what this book sets out to trace, is the distortion of particular features of Muslim life and custom, reducing the diversity of Muslims and their existence as individuals to a fixed object—a caricature in fact. The body of the Muslim, as it appears in these representations, veiled, bearded, or praying, is made to carry connotations far beyond the intrinsic significance of such externals and rituals. Time and again, behavior, the body, and dress are treated not as cultural markers but as a kind of moral index, confirming non-Muslim viewers of these images in their sense of superiority and cementing the threatening strangeness of the Muslim Other.

The reach of today's global media conglomerates and the tangled machinations of international politics give the structures of representation we describe a fierce power and extensive reach. Of course, contemporary forms such as mobile telecommunications and the Internet allow for different kinds of ideas to circulate and opposition to organize and disseminate alternative images. The adaptation of such channels to carry different—although sometimes chaotic and contradictory—messages about Islam and its adherents is now rightly drawing the attention of academics. However, our focus here is on the mainstream or mass media and those political forces that habitually use its channels of communication. This book attempts to trace the proximity and tensions between the nation-state and the types of media most often used as the main vehicles for its agendas when it comes to the representation of Muslims. It is still the case, even in the age of diffuse and multinational media forms, that governments will seek first to establish agendas through the tried and tested (and perhaps more controllable) vehicles of the imagined community, television, and the press. One of our key arguments is that the frequency with which Muslims are "framed" in such discourses has a complex but definite relation to lived experience. The framing of Muslims amounts to a refraction, not a reflection of reality. Nevertheless, it would be wrong to dismiss the connection such mediated images have with intercultural relations. Like a fire, racism needs constant feeding and stoking. We might say that easy, "secondhand" images of Muslims as threatening, untrustworthy terrorists—even when placed in contexts where such stereotypes are called into question—nonetheless repeat the association and, arguably, add fuel to the backward-looking arguments of cultural and national purists.

Of course, the framing of Muslims requires that one engage in some quite egregious generalizations. While that is obviously true of those who would cast aspersions on an entire faith—and a sizeable percentage of the world's population—on the basis of the actions of a politicized faction, it is also inevitably true of books like this one, which claim to offer a critique of such phenomena. So, although producing discourse about the vast multitude of individuals who make up the Muslim world places one in the invidious position of adding to a horde of images, the majority of which are problematic and simplified, this book tries to keep in focus the channels by which such images circulate, rather than their referents. There are no easy diagnoses to be had here. Of course, "representation" as a concept encompasses not only visual, narrative, and other forms of mimetic expression but also political channels of empowerment. At a time when access to the former is beginning to fragment—for example, with the arrival of channels such as Al Jazeera and Internet news providers to break the monopoly of Western multinational news media—the power to represent on a political level has become more fraught than ever. This is often understood through crude notions of opposing "civilizational" or national power blocs, for example "the Muslim World versus the West." However, the spread of communities identifying as Muslim—now sometimes recognized as a diaspora—is such that the idea of sealed compartments suggested by "clash of civilizations" rhetoric is more than ever exposed as a political strategist's daydream. That said, the hostile imagery repeatedly associated with Islam and Muslims does have a self-fulfilling power. It drives a wedge between worlds that are intertwined, indeed interdependent. Just as the framing we describe has a severely limiting effect on the cultural understanding of Muslims and their religion, the process of constructing such stereotypes becomes a self-fulfilling prophecy. Intolerant images and pronouncements breed a kind of self-fashioning that operates as the other half of a distorted dialogue. Muslims are positioned as an irretrievably Other presence, both in communities living in the West and in the broader global geopolitics of an ever-shrinking world. But at the same time, when certain Muslims position themselves, often in direct answer to these images, as the pure antithesis of a corrupt, materialist modernity, they both stereotype the West on its own terms—take it too much at face value, shall we say— and stereotype themselves too. The result is a warped and stifled dialogue, an uneven exchange, impacted by inequalities in economic power and access to the means of representation itself, and characterized by mutual suspicion and belligerence based on fear.

Of course it would be facile to suggest that complex and long-standing geopolitical formations, and their development over time, could be collapsed into matters of mere (mis)representation, as if all that were needed to set the world to rights were more accurate images of other people. Like all politically aware citizens, we are conscious that present intercultural tensions are simply the latest phase in a much longer story. The detailed history of strategic move and countermove— between West and East, the American and Soviet blocs, the European empires of the nineteenth century, their colonial subjects, the Ottoman Caliphate and so on, as far back as the Crusades and beyond to Europeans' rather bemused first reflections on the new religion of Islam in the seventh century—all these phases may be more or less well known, but each still forms part of the intertwined histories of cultural exchange between what are often billed as "Islam" and "the West" and their attendant misrecognitions. Nevertheless, we will argue in the following pages that those stereotypes of Eastern treachery, malevolence, and fanaticism that have accompanied relations since the beginning have received a new lease of life post-9/11, to the extent that they become the (sometimes unconscious) default setting for almost any crosscultural investigation. More disturbingly, such clichés have in some quarters been used to extenuate policies and attitudes of blunt and simple prejudice in the realms of both foreign affairs and "homeland security." In dealing with the Muslim "Other," Western nations have employed a complex and precise set of surveillance systems designed to profile, track, and when necessary exclude the problematic Muslim subject. It is our contention that such developments are not merely the natural response to terrorist activity or a supposed "global jihad." Instead, they can be seen to place cutting-edge technologies and information networks at the service of some of the oldest and most readily available tribal instincts, including retrenchment and scapegoating. Thus, while not suggesting a simplistic relationship between political or media images and enacted realities at home or abroad, we would nonetheless argue that the kinds of images traced in this book work to create an environment—an atmosphere, if you will—wherein Muslims can at a moment's notice be erected as objects of supervision and discipline, and used to obscure more troubling questions about "us," our group identities, our social structures, and our motives for action in the world.

There is always a danger, of course, that in invoking terms such as the "Muslim Other" and "the West"—even to criticize or deconstruct them—one is reinforcing the notional homogeneity that is thrown like a smothering blanket over current intercultural debates. When we use these terms we do so in a critical way: assuming that the phrases themselves, those who utter them, and the contexts in which they are used form the *really* interesting subject. This is not to imply some superior knowledge that allows us to stand aloof and coolly unmask the loaded words and images of the stereotype. Instead, what we would emphasize is the investment in certain quarters in maintaining such ideological fictions as the unified nation and the sealed-off civilization. It will also be noted that our examples are almost all taken from the British and American cases: more so the British, in fact, since this context forms the bedrock of our own experience. While unique cultural histories and mindsets are at work in different nations, we would contend that the similarities between British and American responses to post-9/11 challenges—based on a much-vaunted shared secular polity—make the representations that emerge from their cultural and political elites illustrative of a discourse that spans many Western countries. Of course, an historical sense is invaluable in understanding such contexts and images.

## The Uses of History

As a matter of historical record, the Muslim presence in Britain and the United States is a product of the stories of colonialism and slavery. Muslims had been in Britain for hundreds of years, mainly as individuals from England's trading partners in the Mediterranean and North Africa, often mariners, whose presence was confined to port cities such as London, Cardiff, and Bristol. It was only in the late nineteenth century that the beginnings of anything as definite as a Muslim community can be seen, with the establishment by William Quilliam of a "Church of Islam" in Liverpool and the foundation of the Shahjahan Mosque in Woking, Surrey, in 1889. The story of an organized Muslim presence is generally taken to have started at the moment of mass migration to the West that followed hard upon the decolonization of South Asia. Pakistanis from Mirpur in Kashmir, Bangladeshis from Sylhet, and Gujarati Indians brought their cultures and beliefs with them, accounting for the wide variety of Islam to be found in the United Kingdom, including Barelwi, Deobandi, and Ahl-i-Hadith traditions. Today there are estimated to be around two million Muslims living in Britain.[1] In the United States, Muslims have historically belonged to one of three categories: Muslim immigrants to the United States—many of whom arrived in the waves of immigration that took place in the late nineteenth century, and after the global Islamic revival in the 1970s and 1980s that resulted in a large number of exiles and refugees; the descendants of slaves, among whom can be numbered adherents to the Nation of Islam, drawing on southern black traditions, Garveyism, and North African Islam; and white Muslim converts. Estimates suggest that there are around seven million Muslims currently in the United States.[2]

Yet such developments are only the latest stage of a much longer story of contact between Islam and Western countries. Our interest here is in the uses to which narratives of such contact have been—and continue to be—put. The roots of negative representations of Muslims go all the way back to the early Middle Ages and the arrival of Islam on the radar of an unsuspecting and recently consolidated Christian world in the seventh century. At once, with this rival from the East, there was a need explain the sudden rise and spread of Islam, through North

Africa, eastern Europe, and then southern Europe in the seventh, eighth, and ninth centuries. As John Tolan has pointed out, the early Christian church's efforts to understand its new competitor took their shape from pre-existing, biblically sanctioned categories. Since, for the early Christian theologians, God was the moving force in history and everything was part of his plan, ways were sought through scripture to explain Islam's expansion and, in particular, its success in gaining new converts. Tolan describes a worldview and an intellectual framework that only really changed with the Reformation, when he says: "Authoritative explanations of the world around one are to be found in revered books. These books are timeless, never out of date; if the reality one sees around oneself does not seem to correspond to the models described on parchment, it is the evidence of the senses that must be questioned, not the authorities."[3] Thus, an apocalyptic role was ascribed to Islam in medieval theology. Mohammed was denounced as the false prophet foretold in St. Matthew's Gospel, and as the Beast of the Apocalypse, while texts such as the late seventh-century *Apocalypse of Pseudo-Methodius* saw the "Ishmaelites" (or Arabs) as heralds of the Antichrist, providing evidence that the world had entered the Last Days.[4] Limited knowledge of Islam's tenets led to accusations that Muslims were idolators and pagans, although the notion that their religion was actually a Christian heresy, given the derivation of many ranic stories from biblical sources, was reflected in the work of John of Damascus—who had at least studied the new religion—and whose views were effectively canonized at the Council of Nicaea in 787. Such early refutations of Islam form the staple source for later Christian polemicists, and their outline can still be seen in Martin Luther's writings on Islam 750 years later.

Of course, representations of and from history are always imbued with questions of power. Tolan interestingly ascribes to those early writers of the Eastern Christian church, startled and perplexed by the sudden rise of a new imperial power, the role of what would today be called anticolonial or resistance writers. As a beleaguered minority, they were struggling to keep their worldview alive in the face of an alien ruling culture. As such, according to Tolan, those negative portrayals of Islam that later underpinned Orientalist and colonial ways of seeing—

and arguably resurface in War on Terror discourse—originally stem from the defensive reactions of the newly subject peoples of ninth- and tenth-century Europe; "the *Pseudo-Methodius*, Alvarus and Eulogius oppose the Muslim triumphalist view of history with an apocalyptic vision promising Christian vengeance."[5] This is an important point and works as a caution against any sort of postcolonial ahistoricism, which simply equates domination with race and European hegemony. It reminds us that power dynamics shift radically across history. It is not just that yesterday's colonizer might become today's colonized, but that the sources we choose in making up our accounts of "our" history, how "we" reached this point, and so on, are themselves always selective and partial. Writing about the early modern period, Nabil Matar has similarly remarked how, with the Ottoman Empire at its height, Islam could never be safely domesticated nor its threat be neutralized by writers from Christian western Europe: Islam, he says, "was self-sustained and self-representing."[6]

The view of Islam as the main "civilizational" enemy, and its adherents as little better than animals, was sustained and projected in the literature of the Middle Ages, and later the Renaissance. For example, the *Chanson de Roland* (c. 1100), a tale of the Crusades that helped set the pattern for medieval chivalry, depicted most of the hero's adversaries as bloodthirsty and idolatrous. Renaissance writers such as Thomas Kyd, Thomas Heywood, and Philip Massinger were concerned to depict the dire consequences of conversion to this sinister creed.[7] That Muslims appeared largely impervious to the ministrations of Christian missionaries had long been a source of bafflement to writers and clerics. The result was the establishment of the stereotype of the "irrational Oriental," who refused to avail himself of God's grace even when the true path was pointed out to him. This view was boosted by the ascendancy of Renaissance humanism in Europe, which sought inspiration in Greek and Roman cultural achievements at the expense of Arab knowledge and the legacy of centers of art and discovery such as Moorish Spain. Whereas once philosophers such as Averroes (Ibn Rushd, 1126–1198) and Avicenna (Ibn Sīnā, 980–1037) had been lionized, now Arab knowledge was marginalized, ignored by the early modern scientists and confined to worlds of magic and pseudoscience such as alchemy and Rosicrucianism. Later, with the triumph of New-tonian science in the second half of the seventeenth century, Islam became equated with stasis, traditionalism, and a decayed civiliza-tion: a view that was accentuated after the Ottoman defeat at Vienna in 1683, which marked the beginning of the eclipse of Muslim power in Europe.[8] In the field of politics, the same era saw the beginning of European colonialism, which would bring Muslim and European civi-lizations into contact once again, albeit with a radically altered power dynamic.

The idea of a backward and irrational Orient struggling under the yoke of Islam was useful for British colonial ideology in the eighteenth and nineteenth centuries. Along with this went feminization of the East: a trope that goes back at least to the thirteenth century, where it takes the shape of Christian polemicists urging crusaders and mission-aries to rush to the aid of the Mother Church. Over time the image became focused on the Muslim woman herself. Mohja Kahf has shown how depictions of Muslim women have changed through the centuries, from a medieval fascination with the symbolic figure of the powerful Eastern queen to post-eighteenth-century Romantic notions of the passive Oriental female, cooped up in the harem or behind the veil, waiting to be rescued by the Western male hero. Kahf points out how this shifting view of the Muslim woman coincides with changes in European models of femininity, which themselves came more to em-phasize the chaste middle-class woman inhabiting domestic space.[9] Yet, as we know, the idea of "freeing the Muslim woman" from Islamic male tyranny is a trope with tremendous emotional appeal and longev-ity. It was used to justify military interventions in the Gulf in 1991 and, more recently, the rescue of oppressed women has been behind femi-nist support for the invasions of Afghanistan in 2001 and Iraq in 2003.

Indeed, this contemporary reheating of old Orientalist images with respect to Islam should give us pause whenever we hear cries of "Save the Muslim woman" or "Our civilization is under threat." This is not to deny that Islamic regimes in the Middle East have often forced women into more circumscribed roles and punished deviation from accepted societal norms with violence and death. Instead, it is to redirect our at-tention toward the imagery used in such calls and the cultural assumptions of safe superiority, often deep-rooted and tenacious, they draw on. Of course, our main concern here is with the use of stereotypes, but that means not simply identifying them with a disapproving scowl but thinking about their genealogies and the purposes they serve. In this book, that will also mean critically examining texts that appear to have a more sympathetic approach to Islam and Muslims. For example, Ridley Scott's 2005 movie *Kingdom of Heaven* was widely praised as a corrective to the more jingoistic films that appeared in the wake of 9/11. At a time of widespread hostility and mistrust toward Muslims, it sets out to offer a distinctly post-9/11 reworking of the Third Crusade, but does so in such a way as to avoid showing the Islamic army of Saladin as merely bestial or motivated by bloodlust. *Kingdom of Heaven* won plaudits for its evenhandedness and sensitivity: particularly laudable was the scene where Saladin reverently replaces an ornamental cross on the altar of a ransacked church during the battle for Jerusalem. However, these readings—like the movie itself—implicitly posit an anachronistic and politically expedient historical correspondence that we might want to question. Readings of *Kingdom of Heaven* as post-9/11 commentary work only if the factional Catholic militias who responded to the call to arms by Pope Gregory VIII, and their Muslim opponents, only recently brought together as a unified force by Nur ad-Din, can be taken to correspond symbolically to the twenty-first-century secular "West" and the modern "Muslim world." This is not a criticism of the film as a narrative; all fictions rely on some sort of symbolic equivalence to the real world. However, a serious distortion, a flattening out of historical differences and specificity, takes place if an action-packed and necessarily fictionalized retelling of a contentious historical event is turned by its viewers into an allegory meant to address present dilemmas.

This kind of ahistorical search for a consistent geo-ideological divide has been criticized by Mahmood Mamdani, who berates those who attempt to "read back in" to the historical record the idea of a continuous "clash of civilizations." Even those ideas taken to have a clear and bounded meaning, for example "Islam" and "the West," are temporal constructions. Drawing on the work of Marshall Hodgson, author of the three-volume *Venture of Islam,* Mamdani points out that the

definition of the West itself has changed through time: "The very notion of an uninterrupted 'Western civilization' across linear time is an
idea that only arises from the vantage point of the power we know as
the West."[10] Efforts to equate the modern world with the Middle Ages,
or to suggest that we are witnessing a collision between Islam and
something called "Judeo-Christian civilization," require (almost literally) a willing suspension of disbelief; it is as if the European Enlightenment and secularization never happened, or at least that it has been
a temporary intrusion on deeper, more fundamental differences. This is
how those various manifestations of religiopolitical violence—from attacks on people and places of worship to acts of desecration and hate
speech that have occurred since 9/11—come to be framed: as part of an
inevitable and ongoing struggle from which we should not be distracted. Of course, such universalizing positions in the so-called War
on Terror are favored by both "sides."

The point is that historical knowledge is one thing, what you do with
it is quite another. Attitudes to cultural difference that were valid in the
Middle Ages ought not to go unchallenged as adequate representations
of our current dilemmas, particularly when they are harnessed to im-
perialist and "civilizational" ends. One final example may serve to illustrate these connections and disconnections. In a lecture at the
University of Regensburg, Germany, in September 2006, Pope Benedict
XVI caused outrage by quoting an unfavorable remark about Islam
made by the fourteenth-century Byzantine emperor Manuel II: "Show
me just what Mohammed brought that was new and there you will find
things only evil and inhuman, such as, his command to spread by the
sword the faith he preached." However, what is more interesting than
the headline-grabbing line itself is that the theme of Benedict's speech
is the relationship of faith and reason. The argument the pope is pursuing is one that equates Christianity with reason—stating that not acting
reasonably is contrary to God's nature—which is contrasted to the supposed Islamic view that God transcends concepts such as rationality:
the latter view being taken to open the door to forced conversion and
violence in the name of religion.[11] This is the exact same line of argument that was used to berate Muslims who refused to see the light and
convert in medieval times. Benedict merely transposes it into the pres-

ent day, albeit as a debating point, as if what was philosophically and theologically held to be true then somehow helps to explain the world today. The Pope was at least honest about his sources. Too often while saying Islam is "medieval" its critics overlook the fact that they themselves are indulging in stereotyping that has its roots in the Middle Ages. Timeless truths or truthless signs of the times: it is between these two rocky promontories that this book must navigate.

## Our Own Representations

Turning the spotlight on stereotypes and repeated imagery does not mean that we are unconcerned with the very real human problems in which such representations are rooted and of which they offer a distorted yet telling echo. Whether it is the human cost of atrocities in New York, Madrid, London, Bali, Mumbai, or any other parts of the world blighted by indiscriminate violent acts inspired by a warped religious ideology, or the perhaps even more devastating impact of vainglorious military adventures undertaken seemingly in a fit of nostalgic imperial hubris and, in some cases, with dubious international legality, the tense political context everywhere informs the images with which this book is concerned. Nevertheless, we feel that to isolate those images for the purposes of critical scrutiny—to examine their shape and makeup as well as the contexts from which they emerge—is not simply profitable but essential if the twin projects of more accurate intercultural understanding and meaningful antiracism are to be furthered.

In the following chapters we aim to lay out one way of understanding the relationship between the representations of Muslims in politics and those in the mainstream media. However, it is important at this point to scotch any suspicion that the relationship between these two forms is simple or deterministic. Of course the media play a central role in the representation of Muslims. Yet they do not do so simply at the behest of governments. One ought not to simplify or homogenize the complex, contending, and often contradictory manner in which the media fulfil their role. Nevertheless, they are informed, in specific ways, by agendas of power, both at the level of the "messages" they carry and, prior to this, in their professional practices and structures.

Chapter 1 considers the process of stereotyping, both in general terms (as a shared cognitive practice) and in the specific ways Muslims come to be stereotyped in contemporary representations. In examining this process, questions about the motivations and repressions of those doing the stereotyping present themselves. These in turn tie into bigger issues of national identity and practices of inclusion and exclusion that are still playing out today, in debates about restrictions on types of Muslim dress and in legislation proscribing mosques and minarets. If, as we argue, the nations of the West have lately been thrown back on a preglobalized form of introversion in an attempt to assert a unified body politic, the contradictions of such efforts always present themselves in inconsistencies and selective double standards.

In Chapter 2 we explore those discourses circulating around Muslims and the challenge they currently pose to ideas of multiculturalism. We suggest that one cannot understand the parameters of this debate—particularly as it is played out in Britain—without understanding the forces of mediation through which certain versions of the discussion are disseminated. A brief comparison of the different developmental trajectories of multiculturalism in the United States and in Britain reveals that, while one became embedded in the common sense articulation of Americanness and thereafter in political structures, the other is taken to be a latter-day challenge to a long and ethnically sealed history. Moreover, in Britain, a crucial distinction must be made between multiculturalism as lived experience and multiculturalism as a semi-official "policy": something that is not always observed by participants in the argument. The result is a discourse that slides around, admitting simplistic prejudice, as it were, by the back door. Such a slippage can be traced to early responses by media and politicians to 9/11 and the 7 July 2005 attacks on London (7/7). Criticism of the supposed enervating effects of a lax multiculturalism (understood as imposed from above by a liberal elite) were juxtaposed with embodiments of "good multiculturalism": individuals who had proved their Britishness by their life choices but whose integration could only be guaranteed at the cost of their lives. The fascination with violence and death in discourses about Muslims is here followed through in the reporting of "honor killings," which in practice often evokes old Orientalist assumptions about Muslim pathology and alien values.

Chapter 3 picks up the question of the representativeness of those identified by media and government as "authentic" Muslim spokespersons. We argue that the fascination with hearing "voices from within" Muslim communities—while it stems from an expressed desire to include these communities in the democratic and civic process—is actually subject to the vicissitudes of government agendas, which in turn are closely related with those of the media. The practices of both politics and the press are characterized by a search for "authentic" representatives, whether to front documentary programs or to act as guarantors of fairness and inclusivity on the political stage. However, we suggest that their room for maneuver is, in fact, extremely limited. Muslim journalists and presenters are required to operate as kinds of native informant at the expense of other affiliations, skills, and interests they might have. Political representatives are subject to the whims of government and are always under pressure to stay "on side" in efforts to promote sometimes contentious policies and pacify potential objectors. The "professionalization" of the role of Muslim representative has, we argue, resulted in further limiting the frame within which important civic questions are debated.

Chapters 4 and 5 mark a shift of focus, examining specific examples in more detail as we move from context to texts, exploring post-9/11 television dramas of various types, before Chapter 6 attempts to bring together the strands of previous arguments and suggest—albeit hesitantly—possible ways of challenging the containing power of the frame.

Our examples in Chapter 4 are taken from those television films and dramas that make the claim of offering a relatively unvarnished, direct window onto the Muslim predicament since 2001. In realist films and drama documentaries viewers are purportedly taken "inside" the experience of being Muslim in the modern West. However, we argue that even in sympathetic instances, for example Kenneth Glenaan's *Yasmin* or Abi Morgan's *White Girl*, there is still an anthropological impulse at work situating the Muslim subjects of the films as passive ciphers, embodying values that are at once different yet reassuringly like "our own." Such films never emerge from the shadow of stereotyping because they never allow their characters to transcend their representative status. The same can be said of that type of docudrama that sees its mission as being to inform the public of a present danger and to dramatize the potential consequences of terrorism. Dan Percival and Lizzie Mickery's *Dirty War* relies on already clichéd signifiers of terror and heroism while affording its simplistically drawn Muslim characters only the roles of would-be mass murderers or unthreatening mouthpieces for Muslim grievances. A more complex instance of the dramadoc form appears in Antonia Bird's *The Hamburg Cell,* which deploys a complex temporal structure to take us into the backstories of the 9/11 bombers, for the most part avoiding some of the more gratuitous reductions and stereotypes that, perhaps understandably, marked the public response to the terrorists.

One might expect the thriller form to be even more deeply scored by the lines of ideology staked out in post-9/11 visions of "homeland security." While some shows—such as *24* and *The Grid*—depart only rarely from the script of a civilizational clash, what they and other dramas like them nevertheless play out in the battle of agents and terrorists are some of the contradictions and repressions that mark this way of thinking. On the other hand, some overtly controversial series, such as, *Spooks* and *Sleeper Cell,* are much more confident in their questioning of post-9/11 truisms about Muslim attitudes: the former by complicating an initially simple seeming dichotomy of good and evil, the latter by sending a Muslim agent undercover among terrorists, turning up some uncomfortable truths about Americanness and the American Dream in the process.

In the final chapter we have allowed ourselves to speculate about what the process of breaking out of the frame might entail. In order to do so, we work through one of the most overdetermined discourses about the difference between Islam and the West: that of gender. Taking the case of the various Muslim dolls designed to challenge the preeminence of Barbie and the values she embodies in the affections of young girls, we claim that the attempt to construct an authentic form of Muslim femininity always takes place through certain required performances of self-presentation through dress. The international success of dolls such as Razanne and Fulla would seem to indicate the profitability of Internet promotion and gesture to a specifically Muslim cosmopolitanism that answers back to the usual post-Enlightenment Western models. However, in merely inverting what are presumed to be equally uniform Western modes of femininity—having to do with the oversexualization of the teenage female body—to what extent do such attempts actually break free of the power of the frame? By contrast, those moments where we can see a deliberate overperformance (a hyperperformativity) of Muslimness—found, for example, in the new comedy emerging from contemporary Muslim experience—often directly challenge simple stereotyping by appropriating and unsettling its assumptions.

In the end, while we argue that the framing of Muslims is still endemic in political and media representations, we acknowledge that the space for other articulations *is* being carved out, quietly and for the most part beyond the gaze of Western power elites, in the ruminations of Muslim bloggers and web users and in everyday practices. Such "outlaw" spaces are not the subject of this book, and we leave it to others to explore them and bring them to the attention of a public generally force-fed a particular line about Islam and its adherents. Instead, we hope to highlight, in more detail than has hitherto been shown, the constituent parts of the mainstream stereotyping of Muslims, as we are convinced that it is only through honest self-scrutiny and a consideration of our practices at every level that the debate—and thus the world—can move forward.

# CHAPTER 1

# Muslims and the Nation-State

## The Politics of Stereotyping

In the last twenty or so years politicians, the media, and concerned public bodies have vigorously debated the impact of global migration and the mixing of cultures and ethnicities. At no time since the 1930s have questions about the position of the "outsider" in Western society been raised so persistently, troubling fashionable postmodern notions of the decline of the nation-state in the age of globalized capitalism and a boundless consumer culture. Along with this, as media forms and outlets have proliferated, has come an interest in the way images of ethnic minority or migrant groups are constructed, circulated, and used in contemporary society. Yet paradoxically, this period of cultural hypersensitivity and relativism has also seen an increase in the tendency to deploy stereotyped imagery in the depiction of some communities: a development that sits uneasily beside the ostensibly "inclusive" agendas of modern liberal politics, where demeaning representations of minorities are officially eschewed.

Since the terrorist attacks of 11 September 2001, the discussion—with all its revealing anxieties and ambivalences—has overwhelmingly focused on the position of Muslims in relation to what is often depicted as an equally monolithic "West." The images that emerge, and are repeated and circulated through modern channels of communication, are often little more than caricatures in which the propensity for extremism and violence of a small segment of politicized Islam is magnified and projected onto Muslim communities around the world. The result is that what ought to be a free and frank dialogue over the sacred and the secular, the role of politics in religion (and vice versa), and how identity politics can accommodate religious self-fashioning instead becomes beset with recrimination and misrepresentation. Negative images of Muslims do not *cause* alienation or radicalization. Nonetheless, substituting simplistic and politically manageable views of a sizeable portion of contemporary global citizenry in place of unwieldy and complex realities must have a detrimental effect on the quality of political decision-making, community relations, and public debate.

We wish to critically analyze such recurring yet reductive images. Most contemporary attempts to address this issue have focused on one or two particular genres of representation to construct an argument for the inherent bias and negative stereotyping such forms are deemed to reproduce. Our interest, rather, lies in attempting to produce a discursive, interdisciplinary understanding of the representation of Muslims in the diaspora, both by various mainstream media and by those invested with the power to speak "from within" on behalf of a notionally homogeneous set of interests. We are interested in how these representations operate within carefully regulated agendas and how they often work to reproduce those ideological assumptions that they are supposedly in the business of interrogating and deconstructing. We must, therefore, pay attention to the processes by which such images are constructed, those features that are used again and again, becoming a default signifier for the mistrusted Muslim, and how their circulation takes place within different cultural modes of practice and against particular political backgrounds.

It has become something of a truism to remark on how stereotyping says more about the person or group doing the stereotyping than it does about the group stereotyped. Yet it might be more useful, rather than leaving this as a self-righteous observation, to try to fill in precisely what it means. In other words, why stereotype? What satisfaction and consolation can be gained from painting people in garish primary colors instead of acknowledging the actual pied beauty of humanity? How are reductive consensual stereotypes constructed and how are they circulated? The search for answers to these questions takes us into the realms of psychology, sociology, politics, and the media and will cause us to think about the relation between what motivates individuals, the groups into which they form themselves, and the cultural expressions to which they give rise. Although this book touches on matters of psychoanalysis and deep structures of belief, our approach has been to prefer breadth over depth; in other words, to display and analyze a range of examples of cultural texts where Muslims have been discursively fixed in limiting ways, from a number of contexts, the better to show both the ubiquity of the practice *and* the subtle variations, hesitancies, and contradictions that inevitably appear. It is as if the attempt to solder together a watertight worldview based on supposedly civilizational difference—whether carried out by those hostile to Islam or those feeling the need to aggressively propagate it—can never really be successful; the vessel in which cultural purists set sail is always, in the end, a leaky one that requires constant bailing.

It could, of course, be argued that the category "Muslim" as an object of discourse is produced by such representations and agendas, as they collide with the experiences and concerns of the transnational body of believers. In pursuing these questions we follow the formidable trail blazed by Edward W. Said, both in *Orientalism* and—with more specific application to the treatment of modern Islam—*Covering Islam*. Events since 9/11 have reinforced the urgency of breaking the spell of easy, age-old generalizations about Muslims that has once again mesmerized much of public discourse, and applying in a systematic and thorough way some of the insights and paradigms Said's work offers us. He describes how Islam is "covered"—in both the representational and smothering senses of that word—by "a handful of recklessly general and repeatedly deployed clichés."[1] Said's seminal work allows us to think about the limited and limiting conceptual framework surrounding Islam in public discourse. What emerges from the collision between government policy, the established conventions of media communication, and ideological pressures having their historical roots in Orientalism, is a consensus within which the perceived "negative," "threatening" features of Muslim belief and behavior are constantly promoted and reinforced. Said succinctly captures what we would call the frame governing representations of Muslims and the resulting attenuation of real knowledge about what is in fact a heterogeneous set of cultural systems, when he suggests that there is an "incitement to discourse" about Islam, which "canonizes certain notions, texts and authorities" confirming its "medieval," "dangerous," and "hostile" nature. In turn, such an idea "furnishes a kind of *a priori* touchstone to be taken account of by anyone wishing to discuss or say something about Islam. . . . It enters the cultural canon, and this makes the task of challenging it very difficult indeed."[2] This is the aspect of Said's work that this book aims to continue.

In the current context, it becomes imperative to engage with such frames, as well as what they contain. As Maxwell McCombs has described (*Setting the Agenda* [2004]) it in relation to news media, the frame is "the central organizing idea for news content that supplies a context and suggests what the issue is through the use of *selection, emphases, exclusion and elaboration. . . .* Frames call our attention to the dominant perspectives in these pictures that not only suggest what is relevant and irrelevant, but that actively '*promote a particular problem definition, causal interpretation, moral evaluation and/or treatment recommendation* for the item described.' "[3] We argue that the twin concepts of stereotyping and framing are applicable beyond the boundaries of individual disciplines and cultural practices, taking different forms in different media, but always staking out the territory within which "Muslimness" and "Muslim issues" are recognized and valorized.

Such framing structures are as prevalent, although more subtle, in supposedly liberal media as they are in the more predictable fulminations of the conservative right. In reportage, for instance, the things to look for, as much as raw content, are the contexts in which news stories are set; the juxtaposition of headline, narrative, and accompanying photograph; the staging of the photograph; and the wider debates to which these elements refer. We argue that rather than being descriptive and neutral, such instances are almost always contained within a framing narrative whose parameters are defined by questions of belonging, "Otherness," and threat. It is to the same perceived Otherness that recent initiatives in citizenship, human rights legislation, and sometimes more ostensibly sympathetic cultural representations can be seen to orient themselves. A small, assumed repertoire of images, freighted with unquestioned cultural and moral implications, comes to inform both government policies in Western nations and, by an almost osmotic process, determines the way Muslim matters are presented to the public—this despite the fact that in the modern global village Muslims are "our" fellow citizens too. This is not to say that heinous repression is not a feature of some states using the cloak of Islam to justify totalitarianism, dynasticism, and oligarchy. It is, however, to question the disinterestedness of those advocating what Costas Douzinas has called "the *sui generis* morality of human rights" discourse that has been used to justify neo-imperial interventions since the late 1990s.[4]

Such literally prejudicial decisions about how we should see Muslims seem fixed and repetitious. In their specific features and sheer persistence they call on us to reconsider the idea of the stereotype: a concept branded outmoded in certain circles within cultural criticism, where the term "Other" is preferred as a means to describe practices of exclusion, owing to its presumed ability to carry within it connotations of both the "Othered" and those doing the Othering.[5] We certainly acknowledge the utility of the "Other" as a critical term embodying a struggle over power, and we use it here ourselves. However, it might also be that the very ubiquity of "the Other"—employed nowadays to describe almost any social power imbalance—may blunt the conceptual precision required to deal with the very specific nature of images of Muslims that so insistently cast them as irrational perpetrators of religion-inspired wickedness or as passive embodiments of exotic suffering. While taking on board existing paradigms for understanding the stereotype, we argue that the time has come to examine closely the *process* of stereotyping: how certain images are deployed and circulated and, crucially, how they anticipate an answer from the group being stereotyped. Such processes are complex and uneven, but have the effect of also forming the "frame" with which we are concerned.

Perhaps this is a good point to consider an example and one of the possibilities for understanding its meanings and resonances.

### Islamic Rage Boy and His Meanings: A Case Study in Stereotyping

He appears, with burning eyes and straggly beard, mouth always open, seemingly in the midst of bellowing some anti-Western curse, the nightmare image of the mad, marauding Muslim. Pictures of the so-called Islamic Rage Boy—an inveterate protester who has appeared at a number of marches in Pakistan in recent years over such issues as the Pope's comments about Islam, the Danish cartoons, and the knighthood given to Salman Rushdie—have circled the globe in the age of the Internet, taking on a life of their own as the de facto image of an all-purpose enemy. Islamic Rage Boy has taken his place on mugs, bumper stickers, t-shirts, underwear, and a range of other merchandise. His likeness has been digitally altered to show him as a vampire, as Hitler, as a naked woman, being force-fed pork, and with that distinctive shaggy head superimposed onto the body of a pig. On numerous web and blog sites Islamic Rage Boy's visage is the cue for a huge vomit of invective, often aimed less at this particular protester than at a notion that he in some sense accurately reflects the antipathy towards the West of the Muslim world as a whole, the breeding ground for mass murderers and brainwashed (and unwashed) defectives.

Islamic Rage Boy is, in short, probably the most immediately recognizable of all widely circulated Muslim stereotypes, owing to the viral connections of Internet communication. As such, he provides a useful test case for some possible readings of the process of stereotyping. We need, then, to consider the ubiquity of the image *as an image:* in other words, the fact that, as commonly used, it is essentially a grand, severed head frozen in a convulsion of fury. The head can be detached from the body—in the same way that, as we will see, the man can be conveniently detached from both his personal history and the political background that go to create him—and attached to any number of corporeal shapes. These shapes, the bile with which images of Islamic Rage Boy are inevitably greeted, and the fears that can be hidden behind these transformations but that nonetheless peep through all provide a fascinating insight into what is being expressed by the stereotypers and—no less important—what is being *repressed* at the same time.

The customization of the Islamic Rage Boy image tells us something about the modern mutation of what would, in other times, have been the raw material of the propaganda poster. There is more than a notional connection between the uses of Islamic Rage Boy and the places where his cannibalized image appears and the propaganda posters produced in the two world wars. One ought not to be surprised by this, since the iconic figure of Islamic Rage Boy stands in for a particular enemy, as in their day did the ubiquitous toothy, bespectacled Japanese soldier, grinning as he plunged a dagger into an innocent American woman and the jackbooted, militaristic German Nazi. Of course, in the two world wars such images were produced by highly talented graphic artists, whose skills augmented but in some ways perhaps also distracted from the crude nature of the slogans with which they appeared. In the digital age, when anyone can Photoshop anything into an image of anything else at the click of a mouse, much of the artistry is lost, while the raw hostility often remains. Nonetheless, as a straightforward manifestation of the highly ideological notion that there is indeed a "War on Terror" in a meaningful sense, that we are all part of it, and that we must all choose our side, Islamic Rage Boy, in his various disposable, manipulated guises, will serve just as well as the more craftsmanlike productions of Ben Shahn, Philip Zec, or Reginald Mount.

In the field of postcolonial studies, the most immediately familiar paradigm for understanding the stereotype is probably that constructed by Homi K. Bhabha in his essay "The Other Question: Stereotype, Discrimination and the Discourse of Colonialism."[6] Here Bhabha suggests the psychoanalytic coordinates of the stereotype, which simultaneously articulates both fear of and desire for the Other. He also makes passing mention of the elements of ambivalence in the projection and recognition of such images *as* "stereotypes," and the ever-changing historical context in which the meaning of such images is constantly being made, broken, and remade in different ways. Like the fetish as identified by Freud, the stereotype substitutes for an attribute of power that has either been lost or whose loss is feared. In classic psychoanalysis, a fetish object takes the place of the mother's penis, which the young boy recognizes to be absent in the female but which, for reasons having to do with narcissism and fear of his own castration, he must imagine to have been replaced by something else. Just as the Freudian fetish must always be present for sexual satisfaction to take place, in stereotyping that which is supposedly "already known" must nevertheless be anxiously restated time and again: "the *same old stories* of the Negro's animality, the Coolie's inscrutability or the stupidity of the Irish must be told (compulsively) again and afresh."[7] Such repetition requires for maximum impact the procedures of cultural representation. With its global reach and instant access, the Internet offers itself as the preeminent space where modern stereotyping can be rehearsed. However, in the case of stereotypes of Muslims such as Islamic Rage Boy, two overlapping and contradictory forms of satisfaction are being indulged at the same time: two types of fetishization are in evidence.

In his essay "Fetishism" from 1927, Freud suggests that the male child's disavowal of the perceived anatomical distinction between the sexes results in a splitting of the ego. The fetish object then becomes "a token of triumph over the threat of castration and a protection against it." In keeping with later works, like *Civilization and Its Discontents,* where such connections are worked out more fully, Freud points out that seemingly nonsexual foundational elements of identity can be the object of similar fixation: "In later life the grown man may perhaps experience a similar panic when the cry goes up that Throne and Altar are in danger, and similar illogical consequences will ensue." Thus, perceived or threatened loss of power results in particular psychic formations and impulses, many of which can also be descried in contemporary anxious alarms raised about the threat to Judeo-Christian civilization by the Muslim hordes at the gates. At the same time, "affection and hostility in the treatment of the fetish—which run parallel with the disavowal and the acknowledgement of castration—are mixed in unequal proportions in different cases, so that the one or the other is more clearly recognisable."[8]

There are implications here for our understanding of the reception of Islamic Rage Boy. On one level, what is being fetishized by those expressing their loathing of the figure is their sense of an inviolable-yet-vulnerable Western identity: inviolable because it is ineradicably different and superior in every way to the menacing irrationality projected onto the wild-eyed Muslim militant; vulnerable because the Twin Towers attacks, the agendas of world politics, and the logic of global population movement make it so. At the same time, Islamic Rage Boy himself becomes a fetish object. It is necessary to have his face—glued on top of various parodic deformations—constantly before you, both to remind you of what you are not *and to allow identification with others like you* who can indulge their own contumely by adding comments on websites or, like dutiful consumers, purchasing the merchandise on which the Difference is emblazoned. One only has to glance at some of the vituperation directed at Islamic Rage Boy, as recorded by Patrick French, to see what anxieties are being paraded behind the convenient masking pseudonyms. " 'The Goobs' writes: 'can you imagine how nasty it would smell standing next to this nutter? Whatcha wanna bet he hasn't ever owned a can of Right Guard?' " "Johndoe parades the homogenizing essentialism characteristic of the framing of Muslims: a colonial pseudo-psychopathology against which the discriminating individualism of his Western identity can be implicitly vaunted; "Rage Boy will never rise from the madness that enslaves him. Never. He is past the point of no return—irredeemable like millions of his fellow psychotics." "MoBlows," by contrast, intriguingly conflates the mix of repressed desire and extreme violence that are the flip sides of the stereotype-as-fetish when he invokes the gaping, hair-fringed orifice that has become Islamic Rage Boy's most distinctive feature: "I just want to put my fist down his throat."[9]

French tracks Islamic Rage Boy (otherwise known as Shakeel Ahmad Bhat) to his home in the disputed Indian state of Kashmir. His mission is to try to understand the man whose face has launched a million Internet hits. French tells of a young man, of limited schooling and opportunity, whose family were terrorized by police in search of militants; his sister was allegedly thrown out of an upstairs window at his home and died of her injuries; his grandfather was left bedridden after a beating; and Bhat himself was supposedly detained and tortured by the authorities. In this context, his decision to join the anti-Indian insurgency that began in the 1990s becomes more understandable, although he proved a singularly unsuccessful insurgent, his natural pacifism proving an obstacle to wreaking the necessary carnage and destruction.[10] In this account, Bhat becomes a human being, with loves, hates, and motivations like anyone else, instead of a mere token of fanaticism. And, crucially, this not untypical family history takes its place as part of the long-running tragedy of the struggle over Kashmir, the state controversially granted to India at Independence despite having a majority Muslim population. Here is the history at which the stereotyper balks.

If, as is often remarked, the stereotype seeks to fix an image of the Other, to freeze it at a particular present-centered moment in time, then the eradication of the historical perspective—both personal and cultural—becomes crucial. We must not concede to the stereotype any existence or prehistory outside the straitjacket of representation in which it is encased. (Interestingly, below the online posting of French's essay, which allows for reader comments, a certain Edwin Rowe of Chicago waves away French's actually rather limited attempt to human- ize Rage Boy: "There are millions being brainwashed, raised up to be suicide bombers, and they want to kill, kill, kill . . . I frankly don't care what motivates them."[11] How much easier to deal with our stereotypes of undifferentiated automata and brainless bogeymen?) In view of his experiences, Bhat's decision to turn himself into a sort of professional protester is not only made understandable—it might also be a course of action laudable in the West, where the right to protest is enshrined, al- beit rather tenuously, in constitutions both written and unwritten.

But, of course, Bhat is not protesting about the things "we" feel he ought to be protesting about. However jaundiced the news outlets to which he has access, however fantastical the rumor mill by which his sense of international affairs is informed, it is the vehemence of his protests and the orchestrated effigy and flag-burnings to which such gatherings often lead that turns the delicate stomachs of social demo- crats as they look on. Such is certainly the case when it comes to Christopher Hitchens, the cultural commentator and latterly cheer- leader for George Bush's interventionist policies in the Persian Gulf. In a direct comment on the Islamic Rage Boy phenomenon, Hitchens— like the most vitriolic stereotyping bloggers—pays scant attention to the regional and global contentions that might prompt Islamic Rage Boy to take to the streets, instead preferring to focus on the pathologi- cal anti-Western fanaticism of Bhat and his ilk. (In the process of play- ing along with the stereotype, one might suggest, Hitchens reveals something about his own deeper preoccupations too.) He sees Islamic Rage Boy as a "religious nut bag," a creature of "yells and gibberings," liable to incitement by whatever recent Western abomination has shown up on the finely tuned insult radar of Muslim hypersensitivity. Of course, Hitchens understands that Islamic Rage Boy is a cipher, a symbol of a broader worldview that pits what he sees as the self-pitying and self-hating Islamic East against the usually reasonable but sometimes crass and insensitive West. However, it serves the purposes of Hitchens's polemic to play along with the reductive totalization of the stereotype. Using a coy paralipsis he notes how "our media regularly make the assumption that the book burners and fanatics really do represent the majority, and that assumption has by no means been tested. (If it *is* ever tested, and it turns out to be true, then can we hear a bit less about how one of the world's largest religions mustn't be confused with the lunatic fringe?)"[12]

In fact, any attempts to understand what lies behind the mindset of Islamic Rage Boy and his fellow protesters were absent from Hitchens's consideration of the case. They are signs of weakness and "mental and moral capitulation." Interestingly, in view of his own much-publicized (and criticized) support for the Bush invasion of Iraq, Hitchens aims to perpetuate the long-discredited connection between Saddam Hussein era Iraq and al-Qaeda: "We are incessantly told that the removal of the Saddam Hussein despotism has inflamed the world's Muslims against us and made Iraq hospitable to terrorism, for all the world as if Baathism had not been pumping out jihadist rhetoric for the past decade." Yet he does so by a series of conflations whose cumulative effect is to misrepresent liberal opponents of the war and homogenize and stereotype "the Muslim world." Who has suggested that the removal of a vicious dictator would set the world's Muslims against us? And why? (The dubious justifications and legality of the processes leading to that war that might actually have inflamed opinion across large areas of the non-American world can here be conveniently set aside.) And by inference, a Muslim world that can be roused to rage at the *fall* of a hated tyrant must be a seriously mixed-up place, in need of just such intervention and correction. The instantaneous conflation in the argument of Baathist and jihadist rhetoric serves the same purpose: to evacuate the historical grievances—justified or otherwise—that set Saddam against the West (and most of his fellow Middle Eastern leaders) and to continue insidiously to suggest a link between Saddam and 9/11, evidence for which was never found despite the carefully directed efforts of American and British intelligence agencies. Interestingly, another example of Islam's perfervid touchiness is trotted out immediately after this, when Hitchens notes that "a crass remark from Josef Ratzinger (leader of an anti-war church)" in 2007 also set the Muslim world alight. Given Hitchens's conviction that "God is not great" and view of religion as irrational, superstitious nonsense, it is significant that Islam's knee-jerk outrage figures as more objectionable than the forgivable reactionary "gaffes" of the leader of the most powerful social, moral, and political force in the Christian world: both religions must presumably be in the business of peddling opium to their respective masses, but at least the bishop of Rome is one of "us."[13]

However, we should not be surprised to find Hitchens shoehorning his favorite topics into an article ostensibly about something else. He and his fellow framers of Muslims are merely manifesting an extreme form of what can be argued to be characteristic of the construction of all cultural identities. In *Ecrits*, the psychoanalyst Jacques Lacan writes of "the armor of identity," and this phrase suggests that it is the defensive effort to grasp at, construct, and safeguard an identity—particularly at a moment when conventional wisdom laments that discrete cultures (indeed whole civilizations) are under threat—rather than a lack of identity that is at the heart of the stereotyper's anxieties.[14] Identity is most often constructed so as to exclude from the self all that is deemed "Other" to it. The subject must be sealed off from Otherness in order to arrive at a confident sense of itself. However, in practice this is impossible: identity is something that is always being carved from the category of the "Other," in such a way that the subject ends up making a fetish of its own perceived separate existence in the absence of an original guarantee of power. Therefore, we need not be too harsh on Hitchens or those other Cassandras who declare the fall of "the West" and the imminent return of the Caliphate. They are, after all, doing what comes naturally. In later chapters, we will see how this construction of a threat to "our" culture, nation, and ultimately sense of self is a recurring presumption lying behind the framing of Muslims in political and cultural forms. The distinctive outline of such constructions, having to do with matters such as visible difference, cultural practice, the role of religion in personal life and motivation, and alien moral bearings, is what persuades us that thinking about stereotypes and stereotyping is legitimate—indeed essential—as well as timely. To frame a Muslim, you must first assemble a quite specific set of representational materials, and in the current climate you will never be short of supplies.

## Dialogic Framing: The Mutuality of Stereotypes

So, although stereotyping the outsider might seem an appealingly simple strategy, it is in fact, fraught with self-betraying contradictions. Indeed, despite appearances, the stereotype can in fact be recognized as an inherently dialogic structure. The "same old stories" are constantly born and reborn from the constructed consensus shared within given speech communities. Mikhail Bakhtin reminds us of how the word (or the text) exists in specific social contexts, registers, and moments of utterance and reception.[15] Languages (and texts) carry the imprint of institutional, national, and group interests. So there is no such thing as neutral language. From this it follows that the negative stereotypes that have been reanimated in the last five years or so and the frequent cries for "positive representation" are both inherently dialogical. They call out to each other and answer each other antiphonally. However, it should be understood that this relationship at the present time cannot be said with any certainty to be dialectical. We are not talking about a situation where bad stereotype clashes with good stereotype leading to a synthesis (that is, accurate, "realistic" representation). One would hope that, in due course, some kind of synthesis might emerge whereby Muslim priorities are at least acknowledged rather than ignored. It will only be then that real progress can occur. At present, however, there are willed blind spots in Western politicians' dealings with Muslims and a determination not to seriously consider Muslims' concerns about the questions of Palestine, Kashmir, and what is often perceived as the West's rapacious desire for the mineral wealth of Muslim lands. This book aims to trace the effects of this strategic myopia and how the necessities of certain political discourses help to give form to stereotypical representation.

Yet, while recognizing the invidiousness of negative, prejudiced stereotyping, we also need to acknowledge stereotyping as necessary to meaning, to making sense of the world: something that applies to all groups, whatever their origins or ethnicity. It is there in our initial attempts to make judgments about other people the first time we meet them and to fit them into the categories by means of which we understand the world. While this has caused some discomfort in cultural studies circles, where stereotyping has become synonymous with disrespect and conservatism, the social utility of stereotyping has been more readily acknowledged and explored by social identity theorists. Of particular use in helping us think about what is at stake in stereotyping is Henri Tajfel's notion of the three functions of the stereotype propounded in his book, *Human Groups and Social Categories.* He points out that stereotypes have three overlapping functions: a "social causal" function—the stereotyped group is seen as the cause of an event (such as an economic recession or acts of terrorism); a "social justificatory" function—stereotypes are created to justify behavior toward a given group (as in the denigration of the Other in colonialism, slavery, or official rhetoric about the detainees at Guantanamo); and a "social differentiation" function—differences between groups are accentuated in favor of one group over another. Interestingly, the social differentiation function is particularly noticeable at times when the distinction between groups appears under threat, as in the present multicultural Western world.[16]

In the current climate, the dialogic nature of stereotyping takes on an added edge when Muslims see themselves constantly portrayed as having some indefinable propensity to barbarism. It is unsurprising if, in the face of such vilification, particular embattled and defensive types of group identity emerge. For instance, Haideh Moghissi and her colleagues argue that the Muslim diaspora with its collective sense of itself as a minority has come into existence as a result of "persistent and dominant stereotypes about Muslims in the West as an essentially different, unified and devout religious group."[17] They argue that 9/11, the U.S.-led invasion of Afghanistan, the Iraq War, the 2006 war in Lebanon, and the continued suffering of Palestinians under Israeli occupation have all brought vast and disparate Islamic communities closer and increasingly politicized them. It is now common for public figures to speak of "the Muslim world." What is less often considered is the way that such a "Muslim world," if it exists at all, might actually have been brought into being through transnational solidarities provoked by Western actions.

As well as being dialogic, mutual stereotyping often takes place using critical categories forged in what one might call enemy territory. As such, it reveals an interdependence of values even as it appears to insist on absolute difference. Ian Buruma and Avishai Margalit have described as "Occidentalism" the tendency of antagonists to construct particular stereotypes about the iniquitous West. Occidentalism berates the West as materialistic, soulless, hedonistic, urban, cosmopolitan, decadent, overrational, and bourgeois—all terms of abuse. However, the specific coordinates of such Occidentalism were actually developed in Europe, in the German Romantic idealism manifest in the notions of the *Volk* that, when followed through to its increasingly grim conclusion, provided a rationale for National Socialism in the 1920s and 1930s. The same truisms about the softening effect of mercantile individualism and democracy (in contrast to martial discipline and a willingness to sacrifice oneself) are a feature of, for instance, the Japanese backlash against creeping Westernization in the early twentieth century, long before Sayyid Qutb railed against the idolatrous materialism of the West or Osama Bin Laden sanctioned "anti-Crusader" martyrdom in the 1990s.[18] Despite its obvious attempt to write back to Said's famous 1978 tract *Orientalism,* Buruma and Margalit's reading lacks the ability to link the worldview they describe to any global system of thought as powerful as colonialism, and they have a besetting tendency to simply assume the self-evident rightness of Western liberal capitalism. That said, they offer an important genealogy for the rhetorical flourishes of everyone from Mullah Omar to Saddam Hussein to Mahmoud Ahmedinejad. It seems that synchronous with the rise of the modern nation-state in Europe came a hostile critique that insisted on cleansing blood rituals as a way to reinvigorate a stock made flabby by the comforts accruing from liberal individualism. This happened long before al-Qaeda or the Muslim Brotherhood were thought of, and emerged from within the heart of Europe itself.

The way certain words take on a vast symbolic connotative meaning when used to concoct a "clash of civilizations" view of the world ought to alert us to the centrality of language in setting people against one another.

## A War of Words

Almost the first question fielded by Base Commander Lieutenant General Bob Cone after Major Nidal Malik Hasan had gone on his shooting spree at Fort Hood, Texas, in November 2009 was whether the shootings were a terrorist act. This was not so much a rush to judgment on the part of the press and officials as a predictable response to the congruity of elements in the story: the U.S. military, a Muslim officer, divided loyalties, and lurking in the background the "War on Terror" in the form of Hasan's imminent deployment to Afghanistan. The question was greeted with an equivocal answer; it was too early to say if terrorism was involved. Yet newspaper websites in the United States were immediately inundated with hate-filled messages questioning the national loyalty of Muslim Americans.[19]

The Fort Hood shootings, in which thirteen people were killed and twenty-eight wounded, provide an interesting measure of the condition of discourse on Muslims and its shadow debate about integration and cultural sensitivities. In the subsequent edition of *Time*, Nancy Gibbs tried to disentangle fact from rumor and explore the conflicting forces that were in play not just in Hasan himself but in official responses to his increasingly overt Islamist views. At the heart of her piece was a consideration of the definitions of terrorism. The gunman's apparent isolated self-radicalization appeared to make older definitions of terrorism, having to do with organized conspiracies, redundant. At the same time, there was a danger that revised definitions could become too elastic. However, most revealing was the definition offered by the FBI: "it counts as terrorism if you commit a crime that endangers another person or is violent with a broader intent to intimidate, influence or change policy or opinion."[20] The article went on to question whether "politically correct" cultural sensitivities and fear of equality legislation had allowed Hasan to develop Islamist links and espouse extreme views without being challenged. What Gibbs failed to explore was the extent to which the FBI definition, with its second half emphasizing the *motivation* of changing policy, might jeopardize space for other kinds of dissent and locate terrorism solely in the realm of the political actions of a particular ethnicity.

For the most part, terrorism has conventionally been understood as a tactic, requiring an audience whose outlook and behavior will be affected by the act they witness. (In that sense, the "War on Terror" is a war on a tactic rather than on an identifiable enemy per se.)[21] Of course, it can be argued that terrorism has always been understood to have political aims, ever since the days of anarchist direct action in the late nineteenth and early twentieth centuries. Nevertheless, something subtle has shifted in the lexicon of violence, to the point where incidents with manifestly the same immediate objective and outcome, the spread of terror, can be classified differently according to the ethnicity of the subject in question. Steven Salaita has noted how the term "terrorist" is never used of incidents perpetrated by white Americans, for example the Virginia Tech massacre of 2007, despite similarities in the execution and end result. He notes that "in American usage terrorism must be coterminous with a particular ideology. The identification of this ideology isn't a neutral or natural act. It is one that arises from a series of American geopolitical engagements. . . . Terrorism is usually identified in the United States based on outlook and ethnicity rather than on the actual perpetration of unjustifiable violence."[22] He would agree with Mahmood Mamdani that this new contraction in the meaning of the word "terrorism," aligning it with specific ethnicities, is an example of the "culture talk" that has proliferated since the end of the Cold War; "culture talk assumes that every culture has a tangible essence that defines it, and it then explains politics as a consequence of that essence. Culture talk after 9/11, for example, qualified and explained the practice of 'terrorism' as 'Islamic.' 'Islamic Terrorism' is thus offered as both description and explanation of the events of 9/11."[23]

The branding of terrorism as "Islamic" is bounded by the bigger question of who is empowered to do the defining. After all, *Time's* FBI definition, emphasizing violence to bring about political change, could equally apply to U.S. foreign policy around the world over the past sixty years or so, in places such as Korea, Vietnam, Iraq, and Afghanistan. But, of course, the term is not used in that way. As long ago as the end of World War I, the sociologist Max Weber identified a monopoly on violence as being one of the foundational claims of the nation-state. All nations, including liberal democracies, are carved out through acts of violence in history, for example civil wars, wars of secession, ethnic struggles, and so on. Moreover, if the nation-state can define the difference between legitimate and illegitimate violence, then it also has the power to decide on the terms under which those distinctions can be set aside. Arguably, in the contemporary context it is this ability to decide on exceptionality that has opened the door to practices used against Muslim subjects such as the creation of paralegal categories, torture, and rendition: activities that, in themselves, liberal democratic governments are at pains to denounce. This ability to delineate the difference between so-called legitimate violence carried out by the state and acts of terror means that official discourses always depict the violence of outside agencies or the dispossessed as irrational and without context. This then excuses the wholly reactive violence of the state in pursuing and suppressing such violence. In this view, the liberal democratic state is always vulnerable to attack from less scrupulous groups from "outside." The result has tended in recent years to be the rise of what Philip Schlesinger has called the "'strong state,' 'authoritarian statism' or the 'national security state,'" including curbs on freedom and an "expanded category of subversion."[24]

But we are concerned here with words. The word "stereotype," meaning "rigid trace," stems from the printing trade, where letters were fixed prior to being imprinted on paper. Stereotyping people similarly works to fix them and mark them indelibly with a set of projected characteristics. Muslims in particular now carry the rigid trace of an increasingly tendentious and narrow number of attributes. Karim H. Karim has described how "Islam" has become a term "that is manipulated according to the needs of the particular source discussing it. Among other things, it has come variously to refer to a religion, a culture, a civilisation, a community, a religious revival, a militant cult, an ideology, a geographical region and an historical event."[25] It goes without saying that all these understandings tend to be interpreted negatively. Religious, cultural, ethnic, and political differences are all conflated under the sign of Islam. And anything so irredeemably different on so many levels must be a threat.

By contrast, just as the meaning of "Islam" and "Muslim" has contracted, the investment in what are taken to be its opposite terms—for example "Britishness" or "Americanness"—has expanded along with the possible, always virtuous, qualities identified with these terms. Of course, the notion that something is "American" or "un-American" has long been a standard part of U.S. political language—the most infamous deployment of the latter epithet coming in the era of the McCarthy anticommunist witch hunts. These two terms are used about everything from presidential initiatives on healthcare to the merits or otherwise of genetically modified foods. Americanness comes to define all that is positive for those who recognize its call. And it does so without ever troubling its users to specify what particular quality makes a practice or opinion American (or otherwise). We would argue that with the "War on Terror" has come an increase and spread in this conceptual elasticity in the usage of words such as "American," "British," and "Western." They can be used to invoke at a stroke a range of attributes that, while foggy in themselves, are nevertheless felt to carry the warm glow of cultural familiarity. So, at the same time that "Islam" and "Muslim" are narrowed to mean all that is threatening and foreign, "American," "British," and "Western" swell to operate as what semiotics would term "floating signifiers": words that have no single agreed-on definition and therefore can mean whatever their interpreters wish them to mean. The point is, of course, that such distinctions are always highly ideological and never a natural outgrowth or inherent in the dictionary definitions of such words.

## Muslims and the Western Nation-State

The ambivalence produced by the idea of the Muslim in contemporary Western attempts to articulate homogeneous national and civilizational narratives calls our attention to the shortcomings of such a project, as well as the exclusionary zeal of the effort and its potential to generate violence. It tends also to be the case that the resulting "difference" is understood racially—as a phenotypical schema in which the Other-who-disrupts-the-nation can be recognized and marked out as visibly different on the grounds of ethnicity. Hence the tendency to focus on diaspora communities, rather than white converts, who are at best seen as anomalous and at worst misguided. This racialization is part of a deep and long-standing discomfort about the supposed contamination brought by immigrants to the West, in particular those whose cultural practices appear to compound their ethnic difference.

In fact, the status of Muslims in this discourse can be read as being similar to that of the "stranger" figure of modernity, as described by Zygmunt Bauman in his *Ambivalence and Modernity*. Bauman's book is a description of how the stranger invades and disrupts the cozy insider-outsider binaries through which modernity constructs its social order. Similarly, the Muslim presence in the West has for some years now—at least since the Rushdie affair—operated to trouble the self-image of normalized liberal secular society. In this way, Muslims might well be seen to act as "strangers" in Bauman's sense: those who "commit the unforgivable sin of late entry," who did not belong to the "life-world," as he calls it, of the host community, "originally," "from the very start," "since time immemorial."[26] Their presence, like that of other migrant communities, works against nativist myths of a timeless national past. Moreover, as a supposedly unassimilated interloper, the Muslim stranger's allegiances are always in question. In Europe putatively liberal political discourse responds to this with an obsessive insistence on integration or assimilation. However, beyond and beneath such efforts at domesticating the Muslim stranger lie the harsher solutions of cultural separation and stigma.

The response to this stranger's troubling presence has been a reinvigoration of the desire among "host" nations to define and contain the parameters of national belonging: a move frequently having to do with the delimiting of Muslim identity around questions of citizenship and practice. This phenomenon offers a partial explanation for a variety of important current discussions and moves, including calls for the introduction of identity cards in Britain; the tightening of border controls and entry criteria in the United States; questions of freedom of expression in the Netherlands and Denmark; the wearing of headscarves in

French schools; and debates around the history syllabus at the second-ary school level in various countries. In each instance, stereotypes of both insider and outsider groups in relation to a given nation-state are created partly through the use of frame issues wherein Muslims are constructed as unassimilated interlopers whose practices and beliefs emerge as a challenge to a presumed existing consensus. One might wish to speculate about the extent to which this anxious activity reveals the presence of what Anthony Easthope calls a "national imaginary" where, as with stereotyping itself, the urge to fix a secure and com-pleted national identity can be seen as the manifestation of the desire for a unified ego and the attempt to overcome a perceived lack.[27] While the national collectivity is always by necessity incomplete, post-9/11 and post-7/7 attempts to invoke "Britishness" or "Americanness," for example, are actually symptoms of a desire for origins, for a return to the mythical unified state before the sundering caused by the arrival of the Other. The images of Pearl Harbor invoked after 9/11 and the "Spirit of the Blitz" after 7/7 are marks of such nostalgia and at the same time serve to reanimate the rhetoric of freedom and self-determination by which both Britain and the United States, as nations, understand them-selves to have come into being.

In practical terms, such concerns intersect with questions of secular-ism versus religion, and national versus international modes of identi-fication, for example the way the Muslim concept of the transnational community of believers (or Ummah) problematizes the very idea of the sovereign Western nation-state. Tensions between national and trans-national allegiances have been played out in different ways in Western countries according to their preferred strategies for accommodat-ing immigrants. In the Netherlands, the tussle between proponents of individualist integration and those suggesting that the country's tradi-tional "pillarization"—social and political power blocs based histori-cally on Christian religious groupings—offered the best means to extend collective rights to Muslims was decisively altered by 9/11 and especially by the murder of the filmmaker Theo van Gogh in 2004. The Dutch notion of "contained pluralism"[28] has come under attack from a rightist discourse based on a "homogeneous, static, coherent, and rooted . . . 'cultural fundamentalism'" that advocates "one rule for the 'real Dutch' and another for the 'unwanted Dutch' who need to 'integrate,' 'be saved from their husbands,' or 'learn the language.'"[29] In France, the controversy over veiling is merely one example of an ongoing French debate about religion and the public sphere: an argument that led to the banning of the *niqab* in 2010. Other notable moments have included the headscarf affair of 1989 and the passing in 2004 of a law prohibiting the wearing of religious emblems in schools. Suddenly *laicité*—the principle of privatized religion and governmental noninterference—seems under pressure. However, as Valérie Amiraux has shown, the actual implementation of laicité has always been marked by ambiguities and compromises.[30] This indicates that the heat in current controversies over accommodating Muslim demands might have more to do with suspicions about a culturally different "fifth column" posing a challenge to core Republican values. In Germany an ethnic model of citizenship based on blood ties and descent has increasingly had to contend with a sizeable Turkish immigrant population who can no longer be seen as temporary "guest workers." However, to group these instances as we have here may in itself be misleading, since each can only really be understood in its particular national and historical milieu. That they have been seen by some as providing evidence of an international upsurge of Islamic political extremism testifies only to the power of a certain post-9/11 universalizing tendency remarked on by Gilles Kepel: where, "local skirmishes transcend their specific context and become battlefields for waging a global war on terror."[31]

The tension between the nation as state (making laws, governing, including and excluding would-be citizens, and so on) and as culture (an accumulated body of customs, traditions, and creative expressions) can be seen behind several recent "scares" around Muslim social practices such as veiling and gender segregation. That Muslims may assert different values from those of national normativity in areas such as education and law is seen as a challenge to the jurisdiction of the nation-state.

In fact, one of the key strategies for creating normativity in Western nations since 9/11 has been the requirement to perform national belonging. Here, Britain has followed the United States in introducing citizenship ceremonies for those wishing to become British. In that respect, performing national identification is not in itself something required of Muslims alone. Instead, performing national allegiance has become the endemic signifier of absorption: something, paradoxically, not required of those "born here," whose allegiance is taken for granted. The difference for observant Muslims in Western nations, however, is that their religion requires of them the outward performance of certain visible rituals—praying five times a day, a certain mode of dress, dietary obligations, and so on. Thus, they find themselves in what we might call a double bind of performativity: called upon to demonstrate through performance their national identities, while at the same time performing what is sometimes viewed suspiciously as a conflicting allegiance to the overarching Ummah. It is here that the tensions over loyalty and belonging occur, since secular Western nationalism will not recognize religious national identity as a legitimate form. Thus, Muslims in the West may find themselves overdetermined by the requirements of conflicting performances. (One of the questions we might then want to ask is what spaces exist outside this double bind, and whether its strict obligations can be subverted or treated parodically, to clear a space outside "the frame"—something we take up in the last chapter.)

All these pressures—over dress, loyalty, opportunity, and so on— seem in many debates to be concentrated on the body of the Muslim woman. Muslim women have been at the center of headscarf debates across Europe that have served to reiterate their supposed difference from women of other diasporas and to confirm their supposed position as victims of an oppressive religion. They retain the status of mere objects, looked at and commented on either by traditionalist Muslims who see them as carriers of piety and paragons of virtue or by liberal Western feminists who wish to rescue them. Their own view of the matter is seldom taken into account. They seem to be the silent carriers of tradition. Against this background, innovations in Muslim lifestyle and fashion may represent an interesting form of street-level personal empowerment but one that is seldom reflected on the larger political stage. As in nationalism, so too in religion: women are made to carry the burden of representation, symbolizing far more than their male coreligionists.

## Muslims and Modernity

In his 2003 article "Muslims and the Politics of Difference," Tariq Modood succinctly identified the political roots of the view of Muslims as a "problem" community. He pointed out that "Muslim identity" is considered by some secular multiculturalists to be "the illegitimate child of British multiculturalism."[32] Over the years Modood has consistently argued for the recognition of Muslim cultural identity, but such pleas have been countered by commentators and politicians who view religion as something one adheres to voluntarily, rather than as a cultural identity in its own right.

Along with David Theo Goldberg and others, Modood has also pointed to the emergence in the last twenty years or so of a "new racism" based on cultural rather than biological factors, in which "cultural differences from an alleged British or 'civilised' norm [is used] to vilify, marginalise or demand cultural assimilation from groups who also suffer biological racism."[33] Modood argues that Muslims, owing to their seeming failure to identify with valorized aspects of Western life, are the main recipients of contemporary cultural racism. We would suggest that such cultural racism is manifest in the way the Muslim communities are further circumscribed and "framed" by a political agenda that recognizes their subjectivity through a split register: both as performed identity and, at a deeper level, as based on an essential ontology characterized by difference. Numerous instances of this schizophrenic construction may be found. It inheres, for instance, in the rhetoric of the then prime minister Tony Blair's foreign policy speech in March 2006, where a call for Muslims to join "us" in "modernity" was embedded as a requirement for performed action: in part an applied reformation of interpretations to bring communities into the fold of modernity. Seeking to defend his government's "interventionist" foreign policy from its critics at home and abroad, Blair aimed to distance himself from the idea that Islam and its adherents were inherently antipathetic to the West. In an argument nevertheless replete with well-established binaries, the prime minister insisted: "This is not a clash between civilizations, It is a clash about civilization. It is the age-old battle between progress and reaction, between those who embrace and see opportunity in the modern world and those who reject its existence . . . This is, ultimately, a battle about modernity. Some of it can only be won within Islam itself."[34] Yet, despite the evident intention here to acknowledge Muslims as active agents and coparticipants in modernity, just a few months later a security officer detailed to protect the prime minister was relieved of his duties because his "Muslimness"—suddenly perceived as an essence when it was discovered that his children had attended the same mosque as an imam suspected of having links to terrorism—was deemed to constitute a possible security threat.[35] It seemed as if Muslimness had suddenly taken on the quality of a genetic fault, making one susceptible to infection in the event of exposure to an environment in which extreme opinions might once have been murmured.

Indeed, closer inspection of the habitual discourse of politicians at this moment reveals that such essentializing was a key theme, despite claims to the contrary. Blair's rhetoric on Muslims, like that of his mentor George W. Bush, constantly vacillated between a notion of "improvement" and a latent conviction of inherent regressive characteristics. In this respect, as Paul Gilroy has shown, that rhetoric directly inherits colonialist tropes wherein the native is at one and the same time the object of the improving intervention of the colonizer *and* a hopelessly recidivist type whose very ontology negates this missionary project.[36] As in colonialism, so now social development is read in temporal terms, through an evolutionary sequence and a posited clash between "advanced" and "backward" civilizations. In his classic anthropological treatise *Time and the Other,* Johannes Fabian has called this the "denial of coevalness": "a persistent and systematic tendency to place the referent(s) of anthropology in a Time other than the present of the producer of anthropological discourse."[37] A similar developmental schema can also been seen operating in the frequent calls for a "Muslim Reformation" that conveniently ignore the debates currently going on within Islam between proponents of *ijtihad* (critical reasoning) and traditionalists for whom a definitive interpretation of all Koranic injunctions has been achieved. Such glib demands manage to repeat colonial injunctions by both imposing a linear, Eurocentric model of historical development on Islam *and* conflating a process that, in the European context, took two hundred years of war, torture, bloodshed, and murder to resolve.[38] This view reflects a secularist fantasy of historical process that casts Muslims outside the Enlightenment project, conveniently overlooking the vital contribution that existing Muslim scholarship made to that very project.

Flexible "smart power" may now be preferred to the "War on Terror" in official rhetoric, as a new generation of politicians has succeeded Bush and Blair. Yet, as we write, troop withdrawals in Iraq are being balanced by a surge in Afghanistan and unmanned drones continue to wreak havoc in northwestern Pakistan, killing civilians as well as Taliban insurgents. Therefore, while the language may have softened and become more accommodating, the global project it serves continues unabated. The persistence—indeed reinvigoration—of colonial ways of looking thus sends us back to examine the means by which such structures of representation are created and circulated to take account of this double bind within which Muslims find themselves framed and already read.

# CHAPTER 2

# Muslims, Multiculturalism, and the Media

## Normalization and Difference

"Cultural diversity." "Multiethnicity." "Multiculturalism." Call it what you will, nations and their politicians have been debating its viability or failure ever since 9/11. The crucial question being asked is whether cultural difference can be harmonized and a multicultural society created or sustained, or whether the experiment of respecting and attempting politically to include identity positions with values that may jar with those of the majority is a doomed enterprise. This is by no means a new debate but one that is automatically promoted to the top of the political agenda whenever there is a perceived conflict between cultural diversity and the requirements of the majority, or "host," community within nation-states.

This chapter explores the mutually reinforcing dynamic that exists between political debate about multiculturalism, conventions of reporting in both electronic and print media, and deep-seated and often implicit assumptions about the contiguity of race and national belonging, which are particularly strongly held in Britain. The newspaper and television reporting of the lead up to and aftermath of 7/7 provides us with some appropriate instances that can help us understand this phenomenon, as does the feeding frenzy that accompanies the very real tragedies that have come to be identified by police, policy-makers, and the press as "Honor Killings." How these issues are reported always ends up transcending the local parameters of the case in question, as often-tenuous connections are claimed to the wider "Muslim issues" of terrorism, the mistreatment of women, and a perceived incompatibility with Western family values. The resulting curious but recurring nexus brings us face to face with several central aspects of the framing of Muslims both in terms of what images and tropes are acceptable and in terms of the sanctioned positions Muslims are allowed to take up in defending themselves against the always-lurking charge of disloyalty.

## Muslims, Britishness, and Multiculturalism

In the case of Britain, it is usual to take the story of multiculturalism to be a post–Second World War one, ignoring the much longer gestation period in which the nation was forged out of competing (and often migrating) tribal groups. Such a preference immediately gives the term a racial tinge, identifying multiculturalism with an influx of nonwhite peoples from various parts of the former British Empire. Organized antiracism, of the kind that would later lead to claims for multiculturalism, followed in the wake of postwar immigration, as immigrants settled and, along with their offspring, began to agitate, in the face of intransigence and hostility, for better rights and acknowledgment of their equal status.[1] From an initial focus on immigration and workplace rights, new solidarities emerged in the 1970s when such diverse groups as the Anti-Nazi League, the Southall Black Sisters, the Asian Youth Movement, and the Bengali Workers Association fought for social justice and against the extreme right. Tariq Modood has described this period and how British antiracism was inspired by post–civil rights movement political activism in the United States, which had moved from the "color-blind humanism" of Martin Luther King in the 1960s to the "color-conscious anti-racism" of Black Pride in the 1970s. Out of this came "a new black identity or black political ethnicity."[2] However, as Modood tells it, this strain struggled to "take" in the very different soil of the British nonwhite experience to which it was transplanted. This was owing to a "second cleavage," between West Indians and Asians, whose historical experience and cultural backgrounds sometimes made them uneasy bedfellows. The tactic of denying the significance of this schism led, according to Modood, to a difficulty in mobilizing many Asians for the antiracist struggle. Since the model being followed was an American one, Afro-Caribbean experience tended to be privileged as *the* authentic nonwhite paradigm. This took insufficient account of the inflections of identity (national, regional, and religious) that animated the British-Asian community. Modood, quoting I. M. Young, links this to broader trends in left politics in the last thirty years or so, "in which solidarities of class and social citizenship have been superseded by an idea of equality based on the view that 'a positive self-definition of group difference is in fact more liberatory.'"[3]

The defining moment in a specific sense of British-Muslim identity is often taken to be the controversy over Salman Rushdie's novel *The Satanic Verses* in 1989, which brought Muslims onto the streets to protest the novel's alleged blasphemy. Instead of ethnicity or nationality, religion was, for the first time, being seen as a major identity marker around which to organize. That this was a troubled birth, however, should be clear from the fact that to the broader population, this "new identity" was born amid calls for censorship and, from some quarters, the murder of an author. Therein began the difficult relationship between "Muslim" as a political category and the perceived values of civil society that is still being played out today.

Thus, in Britain, multiculturalism has had a somewhat fraught history, even before the current debates. To that extent, it has never won as widespread general acceptance as when it has been expressed in the United States. This must partially have to do with the United States' acknowledgment of itself as a nation born through immigration and Britain's corresponding fantasy of a comparatively seamless ethnic history troubled only in recent years by postimperial arrivals. Yet here we encounter one of the key fractures in the understanding of the term "multiculturalism"—what it ought to mean and what action it requires states to take if they subscribe to it—a fracture that determines and perhaps diverts all subsequent debates. According to David Theo Goldberg, in the United States multiculturalism can be understood as a reaction that took place, beginning in the 1960s, against the ethno-racial, Europeanized monoculture prevalent in the Cold War era, when a particular white construction of America was elevated and promoted. Multiculturalism is, in this reading, "a *policy-oriented* movement that promotes a 'multicultural society' marked by racial, cultural, and ethnic diversity."[4] Modood's account can take us further by distinguishing explicitly between the European and American models of valuing difference. The U.S. model resulted in "a politics of identity: being true to one's nature or heritage and seeking with others of the same kind public recognition for one's collectivity. One term which came to describe this politics, especially in the United States, is 'multiculturalism.'" By contrast, multiculturalism in Britain and Europe can be said to have a more restricted meaning, being seen as the product of immigration "from outside Europe, of non-white peoples into predominantly white countries."[5] The U.S. model, then, most famously summed up in Charles Taylor's 1994 phrase "a politics of recognition," requires that society at large make legislative changes to incorporate minorities now recognized as legitimate identity-centered lobbies in their own right.[6] Multiculturalism in Britain and Europe, having to do with the movements of peoples, seems to bear more relation to lived experience *before* it is necessarily organized for political purposes. To some extent this may seem an artificial distinction to insist on. Yet the split in popular attitudes toward multiculturalism tends almost always to articulate itself through a stated preference for the empirical, day-to-day practices of different communities rubbing along together over what is felt to be the intrusive and coercive imposition of multiculturalism through legislative interventions. Of course, this preference may have something to do with a desire to preserve a secular (and white) existing hegemony, but few would ever admit as much.

"Multiculturalism" as a term is often traced back in Britain to the education policies of the 1960s and 1970s that culminated in the 1985 Swan Report, advocating adjustment in education provision and the national school curriculum to take account of Britain's changing population. However, Swan's recommendations appeared at a time when the Thatcher government was in principle hostile to greater multicultural accommodation. The seesawing fortunes of multiculturalism have remained a feature of the British political landscape ever since. It is certainly the case that the most sound and fury is generated in British politics and media by the directly political understanding of multiculturalism. If part of the backlash against multiculturalism can be said to be motivated by an anguish that something essential to the British polity is under threat—from, for example, calls for the introduction of aspects of sharia law—the favored way to blend this anguish into an attack on multiculturalism is to construct a bridgehead where the Muslim minority is portrayed as always engaged in special pleading, creating a din far in excess of its numerical size, and possibly receiving preferential treatment as a result. To move down this path it is necessary also to ignore the fact that no mainstream Muslim representative group has actually pressed for the introduction of sharia law. Instead, one has to execute a neat sidestep and locate one's evidence among fringe elements or in the public pronouncements of figures such as the Archbishop of Canterbury, whose role these days seems mainly to consist of musing aloud about social cohesion in the most general of terms.

In pointing out this contradiction, we do not mean to suggest that there is, or should be, no link between the political and the personal when it comes to Muslims and multiculturalism; that would be simply perverse. The betterment of conditions for British Muslims—which also means a serious attempt to eradicate poverty and social deprivation—requires open channels of meaningful communication among individuals, groups, their representatives, and government. Nevertheless, the way critics of multiculturalism often swerve from a general acceptance that discrimination should be fought to an idea that differences in how people choose to live have somehow ineluctably led to a legalized watering down of Britishness ought to be noted and challenged. *If* a multiculturalism project can be said to exist in Britain, and *if* that project can be said to have turned sour in recent years, then there is a responsibility on us to explore with a little more care than is usually employed the actual trajectory of that "failure" and the interests being served by declaring it.

## The Multicultural Moment and Subsequent Rollback

In 1997, the Runnymede Trust, an independent research and policy agency working on race relations and cultural diversity in Britain and Europe, published a report entitled *Islamophobia: A Challenge for Us All,* using the recently coined term to describe the nature of anti-Muslim prejudice. The Trust's report argued that the need to combat this mutation of prejudice was as urgent as the historical battle against the comparable phenomenon of anti-Semitism. Looking at examples from the media, public discourse, and people's daily experience, the Trust identified the main features of Islamophobia, which, they suggested, takes its cue from a more general opposition to immigration and a view of certain types of racism as natural and unproblematic: Islamophobia is characterized, the report said, by a view of Muslim cultures as monolithic, isolationist, threatening, prone to violence, and inherently hostile to the West.[7] The report arrived at a moment of transition in British political life, when eighteen years of Conservative government, eleven of them under Margaret Thatcher, was giving way to the dawn of a "New Labour" government headed by a charismatic young leader and committed to address the perceived exclusions of the Tory years, including those having to do with the positions of minority communities.

The most persuasive available account of the changing nature of racial discourse in Britain since 1997, particularly as it has affected Muslims, is that offered by Andrew Pilkington. His model identifies a "radical hour" that accompanied the election of Tony Blair, followed by a rollback of radical reform in the light of tensions at home and the international impact of 9/11. On Blair's accession, Britain was rebranded as Cool Britannia, a "young," dynamic country at ease with itself and with the diverse communities that gave it color, who were now encouraged to express themselves in culture, fashion, and the arts. (This is the moment of films like Damien O'Donnell's *East Is East* and Gurinder Chadha's *Bend It Like Beckham,* the popularity of the BBC comedy show *Goodness Gracious Me,* and the critical plaudits given to music acts such as *Cornershop* and *Asian Dub Foundation.*)

According to Pilkington, what galvanized and gave additional urgency to the inclusive impulses of the first Blair government was the 1999 Macpherson Report, into the racist murder in Eltham, South London, of the black teenager Stephen Lawrence six years before. The Macpherson report was noted for its strong assertion that the major institutions of British life—including the police—were guilty of "institutional racism": a collective failure to serve people of color because of their culture or ethnic origin. The report was widely accepted, and its most noteworthy outcome was the 2000 Race Relations (Amendment)

Act, which made it incumbent on all public authorities not simply to prevent discrimination but actively to promote racial equality.[8] However, under the law as it existed at that time, such an extension did not reach as far as tackling Islamophobia, since nonethnic religious identities were not recognized under existing provisions as in need of protection.

Not long after this a backlash began, prompted first of all by the Parekh Report on the future of multiethnic Britain in 2000 whose suggestions for a more plural, inclusive notion of Britishness were met with derision and accusations of political correctness by a press that, Pilkington suggests, was bridling from the Macpherson Report's inferences of "institutional racism" and looking for a way to strike back. The subsequent riots in Oldham, Burnley, and Bradford in 2001 and the ensuing Cantle Report, which ignored economic deprivation and placed the blame for the disorder at the feet of Muslims and their failure to integrate, gave impetus to a retrenchment that was complete after 9/11 and 7/7. Instead of equality and antiracism, the emphasis in press and political pronouncements was now all about the need for common British values, community cohesion, and the prevention of terrorism.[9]

Since then, multiculturalism has come under attack both from critics on the left who might otherwise appear sympathetic to struggles for equality and from those on the right who never had any time for it in the first place. Among the former, antiracist campaigners such as Kenan Malik and Trevor Phillips have attacked what they perceive as multiculturalism's in-built claims to exceptionalism, cultural relativism, and a fetishization of historical differences that, in Phillips's phrase, could take Britain "sleep walking to segregation."[10] In both these cases, behind the carapace of the disillusioned antiracism veteran, the critics make some serious points about the consequences of a perceived political approach that has backfired and now endangers those its gentle benefices were supposed to protect. Among the charges are that political correctness has so hamstrung the ordinary operations of a plethora of public bodies that no criticism, no critical interrogation, of the practices and attitudes of ethnic minorities can be countenanced. This has also resulted in a desperate, defensive timidity and desire not to give offense for fear of violent consequences. In a 2009 radio series, Malik followed up this charge with a number of examples of Western self-censorship prompted by a fear of reprisals should Muslims be offended by something: from the abandonment of a Berlin Opera production of Mozart's *Idomeneo* that featured the severed head of the Prophet Mohammed to the removal of nude figures from a Whitechapel art exhibition, the Danish cartoon controversy, and Random House's withdrawal of the controversial novel *The Jewel of the Medina*, about the love life of one of the Prophet's wives.[11] Of course, here we have a choice of preferred interpretation, since self-censorship and civic timidity played the censoring role in some of these cases whereas in others some direct threat was received. Malik's examples, and others frequently cited, prove only a poisoned atmosphere—created, we would suggest, largely by the limited framing we describe in this book—in which cultural exchange and debate is stifled. These examples may indicate that individuals and groups have become hypersensitized in a context where anything can be misconstrued and any type of offense taken. What they *do not prove* is that multiculturalism is responsible for this sorry state of affairs. As Pilkington remarks, charges of the all-pervading, crippling effects of political correctness are made so often and from so many quarters as actually to undermine the very claim being made: "It is remarkable that this discourse [of political correctness] has become so pervasive. The vitriol thrown at . . . multiculturalism, and indeed the current demonization of Muslims by large sections of the media scarcely indicate an intimidated press. I would suggest that what such coverage indicates instead is the hegemonic position of a right wing anti-PC discourse."[12]

### The Ambiguities of Multiculturalism-as-Law

It has been argued here that a central ambiguity in the common use of the term "multiculturalism" serves to explain how it is so easy to stoke up the heat of the debate: multiculturalism means different things when used by different speakers. For some, it is a system of sinister interventions by government, nudging, directing, and maneuvering laws and cultural practices so as to favor nonindigenous populations. For others, multiculturalism is merely the lived experience of a postcolonial, post-globalized society in which peoples from different backgrounds, working side by side, produce hybrid cultural forms and shape aspects of their environment and practices according to these new forms in what Paul Gilroy has called a "convivial culture."[13] Only extreme cultural purists could seriously attack the latter phenomenon, and it is fair to say that the most sound and fury has been expended on the former interpretation, with critics seeing multiculturalism either as a conspiracy or as a kind of well-intentioned blundering into dangerous waters wherein "real British values" are being actively downgraded. For example, the Conservative Party's Home Affairs spokesman, Dominic Grieve, used his party's conference in 2008 to make the claim that multiculturalism—which remained frustratingly undefined throughout his speech—had wrought a "terrible legacy" in Britain. Invoking Britain's supposedly now neglected Christian tradition, Grieve stated: "We've actually done something terrible to ourselves in Britain. In the name of trying to prepare people for some new multicultural society we've encouraged people, particularly the sort of long-term inhabitants, to say 'well your cultural background isn't really very important.'"[14] The well-meaning but pusillanimous relativism that had supposedly led to this situation was then directly connected to the rise of fundamentalist Islamic sympathies—a claim likewise made with no statistical backup but relying on the moral panic mentality for its effects.

It is common to go on, as Grieve did, to suggest that it is dissatisfaction with the mealymouthed equivocation of politicians that, in turn, feeds support for parties of the extreme right, such as, the British National Party. This claim, that *not* talking about immigration and assimilation breeds extremism, has become a standard tactic since 7/7. However, it deliberately omits a key stage in the process it professes to describe by assuming, first of all, that vast swathes of its target audience feel squeezed and marginalized by the supposed favoritism shown to newcomers, without making reference to the framing process with which the press and political elites have kept this version of the story permanently on the agenda, regardless of the degree to which it reflects (or doesn't) most people's lives. In addition, attributing the rise of support for extreme right parties to a chimerical misguided "policy" is a useful "get-out-of-jail-free" card for all the main political parties, efficiently distracting attention from the economic and social disadvantages that neither has been willing or able to alleviate. The "blame" for multiculturalism can be shifted around in space and time: to the various immigration acts that, in fact, have made it progressively *harder* for people to enter Britain; to the liberalism of the 1960s, when so much of what was previously held sacred was challenged; or to the failure to manage the population movements of the global economy. So each of the main parties gets its chance both to be blamed and to blame the other side. The practical effect, however, ends up always being the same; when in doubt, finger the newcomer. The politics of scapegoating has become so ingrained that most politicians would not recognize— indeed would vehemently deny—that this is what they are doing when they set afloat the same convenient decoy. Multiculturalism's catastrophic impact is taken to have dropped on Britain out of a clear blue sky, and no possible precedents are investigated. It is, therefore, conveniently forgotten that the same South Asian Muslim community whose members are now widely vilified for breeding sedition and terrorism were only a few years ago taken as models of hardworking, family-oriented integration juxtaposed against the rioting, criminally minded young Afro-Caribbean males of 1970s racist mythology. Thus, there seems to be a kind of merry-go-round of cultural approval—judged always according to a fairly narrow set of middle-class standards arbitrated by the "host" community—on which ethnic minorities are obliged to ride, waiting for their time in the sun. Were the debate on multiculturalism and the criteria for cultural acceptability to be at all consistent, arguments for proactive integration by minorities might carry some weight. But then, a skeptic might argue, there would be no need for such arguments in the first place. The political convenience of vagueness in talk about multiculturalism ought not to be underestimated.

Of course, Britain is not Canada. There has been no Act for the Preservation and Enhancement of Multiculturalism in the United Kingdom. At most, there have been a few rather hesitant and tentative pieces of antidiscrimination law. Yet even these are fodder for those who see a dilution of Britishness as being one of the results of postwar immigration. Such doomsayers seldom bother to provide concrete examples of how central government is foisting a "multicultural agenda" on an unsuspecting population, relying instead on the fear instantly conjured up in the post-9/11 world by the idea that "they"—whoever they actually might be—are over here, diluting "our" prized traditions, refusing to integrate, and in extreme cases threatening our lives. At their most specific, the criticisms tend to be aimed at perceived practices such as "positive discrimination" (also known as affirmative action) and the alleged existence of an unofficial quota system in certain employment practices or in local housing policies. For the most part, the lack of detail in populist attacks on what can be termed multiculturalism-as-law tends merely to assume that everyone knows what "it" is and agrees that "it" (whatever it is) is a bad thing.

In press coverage the scare stories that accompany the paranoid reading of "Britishness under attack" have tended to focus on the perceived misguided zealotry of low-level functionaries in local councils and the civil service. These stories frequently take on the quality of urban myths, having to do with sour-faced mini-Napoleons discouraging the celebration of Christmas so as not to offend those of other faiths or forcing private citizens to remove ornamental pigs from their windows lest they annoy members of minorities with dietary taboos. There is a peculiar element of the absurd in many of these myths, yet they feed a general climate in which news consumers who belong to the majority are encouraged to see attacks on the foundational principles of their collective identity coming from all sides. It is in this climate that the leader of the British National Party can, with a straight face, suggest that London has been "ethnically cleansed" of British people, since such a high proportion of its inhabitants are immigrants or the children or grandchildren of immigrants.[15] The British National Party has in recent years made the strategic policy shift of moving away from an explicitly stated hostility to all ethnic minorities, instead aiming its opprobrium at Britain's Muslims. However, the idea of a foreign, unrecognizable London overrun by specifically Muslim hordes is one that has also been peddled by more mainstream commentators such as Melanie Phillips.[16] If the easy answers offered by the extreme right tend historically to find a more favorable reception at times of economic hardship, we still ought not to ignore how the way is paved for this reception by a powerful phalanx of politicians, commentators, and news media.

Critics of multiculturalism-as-law all face the same basic problem: how to make tangible this new threat to a British nation that has always been encouraged to imagine itself as homogeneous, timeless, and unified. Culture, being the outcome of human practices, provides fertile ground in which to sow seeds of discord. Activities that are unfamiliar or that appear to challenge the value system of the majority often provoke defensive reactions, which in turn open the possibility for misunderstanding and mistrust. To be sure, certain types of alien and troubling acts can be, and are, associated with Islam and Muslims— even though the roots of such acts tend to be in the shared soil of tradition and hierarchical communities back in their countries of origin. However, if mass migration has brought the British such undisputed benefits as cheap labor, colorful textiles, and decent food, there is, nonetheless, a rich vein of suspicion of the outsider that can be summoned at short notice, a connection to long-held fears that is not hard to spark. In the case of the framing of Muslims, cultural joins forces with racial Otherness to create a new template of fear.

## Journalistic Form and the Associative Chain of Images

So why are Muslims seen by the majority as such a problematic group in the multiculturalism debate? At a historical level, this undoubtedly has to do with the transporting of social and religious structures largely unchanged from one latitude and cultural environment into another. However, the Western media has also played a key role in shaping attitudes and, quite often, confirming prejudices about Muslims. To claim this is, of course, to generalize to a certain extent and to downplay the contribution of those scribes who have made it their business to cut through walls of ignorance around the Muslim issue. Nevertheless, an ingrained degree of complicity with power agendas—something that has always been part of political journalism as it attempts to explain the ways of secular gods to men—comes to have particular implications in the world of the "War on Terror" and the persistent low-level murmur of Islamophobic suspicion.

To be sure, there has been a heightened understanding, post-7/7, that Muslims as social subjects cannot and should not be confined to the role of suspicious alien presence. This awareness finds its way into magazine and lifestyle programming, for example the BBC's *Women in Black*—exploring the activities and tastes of Muslim women from a number of national contexts, thereby challenging the stereotype of the passive, oppressed female—and the provocatively (and perhaps unfortunately) named *Shariah TV*, a late night talk show on Channel 4 that takes the opposite line of tackling head-on hot "Muslim topics" such as homosexuality, free speech, and antiterror legislation. The degree to which this show merely confirms the frame we claim as characteristic of cultural productions about Muslims can be debated. However, at least such programs acknowledge the need to nurture a space where important matters can be raised and discussed without necessary recourse to the norms of an encircling ethnic majority.

Indeed, in the case of British television it should be admitted at once that nothing as crass as an anti-Islamic agenda can really be said to exist. Broadcasting strategies tend more toward scrupulous fairness and a balance in the types of show transmitted. We can see this in a few of the programs commissioned and shown in the first decade of the twenty-first century, and especially since 7/7. There have been positive portrayals of Islam in Nasfim Hafique's 2005 BBC feature *Don't Panic, I'm Islamic,* and in Tariq Ramadan's account of a sea change in Islamic scholarly thought: *The Muslim Reformation* (Channel 4, 2006). And there are other programs that display a genuine questing spirit or an attempt, at least, to understand Muslims better, such as Ziauddin Sardar's *Battle for Islam* (BBC, 2005) and Channel 4's survey of Muslim values and opinions entitled *What Muslims Want* (2006). In fact, the sheer number of such programs has led to claims from other minority communities that the BBC in particular is unfairly "favoring" Muslims. Statistics gleaned from the BBC's Religion and Ethics Department claim that between 2001 and 2008, the BBC made forty-one programs on Islam, five on Hinduism, and one on Sikhism.[17] Whether or not these figures are accurate, one can certainly say that this disproportionate attention to Islam is triggered largely by current national and international tensions as they have risen to the top of political agendas rather than by a sudden interest in spirituality. In that regard, broadcasters are certainly not "favoring" Muslims in anything other than a numerical sense. The sympathetic interventions mentioned earlier can only be properly understood in the context of a slew of hostile and negative documentaries with more or less interchangeable foci, in which problematic "Muslim issues" are endlessly recycled, often in sensationalist tones; see, for example, Channel 4's *Edge of the City—Bradford* (2004), claiming that mainly Muslim Asian males were procuring and sexually assaulting white girls; *Panorama: A Question of Leadership* (2005), which challenged the credentials and commitment to peaceful integration of members of the Muslim Council of Britain; and *Dispatches: Undercover Mosque* (2007), which sought, and found, extremist preaching at mosques across Britain. To say that such programs tap into a deep well of suspicion, underwritten by current governmental priorities, is not to suggest that criminality or incitement to violence ought to be overlooked or hushed up. It *is*, however, to say that the relentless depiction of Muslims as a fifth column within Britain provides the underlying "common sense" position against which those more favorable shows must perpetually struggle.

Such a narrow journalistic agenda effectively underwrites the more general criticisms of multiculturalism that are loose in the world today. That agenda at once casts aspersions on the notion that convivial coexistence is a possible or even desirable outcome for a postimperial world and hints that multiculturalism-as-law needs to be rolled back in the interests of future harmony and cohesion. To funnel all efforts toward the scrutiny of those staples of framing, Muslims' failure to integrate and their propensity for terrorism is to shadow the very kinds of instrumental thinking that has produced the government's Prevent agenda, one of the strands of the antiterror strategy known as CONTEST. Prevent ensures that funds and backing are channeled toward the bodies and initiatives that are approved partners in the fight against al-Qaeda-inspired terrorism, conceived as the biggest single threat to Britain today. Yet heavy-handed tactics, such as efforts to persuade higher education institutions to spy on their Muslim students for signs of radicalization, have drawn criticism from civil libertarians and from those who see Prevent as something of a smoke screen, diverting attention from the inconsistencies in domestic and foreign policy that are also at the root of Muslim disaffection.[18] Surprise raids on universities, for example that in which a team of heavily armed police swooped down on a group of suspected radicals outside the library at Liverpool John Moores University in April 2009, provide great copy for newspapers and thrilling pictures for news channels. Given the rather low conviction rate that often accompanies such operations, one could wish that a greater number of journalists might have been exercised by the adjacent questions of whether free enquiry in universities was endangered by intrusive policing or whether such raids actually do more to harm than aid community cohesion. A few correspondents did take up these issues. However, for the most part, the narrative spun was a more conventional one about thwarted conspirators and, by implication, a characteristically British disquiet about universities as sites of intellectual pretension justifying moral relativism. Such coverage serves to keep a hegemonic government viewpoint about threat levels and their sources firmly in the public consciousness. Why should the more troubling fine detail be picked over when the idea of radical Muslims around every corner justifies government policy and expenditure? To this extent Prevent, and other measures like it, are not really so much a consultative exercise as a mechanism for forcing Muslims to take responsibility for acts done in their name, even when they may be separated from such acts by vast distances of space, doctrine, and sympathy.

In this scenario, the idea that all Muslims must be drawn into a battle against violent fundamentalism works on the assumption that religion is the foundational principle animating all actions. Cultural acts derive from religion, and any other impinging factors such as class, gender, or doctrinal or regional differences are considered less crucial to the formation of identity. The trouble with this view— which privileges religious identity above all else—is that by failing to discriminate properly it allows for a resonant chain of association to be set up in which the aberrant activities of Muslim groups (or individuals) in one part of the world are seen as having unavoidable corrupting effects everywhere else. This is a particularly postmodern form of paranoia, since it tends to view the instantaneous crossborder reach of telecommunications and the Internet as the main means of "terrorist" indoctrination. Yet this paranoia also represents a logical consequence of the globalization of capital that we are daily invited to celebrate, even though it is more usually explained by reference to some kind of unspecified propensity for radicalism to spread rapidly among susceptible Muslims like a form of contagion.

As far as the reporting of national and international tensions is concerned, the key agendas known to be circulating among governments at any given moment form the bedrock on which news agencies build. Yet crucially, we would argue, some transformation takes place in phenomena as they are covered by the media; one might even say that a transformation takes place *through the actual process* of coverage itself. Simon Cottle has described the way the media's relation to the conflicts they describe is never simply reflective or neutral. Instead, they have an "active performative involvement and constitutive role within them," for which he coins the term "mediatizing." Cottle shows the way the media rely on an existing "inferential framework of expectations" among their audience, to which they contribute by means of repetition, shaping responses, behavior, and actions.[19] In other words, as actors in the phenomena on which they are reporting, media themselves by necessity change that which they are representing and, by extension, the public's attitudes to it. Taking this idea further, we can see that such transformations have marked ideological results. For instance, far from being a complex story about how and why Western citizens might, in the age of accessible global travel, transport themselves to terror training camps in Pakistan or Afghanistan, the creeping tendrils of the Islamic threat generally are *created performatively*, so to speak, through the tendency of news editing to seek quick and accessible connections between contemporary phenomena. Depth is sacrificed to speed in most cases. Not only do editors have their deadlines to consider, they are also forced to keep an eye on sales figures, viewer and listener numbers, and so on. Twenty-four-hour news channels, which for the most part rotate the same stories every fifteen or thirty minutes, similarly sacrifice the potential depth with which a subject might be treated, preferring instead to deliver content in ways more attuned to busy life-styles and presumed shorter attention spans. The potential for resulting condensation and simplification to also work in the interests of "War on Terror" discourse is a by-product, but one that is hugely important for the way the world is mediated for us. This is a matter of individual texts reinforcing a context predetermined by political agendas: something that happens through the greater meaning emerging from the way a story is presented as well as from its content.

To see an example of form seamlessly dovetailing with content in such a way as to set off an associative chain of presumptive connections between supposed general Muslim secretiveness and group loyalty, criminality, and what President Bush conveniently branded the Axis of Evil, we can take our cue from one particular news story, a BBC *10 O'Clock News* bulletin of 14 April 2005 on the conviction of illegal immigrant Kamal Bourgass for attempting to develop ricin for terrorist purposes. Images of the convicted man were juxtaposed with close-ups of chemicals in lab containers, followed immediately by the standard (stereotypical) shot of Muslim men in a mosque performing their prayers. Yet again, although the spoken report itself avoided suggesting *causal* connections between these elements, in which religion seemed to be privileged, the selection and juxtaposition of the visuals made the link. The surly features of the previously convicted cop killer Bourgass, his toxic weapon of choice designed to spread fear and mayhem, and the Finsbury Park mosque—already known in the popular consciousness as a hotbed of Islamist extremism—all added to the story of immigrant treachery and ingratitude that was being repeatedly embellished during the period between 9/11 and 7/7.

The story of Bourgass's downfall had, by the time of the *BBC News* broadcast, become freighted with numerous other tentacular associations too, the nature of which worked to draw Muslims and Muslim nations across the world into the embrace of politically expedient framing. The drip-feeding of a story that had its beginnings before 9/11, and the traditional British news self-censorship imposed as the case made its way through the courts, allowed certain entirely groundless claims to be made about the nature of the specific threat posed by Bourgass and his accused coconspirators. For instance, the "ricin" supposedly found on a pestle and mortar in the flat used by Bourgass was quickly proven to be no such thing by scientists at Porton Down, the government's biochemical research facility. Yet news of this discovery, which was made well before the attack on Iraq in March 2003, was held back, allowing politicians in Britain and America to imply a connection between Bourgass's cramped, ordinary-looking North London flat and the malevolent influence of Abu Musab Zarqawi, whom U.S. intelligence was seeking to link to al-Qaeda, and Iraqi president Saddam Hussein via a camp in northern Iraq where the ricin had supposedly been made.[20]

Moreover, it emerged that in pursuing the plotters the British authorities had relied heavily on information gleaned from the alleged mastermind of the ricin plot, Mohammad Maguerba, by means of torture in an Algerian jail.[21] Those moral dilemmas raised by the zealous pursuit of the U.S. president's "War on Terror" thus received an early airing, before tactics such as rendition, water-boarding, and other euphemistically termed "enhanced interrogation techniques" fully emerged from the shadows to blight Bush's second term. Moreover, the ability of Bourgass to remain undetected for so long, despite his illegal status, fed into those fears—bordering at times on hysteria—rehearsed in the news media at the time about how Britain's supposedly generous immigration policies were now being abused and its citizens imperiled by overstayers, Islamists, and "bogus asylum seekers."[22] Bourgass's avoidance of detection was even cited by the British home secretary of the time, Charles Clarke, as underscoring the necessity of introducing identity cards in Britain, although he preferred to deflect more awkward questions about why information on the putative ricin trace had not been corrected.

Of course, the fact that such false trails and misleading use of intelligence were subsequently exposed to the world by journalists might be cited as evidence of the definitive fairness and transparency of the news media. Likewise, the Bourgass case being particularly layered and complex, it might be claimed that the BBC's presentation of visual elements in the news report cited above was entirely justified by the need to tell the story. We are not suggesting here that images of mosques or Muslims at prayer ought to be banned from the airwaves because they carry negative connotations. Nevertheless, what is striking is the persistent parading of particular images that, in the "War on Terror" era, came to lose their neutrality and instead became a decontextualized, interchangeable sequence of markers denoting an alien culture in perpetual crisis that had turned on its hosts and taken refuge either in outright acts of war or in more latent forms of intransigence such as denial and insularity. In turn, this then furnished more ammunition to those critical of the multicultural laxity that had allowed such criminality to flourish unchecked. This is a matter to do with frequency of repetition and the overall news context that, for reasons of convenience or laziness, has injected an element of inevitability into the use of such otherwise standard images.

Of course, one ought not to be too churlish about the challenges any news editor faces, working against an inflexible and always looming deadline and having only a fairly standard and limited set of stock images to hand. Nor should one dismiss the proud tradition of questing, investigative journalism that often focuses on the blind spots and double standards of those in power. Still, it is worth considering in more detail the relationship between mainstream news reporting and the agendas of power politics, not least because of the perhaps necessary proximity between politicians and, in particular, the national media.

## Agenda Setting: The "Muslim Issues" Matrix

Political journalists rely on elite sources for their raw material. They need to know the plans, plots, and policies of government at its various levels if they are to convey an accurate image of current affairs to their readers. That is not to say, of course, that personal prejudice and the coloring of the outlets for which they work play no part in the product that hits the newsstands or airwaves. As is well known, particular news providers give a certain slant to the information they disseminate. However, the obvious and rightly criticized cases of gross bias that have been able to poison the wells of public debate since 9/11, as access to globalized media has continued to spread, remain in the minority. Unlike the United States, where, as Barbie Zelizer and Stuart Allan have shown, objectivity was sacrificed in favor of an unquestioning patriotism by most media and journalistic outlets in "War on Terror" coverage immediately after 9/11, the British media in the same period managed by and large to preserve a more critical and interrogative relationship with their government.[23] To understand the framing of Muslims, we need to acknowledge that its roots lie not in journalism's yielding to a simple patriotic urge, but in a variety of forces that have a bearing on the news that is produced and consumed.

Limited framing narratives about Muslims that only identify a small range of newsworthy topics form what we would describe as a "Muslim issues matrix." This matrix can be analyzed with reference to the practice of "agenda-setting," which it has been argued creates a cognitive relationship between the "representation" of the world and how people come to perceive it in their minds. We have proposed that one needs also to take a formal view of the way the frame is constructed— considering the choice and ordering of material, the privileging of one voice or account rather than another, the tone of a story, and the juxtaposition of aural and visual elements. Only limited attention has been paid to these factors in the post-9/11 context. However, it must also be conceded that agenda-setting can never be the preserve of individual journalists, outlets, or media tycoons, be they ever so determined. The media critic James Watson, for example, has emphasized the importance of the often very different agendas of governments, media professionals, corporate entities, and audiences in shaping meaning.[24] Nonetheless, as Cottle points out, "journalism post-9/11 and the reporting of the global War on Terror . . . clearly reproduce agendas and representations that support state interests and policies."[25] When it comes to Muslims, these dominant agendas have to do with radicalism, terrorism, and practices that are seen as a threat to the nation-states that even a globalized media still sees itself as primarily serving.

So we are talking about media practices that allow for and perhaps give respectability to prejudice, rather than dominant or hegemonic messages handed down as unvarnished truth to a dull, passive audience. Indeed, we might say that "public opinion" is both a much-coveted quest object sought by all news providers and something that they themselves see it as their role to influence. However, inasmuch as there *is* such a thing as public opinion—given the diversity of age, sex, race, religion, and so on that make up present-day metropolitan populations— it must needs be brought into existence, given voice, so to speak, by media, and thereafter constantly tended through repetition and elaboration. One should not underestimate the strength of the embrace between news providers and consumers. Even so, nothing as consistent as a unified public opinion has yet emerged from their wrestling. Instead, the media organs' role in relation to normalized and marginalized groups is summed up in Elizabeth Poole's comment that they often "contribute to the material practices of discrimination through their discursive practices, which normalize attitudes towards problematized groups and then legitimate and prefer negative constraining actions above other fairer solutions."[26] Poole's comment comes in her study *Reporting Islam,* a quantitative analysis of British newspaper coverage of Muslim issues mainly in the broadsheets. She argues that "Muslims have . . . entered the frame as the central racialized Other in Britain," an assessment based on persistent coverage reiterating the Muslim community's supposed inability to integrate in various ways.[27] Poole's analysis provides the ballast of sound empirical research, providing a substantive and coherent answer to the questions of how the media normalize certain attitudes toward a "problem group" and how a collection of diverse communities comes to be perceived as a monolithic entity.

Such framing, in fact, long predates 9/11. A sort of postimperial haze seems sometimes still to pervade white British perceptions of their fellow citizens from South Asian cultural backgrounds, perhaps fed and informed by centuries of Oriental romances and decades of cinematic and television blockbusters. Those softer stereotypes of a "gorgeous East" of spices, colors, licentious promise, and mystical spirituality always had as a simultaneously available flip side the brutal patriarch, the bloodthirsty warrior, and the irrational hothead. At certain moments, as multicultural Britain became more widely recognized as a reality, efforts were made to explain the peculiar ways of these new fellow citizens to their contemporaries. Yet always, in the case of Islam, a sense of inherent alienness remained, an idea that Muslims were, in the end, motivated by strange beliefs and subject to a sort of transplanted desert tribalism that could bring them into conflict at any moment with the milder manners of those from a more temperate climate. Such exotic fixations were scrupulously expunged from the 1990s BBC television series *Living Islam,* which sought to explain the faith to the wider population. However, such fixations were very much present in the comments of Hugh Purcell, the executive producer of the series, when he was justifying the British media's penchant for a narrow range of topics on Islam: "I submit to you that what most Britons want to know about Islam is why it appears to give women an inferior position to the extent of possibly encouraging wife beating and polygamy. Why it appears to encourage violent fundamentalism—that's the phrase used—and dictatorship and so on. These are the preoccupations and, let us admit[,] prejudices of most Britons."[28]

Purcell's comments were made in 1993 but resonate as much in the post-9/11 world as they did in the immediately preceding era, marked by major disputes such as the Iran hostage crisis of 1979, Anthony Thomas's controversial 1980 docudrama *Death of a Princess,* and the Rushdie affair of 1989. In the twenty-first century we continue to see issue-led stories focusing on a narrow and repeated series of supposed Muslim misdemeanors. When it comes to such coverage, the kind of global and transnational loyalties represented by the Muslim Ummah come to form the motive power driving suspicion of multiculturalism at home and neocolonial adventures abroad. The *longue durée* of framing means that the task of politicians in bringing the press on board, at least partially, for their projects is already half done for them.

### Race, Reporting, and 7/7

It is fair to say that the 7/7 attacks in London made sullen homegrown *jihadis* and bellicose foreigners big news business. The soul-searching that followed revelations that a group of unobtrusive and seemingly well-integrated Muslim men could have felt so disenchanted and disconnected with their fellow citizens that they deliberately set out to kill and injure as many of them as possible tended (and still tends) not to discriminate much between the geographical locations of the people about whom it is concerned. For a brief moment after 7/7 the media acknowledged that there were multiple "Muslim communities" in

Britain, rather than a singular bloc as had always been assumed; how else could one account for the fact that three of the four bombers came from the otherwise unexceptional and hence overlooked town of Beeston in West Yorkshire? Somehow the surly figures caught on CCTV cameras entering Luton station with their backpacks on the morning of 7/7 had missed out on the jamboree of intercultural fusion and celebration known as "Balti Britain" still being ostensibly celebrated in the nation's capital. However, this revelation of microworlds of disaffected radicalism in areas with more deprivation and racism was quickly subsumed by the louder clamor of voices calling for various ways of enforcing Britishness: each voice having its own quirky version of what it was that was supposed to be being enforced.[29] We can see the 2005 shift from a shocked dawning awareness of the existence of "lost" Muslim individuals and groups to a project of national repair and cultural retrenchment around a racialized Britishness, played out overtly in the way the press covered the London bombings.

In the immediate aftermath of the 7/7 attacks a strong strain of racialization was evident in all types of journalism: blurring together religion, ethnicity, and national normativity in a disturbing repeat of the demonization of "immigrants" in the 1970s and 1980s, when race relations in the United Kingdom were at their lowest ebb. For instance, what was implicit in the racial undertones of the trendy intelligence community shorthand terms for those malefactors with no previous connections to extremism—"clean skins," or "lily-whites"—became explicit in early speculations that "white mercenaries" may have been behind the attacks. The emphasis here on phenotype registers a sense of unease at the possibility that the perpetrators might not be marked out as different from "us" by the decisive external features of race. It was commonly assumed that no "true Briton" could be responsible for the horrors of July 7. As this came to be carried in news reports and media speculation, there was a silent but telling tendency to conflate "true Britons" with the white, non-Muslim population.

Similarly, as the story developed, difficulties became evident over "placing" the bombers in relation to national normalization, despite the fact that they were born and raised in Britain. The question of Muslimness as opposed to British identity was further thrown into relief after the discovery of Mohammed Siddique Khan's video testimony outlining the grievances inspiring his actions, and declaring non-Muslim Britons to be legitimate targets. Yet, if we examine closely the imagery circulating even before this, we find that subtly—often in the space between words and pictures, text and context—the same question is insistently being broached. The result was a series of initial euphemisms aimed at distancing, for example "British born but of Pakistani origin," and "British-Pakistani." This allowed for a contrast with what *The Sun's* front-page headline in the days after 7/7 described as "True Brits": the members of the emergency services and the resilient Londoners clearing up the mess left by the bombings and getting on with their daily lives, and in so doing calling up echoes of the World War II Brits, always a tabloid default mode for evoking unsullied and unified Britishness.

The visible traces of the 7/7 bombers—caught on CCTV cameras and leaving so-called martyr videos outlining the motives for the attack—worked to once more call into question the loyalty and commitment of Britain's Muslims as a whole body. Statements from Muslims distancing themselves both as individuals and as group representatives from the bombers became expected and, as a result, were often forthcoming from those who found themselves boxed into a corner. Few opinion-formers stopped to ask on what basis it was assumed that Muslims en bloc ought to apologize for something almost none of them had anything to do with. While prominent Muslim representatives in the media, such as Yasmin Alibhai-Brown with her weekly column in the *Independent* and Sir Iqbal Sacranie, secretary-general of the Muslim Council of Britain, were drawn into the debate on British identity, their comparatively isolated voices seemed to confirm a token nod toward multicultural inclusiveness, which signals diversity through its ethnic minority representatives but remains firmly embedded in the monocultural landscape of liberal democracy. At the same time, the Muslim media, including the newspapers *Q-News* and the *Muslim News,* were conducting important debates on exactly those issues about Islam and Western values that were preoccupying the mainstream media.[30] However, the very same "marginal position" that allowed them to address and reflect a particular constituency also meant that they were largely ignored by broader agencies. To be sure, "visible Muslims" began to make more appearances as newspaper columnists and television commentators, but their role, in these early days, amounted to little more than explaining possible Muslim grievances. (As we will see later, it is not at all unusual for Muslims, once they have been identified as posing problems, to be spoken about and at, rather than being given much of a role themselves in the definitions of national belonging that they are then asked to sign up to.)

In this political landscape, if Muslim citizens cannot be seen actively to assimilate into mainstream culture, however that might be defined, they can find themselves threatened with the potential loss of their legal right to remain in Britain. The call to return immigrants to their "origins" was conveyed succinctly by the columnist Michael Howard, who urged the government to revoke citizenship rights for those who had been naturalized as British citizens if they were seen to be a threat to national security. Advancing this proposal in an article in the *Guardian,* he spoke of the principles of integration and the "British Dream" as they were espoused by the right kind of immigrants such as his own parents; "they never thought their Britishness was inconsistent with their Jewishness. They would have recognized the difference between integration, which they supported, and assimilation, which they did not."[31] At this stage, what had merely been assumed in some of the reportage post-7/7—that people were choosing *either* their British or Muslim identities—had passed into the common-sense parlance of high-profile politicians. Foreign Office minister Denis MacShane went as far as to call on Muslims to choose the "British way of life" over the way of the terrorists.[32] The reality that any identity, indeed *all* identities, are shifting and provisional—that different aspects of individual and group self-representation might be emphasized at different moments— was conveniently forgotten in the din of demands for the imposition of a clearly defined, reinvigorated Britishness.

However traumatic, 7/7 was in fact only one milestone in a dominant narrative that had already emerged as being about the misguided "policy" of multiculturalism pursued by successive British governments and how it had allowed enemy ideologies to take root. Yet it is crucial to note that this narrative has, as its target, what it takes to be the political concessions granted by multiculturalism-as-law that *then* feed back into isolationist practices and attitudes at ground level. Because minority groups have been encouraged to value and nurture indigenous traditions, with such encouragement being given legislative backing, it is no surprise if separatist ideologies grow. On the other hand, several writers lined up to defend multiculturalism, with reminders that integration might require action from both "sides."[33] On the whole, the immediate response to 7/7 was to point to the bombers as aberrations and, correspondingly, to foreground embodiments of successful ground-level multiculturalism instead.

Two such embodiments presented themselves, each under tragic circumstances, in the fallout from the war in Afghanistan and in the roll call of the dead after 7/7. The first was Shahara Islam, a twenty-year-old bank employee who was killed in the explosion on the number 30 bus at Tavistock Square. The murder of a promising British Muslim by her coreligionists was widely reported, alongside photos of a strong, confident young woman. Headlines such as "For Shahara's Sake Don't Hate Muslims" (*Daily Mirror,* 11 July 2005) and "Confirmed Dead: The Woman Who Embodied Multicultural Britain" (*Independent,* 14 July 2005) suggested that the victim's cultural identity underlined the random futility of her attackers' indiscriminate methods, and that there continued to be potential for a true multicultural Britain lived out every day in the lives of integrated minorities. Alan Hamilton, writing in the *Times* (London) on the first anniversary of Shahara's death, reminded readers that she had been "a devout Muslim girl . . . who straddled the Muslim and Western worlds, going to mosque every Friday while enjoying Western independence and fashion."[34] Behind Hamilton's rather question-begging binary view of Islam and the West lies a sense of a multicultural fusion that is worth preserving.

The other embodiment of positive multiculturalism appeared a year after the 7/7 attacks in the form of Lance Corporal Jabron Hashmi, who was "Born in Pakistan, Raised in Birmingham, Killed in Afghanistan," as the *Independent's* front page told us, under a large picture of the smiling soldier. Inside the paper the first British Muslim soldier to die on one of the fronts in the "War on Terror" was remembered by his older brother as "a Muslim first and foremost, and a British Pakistani . . .

[who] was proud of both identities." " 'Jabron, like me, thought that the majority of the problems in British society came down to the absence of understanding of each other's culture and my brother has, by example, proved the fact that in this difficult time we can bridge these gaps.' "[35] Jabron Hashmi's death led to a sudden awareness of the presence of Muslims in the British armed services and for a moment quieted the voices advancing a pathological reading of Muslims and their behavior. "Muslim Heroes Fight for UK," as the *Sun* reminded its readers in January 2007. And of course, in the case of Jabron Hashmi, Muslims die for the UK, too.

It must betray something deep-seated in the psychology of cultural acceptance that it would take the deaths of two young Muslims—elevated to symbolic status as part of a press-led process of national suturing against an enemy who seemed to know no borders—to legitimize a defense of multiculturalism. In this chapter we have insisted on a distinction between discourses about multiculturalism-as-law and multiculturalism as quotidian experience. Newspapers from both left and right joined together to celebrate the lives of Shahara and Jabron, but what was being celebrated most of all, one felt, was the sacrifice that propelled them to national prominence: a definitive, clarifying rite of blood. No one would have wished their fate on them, and everyone would want them back if that were possible. However, in the wider landscape of press coverage of multiculturalism, the iconic status of these two brief lives suggests that it is *only through death* that a Muslim's right to Britishness can be proven once and for all. This may sound too extreme, yet as we will see later, there is ample evidence for this construction in the television dramas that have appeared post-9/11. With all the imperial and military history at its back, the British press in a time of war called once more on the deepest impulses of group loyalty, sanctioned in the Gospel of John, and applied it as a test to its new population: "Greater love has no one than this, that he lay down his life for his friends."

Shahara and Jabron were frozen in death as "Muslim" representatives—any other affiliations, interests, doubts, and contradictions were effectively evacuated by the press's need to show that Muslims could be good Britons too. This fetishization of "death" through commemoration as the ultimate evidence of one's belonging is, of course, the flip side of the terrorists' own fixation with mayhem and death. The bombers, in their deaths and the death they brought to others, revealed they could not truly be British. Shahara and Jabron, in their deaths, were, respectively, a bright young innocent Briton (who also happened to be Muslim) and a British military hero (who also happened to be Muslim), whose death for a declared "national" cause, "our" cause, confirmed him as one of "us"—while simultaneously shaming all the disloyal Muslims in the country.

We should not be surprised that it is only at the extremities of life, and in the manner of their deaths, that Muslims can prove their Westernness. The neoconservative truism that Westerners cherish life and fear death whereas Muslims embrace death and undervalue human life likewise draws on centuries of Orientalist antagonism. As with all the other examples of "liberal" coverage of Muslim issues cited in this chapter, the defense of Muslims is almost always an attempt directly to refute such myths. More often, though, Muslim attitudes to death—even the deaths of loved ones—provide another stick with which to beat multiculturalism.

## Honor Killings as a "Muslim Issue"

The post-9/11 depiction of honor killings as a minority and often Muslim issue in the British media is symptomatic of the way a certain kind of cultural practice can be held up as an example of the key difference between a civilized Self and an unenlightened Other. It also helps to underline the vulnerable status of women in Muslim cultures and foregrounds the prevailing authority of progressive Enlightenment values in Euro-American cultures. It is this sense of an unbridgeable cultural divide that seems to take center stage in the reporting of honor crimes in the media and the normalization of Muslim values as backward and outside the scope of Western civilization. Our focus here is on the reporting of honor crimes and not the details of individual cases, which are, of course, very real tragedies in their own right.

In Britain, two of the most widely reported "honor killings" cases are those of Rukhsana Naz and Heshu Yones, women from different ethnic backgrounds, the former being of Pakistani and the latter of Kurdish origin. In 2002, sixteen-year-old Heshu Yones was killed by her father who stabbed her eleven times and with such ferocity that the tip of the kitchen knife broke off. Abdalla Yones committed the murder a few days after receiving an anonymous message that his daughter was "behaving like a prostitute." Rukhsana Naz was murdered by strangulation in 1998 by her mother, assisted by Rukhsana's brother. She had become pregnant by an old boyfriend whilst being the married mother of two.

Geraldine Bedell, writing for the *Observer*, noted the inadequate Western response to honor killings. She argued that the British legal system finds it problematic to adjudicate over what is framed as a "cultural practice." In the Heshu Yones case, which went to a murder trial, the judge, in his concluding remarks, reflected that it was "in any view a tragic story of irreconcilable cultural differences between traditional Kurdish values and the values of Western society." Bedell underlines a problem in this reading of cultural difference in British society, where passion crimes are equally prevalent and two women are murdered by their partners every week.[36]

While academic debate has engaged with the problematic representation of honor crimes, it seems to have made little impact as far as policy and reportage are concerned. At a 2007 conference entitled "Gender Politics in South Asia" held at the Institute of Commonwealth Studies in London, Kaveri Sharma, a legal advisor to the Newham Asian Women's Project in London, pointed out the loaded phrases that riddled news reports of the Yones case. Phrases such as "a ghastly way of life" and headlines like "Asylum Dad Murders His Daughter (16) for Being Too Western" serve to confirm the outsider status of the perpetrators of these crimes and the seeming impossibility of achieving cultural cohesion between Muslim immigrants and their "host" society.

After 7/7, the stakes were raised further by certain cases in which the Crown Prosecution Service made links between "honor" violence in Britain and extremist groups abroad. Such connections were in evidence in BBC Radio 4's *File on 4* in a program broadcast in June 2007. The program featured an investigative report into honor killings presented by Angus Stickler. Listeners were treated to a new angle on the subject, with tantalizing references to the involvement of "radical extremists" as well as confirmation from the police that the majority of honor crime cases in the United Kingdom were within the Muslim community. Two Muslim authorities with differing views were pitted against each other in the first part of the program: Nazir Afzal, director of prosecutions for the Crown Prosecution Service in West London and Lead on Honour Crimes for the CPS nationwide, and Dr. Reefat Drabu, a representative from the Muslim Council of Britain. For Afzal, denying any connection between honor crime and Islam pandered too much to cultural sensitivity, whereas for Drabu, honor violence was rooted in "culture and tradition" and not faith. It was Afzal who voiced the link between the radicalization of Asian youths and honor-based violence, saying "they feel very strongly that the way you treat your women is a demonstration of your commitment to radicalism and radical thought and extremist thought and they are proud of the fact that they will treat their women in a certain way. And if charity begins at home, why shouldn't radicalism and terrorism?" In one fell swoop, a linkage has been made between criminality, terrorism, and Muslim machismo.

Stickler went on to suggest evidential links between honor crimes and Islamic, nationalist, and terrorist groups abroad. What these links actually were was never made entirely clear, but listeners were left to draw their own conclusions. Instead certain inferences were made that sufficed to begin the usual chain of association and implication. A tenuous link between radicalization and honor crimes was presented in relation to the Heshu Yones case. According to Nazir Afzal, her father, Abdalla Yones, had been a prominent member of the Kurdish community and had associations with Kurdish nationalist groups who put up a substantial amount of money as security for his release and had plans afoot to spirit him out of the country and into northern Iraq. To Stickler's question "Was this an extremist nationalist group?" came the answer "Yes it was, [a] Kurdish Islamic nationalist group based in Northern Iraq and South Eastern Turkey." "Extremist," "Islamic," and "nationalist" might all have been terms worthy of further definition by Stickler. They represent points on an assumed sliding scale along which one might find ranged a number of not necessarily consonant political positions. Instead, in the absence of any background research into what the group might stand for, the nature of its struggle, and so on, reliance was placed on the horror that such local disputes had spilled over onto the streets, and were raging behind the front doors, of Britain. Stickler was excited to tell his audience that there was more "evidence" of terrorism and honor-based violence connected to another case, that of "Miss B," a woman who had been deemed to have "gone off the rails." She wanted a divorce from her husband, and the police cited evidence that her husband had links with a terrorist group in Egypt: "A group prepared to travel to the UK and carry out executions *on British soil.*"[37] Again according to Afzal, the evidence showed that Miss B's husband was being encouraged by a terrorist group to take action against his wife. While she had been rescued by the British police and was now in a safe house, her husband had been murdered by the group. This disconcerting story pointing to links between terrorism, radicalization, and honor left the matter of proof fairly vague and, on the face of it, circumstantial. In fact, Reefat Drabu voiced her disagreement with the program's central thesis by referring to meetings on forced marriages and honor-based killings that she had had with Mr. Afzal at which it had been accepted that there was no connection between these three phenomena. For Drabu the linkage was "unacceptable," and Afzal's analysis "dangerous and wrong." A clearly skeptical Stickler countered that Afzal was "a Muslim man himself," thereby attempting to trump Drabu's contrary viewpoint. The framing of this dispute was clear: Afzal had confirmed what we had long suspected: that there were links between Islamic extremism and honor crimes. Once the program had established for its listeners this topical chain of association between Muslim extremism and domestic violence, it then proceeded to the real problem: the way the police had dealt with individual cases and their role in bringing the perpetrators of honor-based violence to justice and providing protection to victims. This discussion confirmed problems of communication between Muslim leaders and the Metropolitan Police and the way cultural sensitivity can be a hindrance to investigation. In addition, we were told that Met operations against honor violence had been further hampered by political infighting.

The way this radio broadcast was constructed clearly did more than simply position journalists at the heart of raising awareness of a very real problem for minority communities in Britain. It went as far as to cast this particular reporter as a kind of whistleblower, lifting the lid on an area of crime where cultural sensitivities were said to be hampering the police at a fairly central procedural level. Here, then, was an apparent refutation of the old Macpherson Report line about the police being "institutionally racist." In fact, the police supposedly were now so institutionally antiracist that they were no longer allowed to go about their basic task of solving serious crime and putting criminals behind bars. Whether or not one buys this argument, it seems clear that the frame around Muslims is such that ordinary crime—horrific though it may be—cannot but be represented as linked to the other misdemeanors and backward values "we" know "them" to be guilty of. The softening effect of multiculturalism on British institutions and procedures allows them to get away with it. All in all, when it comes to public discourse around honor killings, humanitarian concerns have become colored with the lens of a nationalist antiterror rhetoric, and the stereotyping of communities has become more pronounced than ever as a result.

This is an instance of the way a kind of cultural racism works its way back into the representation of "Muslim issues." It is not that honor killings should not be condemned and as far as possible eradicated, but that the very classification itself becomes elastic enough to encompass a number of other wrongs associated with what are seen as "Muslim" practices. It seems that if in a multicultural society members of ethnic minorities can be subject to recognition through their religion, Muslims as presented by the media are particularly susceptible to the presumed ingrained heritage of honor killings.

Yet, more than this, the classification of crimes as being based on honor sometimes takes on the tinge of cultural essentialism and double standards. In all the unhappy accounts of truncated lives and wasted potential, a rigid barrier is seemingly erected between crimes perpetrated by those of Muslim (or Sikh) cultural background and the rest of the world. Those all-too-regular stories of husbands prompted by pride, insecurity, or derangement to slaughter their wives—and often their children too—are almost always inflected differently according to whether or not perpetrator and victim are from backgrounds where honor is understood to be paramount. What will pass for cold-blooded murder or a "crime of passion" when taking place among Europeans or Americans will, if occurring in tightly knit immigrant communities, almost automatically carry the whiff of an honor crime and is likely to be investigated (and reported) as such.

Take, for example, the BBC's two-part documentary *Honor Kills*, which was first aired on the digital channel BBC 3 in October 2007. Amid the depressingly familiar accounts of husbands and fathers driven to kill by the unutterable prospect of "losing face" as a result of the sexual misdemeanors or romantic preferences of their wives and daughters, was nestled a far more complicated case that appeared, on the face of it, to have had more to do with a wife whose ambitions for herself and her children no longer coincided with those of her more conservative husband. In November 2006, Caneze Riaz and her four daughters died from smoke inhalation at their home in Accrington, Lancashire. The terraced house in which the family lived was sprayed with petrol, allegedly by the husband, Mohammed Riaz, who also set himself on fire after a night of heavy drinking. While his four daughters and wife died that night, Riaz lingered in hospital for two days before also succumbing. We are told that Riaz was frustrated with Caneze's desire to continue with her own career, her encouragement of her daughters to pursue their education and interests, and her depression over their son's illness with terminal cancer. Apparently he was also depressed himself because of low self-esteem over his own job situation, while Caneze worked for community relations in her locality and enjoyed a good rapport with her colleagues.

In this respect the case sounded, in terms of motivation, more like many other tragic cases from various cultures where a wife is brutalized or killed for getting above herself or displeasing her husband. The extreme emotional distress caused by the son's imminent death might also weigh heavily in the balance as a motivating factor. As it was explained in *Honor Kills*, only the fact that it had taken place in a South Asian and specifically Muslim domestic scenario seemed to justify the crime's categorization as an honor killing. Patriarchal brutality, intimidation, domestic violence: all are endemic to our society and most others too. However, it is only those whose domestic life seems alien, organized according to creeds spawned thousands of miles away and hundreds of years ago, who carry the mark of honor in this way. Such categorizing underscores a whole range of superior value judgments made by the host society toward its minority communities. In public debates, in the formulation of government policy, in police intervention, and in the judicial categorization of honor crimes, ethnic minorities in Britain come to be seen through the lens of tribal values and customs. Issues of honor and shame are nothing new in the debates on cultural difference, multiculturalism, or integration. Yet when it comes to underwriting the "clash of civilizations" discourse, such essentialized markers of difference confirm an unbridgeable divide between Islam and the West.

## Conclusion

There is no conspiracy between politicians and the media to restrict the way Muslims are represented and treated. In this chapter we have suggested that it is, rather, the habitual workings of the mainstream press and news media that lead to a sometimes inadvertent complicity with power agendas. Since 9/11 this has meant elevating the threat from Islamist terrorism to the number one priority impacting both domestic and foreign policy. This political priority is duly reported, but some of its more paranoid implications and inferences, we have suggested, are taken up too in the way Muslim issues are identified and relayed to the broader public. When this is combined with a knee-jerk reaction that indiscriminately identifies multiculturalism as the weakest link in British national identity, the scene is set for obsessive scrutiny of all the aspects of Muslim culture that make "them" different from "us." Such criticisms are also generally aimed at shoring up a British identity that has historically always been in flux but is seen to have come under particular strain since decolonization and the beginnings of mass migration. Attacks on multiculturalism from the antiracist left tend to have more to do with a perceived betrayal of old solidarities through the admission of religious discourse into the previously secular terrain of equality activism. The claim that attacks on multiculturalism are the product of a political structure of representation that fetishizes narrow religious identity is worthy of further scrutiny. When faith becomes the defining marker by which groups are invited to identify and organize themselves, there follows the establishment of an entire industry around authenticity and "representativeness." Our next chapter will look at this phenomenon and how, once again, governmental biases find their way into media handling of "Muslim issues." In other words, in the political and media discourses that help to shape public discourse, who are the representatives and how are they represented?

# CHAPTER 3

# Representing the Representatives

## The Limits of Cultural Identity

We have seen how, since the 7/7 attacks, the nature and parameters of Britain's multiculturalism have come under renewed question. As in the United States after 9/11, so in Britain the nature of the debate over variants of Britishness has been subsumed beneath moves to firm up borders and establish hard and fast definitions. The result has been the requirement for a management of difference that must nonetheless be articulated within sanctioned parameters and reiterate certain commonalities to be recognized as legitimate. While Britain's communities may appear as a panoply of cultural diversity, they must express themselves politically in the narrow, accepted manner, using approved channels, adhering to certain agendas, and so on. Failure to do so means punishment and exclusion. Such monoglot diversity confirms Sanjay Seth's view that liberal multiculturalism often domesticates its Other in order to accommodate it in terms it understands. In short, toleration for other values and opinions only operates within the limits defined by the majority culture in any society.[1]

Where the question of those institutions and individuals recognized as "Muslim representatives" is concerned, another aspect of framing comes into view. Liberal multiculturalism invests much in the notion of "authenticity": imbuing certain spokespeople and organizations with the right to speak on behalf of wider communities. In the case of Muslim representatives, the nature and scope of their "representations" has been severely curtailed in the current climate. It is not so much that certain areas are off-limits. Rather it is that particular voices, representing certain recognized and accommodated strands within Islam, have been cultivated and brought to the fore, while others have been down-played and marginalized, treated as "less representative." Nor does this only apply to those articulating extreme, and therefore unacceptable, views. Censure in the name of patriotism is also a favorite tactic when confronted with any kind of disagreement with government conduct when it emanates from a Muslim source.

"Clash of civilizations" discourse begins from the assumption that cultures and nations are fixed, finished, and stable. This stability would, it is claimed, be jeopardized by the unrestrained and injudicious mix-ing of cultures and peoples. As such, it is in a sense a perfect top-down view, and might be expected to find favor with those who rule, since it emphasizes both obedience and integration with what already figures as the norm.[2] Yet at the same time, the colonial aspirations of interven-tionist foreign policy require the claim to be made that "our" cultural values are superior to those whom "we" are aiming to free/educate/punish. As such, so-called Western values are projected as universal values, once more representing the norm: this time one that all the world aspires to and for which we will receive thanks when the popula-tions we have freed recognize the worth of what they have been given. This kind of bombast lies behind so many policy decisions, so many utterances since 9/11, that its links to a colonial mindset have faded into the background and are seldom mentioned. Similarly, the histori-cally and culturally negotiated nature of these proclaimed universal values also tend to be obscured or—if they are acknowledged—are rolled out as an example of how "mature" nations conduct the pro-cesses of change. All that remains is the growled imputation that dis-sent from these values among immigrant communities is a form of low-grade disloyalty.[3]

## Recognition and Politics: The Fate of the Muslim Council of Britain

The politics of cultural identity, which has been developed, deployed, and finessed by groups coalescing around race, gender, sexuality, and latterly religion, also has its origins in assertively delineated under-standings of culture. This is the case despite their often egalitarian im-pulses and desire to challenge existing power structures. Charles Taylor traces the basis for the politics of recognition to Hegel's phenomenology of self-consciousness in the *Phenomenology of Spirit* (1807), which proposes that it is through intersubjective communication and recognition by others that one gains a sense of self. Taylor sees the same impulse acting as a common denominator in many contemporary political groupings. He says: "The thesis is that our identity is partly shaped by recognition or its absence, often by the *mis*recognition of others, and so a person or group of people can suffer real damage . . . if the people or society around them mirror back to them a confining or demeaning or contemptible picture of themselves. Nonrecognition or misrecognition can inflict harm, can be a form of oppression, imprisoning someone in a false, distorted and reduced mode of being."[4] Although this understanding of cultural identity as separate from, yet reliant on, an Other has been criticized—most notably by Stuart Hall, whose theory of "new ethnicities" emphasizes the multiple and temporary nature of identity—it continues to be the model favored in political practices at both national and international levels.[5]

In the United States, the apotheosis of the politics based on these principles—which, unlike its British cousin, tends to make no distinction between the antiracist and cultural identity phases of its history—came with the election of President Obama in 2008. At that time, the strong strain of reactionary black purism that had questioned whether Obama, with his mixed heritage, was actually black enough to be considered truly black was drowned out by a chorus hailing the victory as evidence of the American capacity for renewal and as the final exorcism of its racialized past. Things may have worked out in rather more ambiguous ways subsequently. We can, nevertheless, point to this moment as one where the potential for a kind of politics appealing to deeply cherished identities came together with sanctioned national myths about immigration, integration, and personal achievement with results that inspired millions around the world.

At the time, there was much speculation in Britain about whether the country was similarly ready for a black prime minister—even though no serious candidates for the role presented themselves. However, the historical separation of identity politics from the structures and systems of power actually makes the question of academic interest only.

As things stand, if there *is* a black prime minister at any time in the future, it is more likely to be because he or she has shown particular personal qualities, played the party system effectively, or is seen to meet some public relations need than because they have tapped into pre-existing power banks based on identity. In the case of Muslim identity, representatives have been sought, and thrust themselves forward, in ways that have bypassed democratic processes entirely. Of course, the *Satanic Verses* affair at the end of the 1980s is taken by all commentators to mark the beginning of a British Muslim political identity. However, the oppressive levels of governmental intervention and direction that have since impacted directly on the shape of that identity—and that continue to do so to this day—are less often remarked on.

A plethora of bodies have sprung up in recent years with a greater or lesser claim to represent Britain's Muslims. These include the Muslim Parliament of Great Britain, the Muslim Society of Britain, Muslim Association of Britain, the Sufi Muslim Council of Britain, the Islamic Society of Britain, and many more. The best known and most powerful of these organizations is the Muslim Council of Britain (MCB), an umbrella group with a national remit, set up in 1997. The MCB has had a privileged position in the bulging portfolio of representative bodies, having direct access to the government, working with them to address specific achievable goals—such as improving the caliber of Imams serving British mosques—and more generally pursuing the interests of Muslims in the cultural and political life of the country. The MCB has, for example, been the first port of call both for ministers and civil servants seeking advice on issues of cultural sensitivity and for broadcasters looking for suitable spokespersons for television and radio news programs.[6] Recently, several newspaper and television exposés have aimed to associate prominent MCB leaders with the supposedly extremist politics of the Jamaat-i-Islami, the organization founded by the twentieth-century Pakistani political thinker Sayyid Abu A'ala Maududi: the most prominent of these efforts being the BBC's *Panorama: A Question of Leadership* in 2005. A rather more intriguing, although less sensationalist and simple, story concerns the way the MCB has been positioned, paraded, and pummeled by those in power, especially since 9/11.

The MCB was founded in response to a 1994 call by the then Conservative home secretary Michael Howard for a single representative body he could deal with. The Muslim professionals who grouped together first as the UK Action Committee for Islamic Affairs and later as the core of the MCB were responding to a specific invitation from the center of power to help populate the political landscape in a new way.

Jonathan Birt has described how after the 2001 attacks the British government was on the lookout for ways of shoring up support for the U.S.-led invasion of Afghanistan, for which it played the part of willing lieutenant and chief cheerleader. It expected the MCB, as its favored representative group, to play its part by smoothing the way among British Muslims, for whom the invasion was potentially a divisive issue. The MCB was promised direct access to the prime minister, and the charm offensive included positive spin stories about Muslims put out in a press still awash with negative coverage. However, under pressure from its supporters and affiliates, the MCB was forced to declare its opposition to the war, a declaration that Birt says led to a swift rebuke from the government and a temporary expulsion from favor.[7] Two lessons emerge from this initial salutary experience of how, in Tony Blair's phrase, the rules of the game had changed: the first being that Muslim transnational loyalties were now expressly disallowed and a war mentality, emphasizing national loyalty, imposed; the second being the extent of the government's belief in the representativeness and power of its own chosen group—and, perhaps, the sheep-like propensities of the Muslim population when handed an official line. There then began a strange love-hate relationship between the MCB and the British government that continues to this day.

This peculiarly tense connection has seen the fortunes of the MCB ebbing and flowing like the tides of the sea. For instance, between 2001 and 2007 the MCB pursued a policy of refusing to send an official representative to attend Holocaust Memorial Day commemorations—suggesting instead the establishment of a day of remembrance for genocides more broadly. This stance resulted in its commitment to multicultural integration being questioned by government ministers, and in 2006 it was threatened with derecognition and a withdrawal of some funds. The following year, the MCB revised its position and sent representatives, drawing praise from the same sources. However, in 2009, in response to that year's Israeli offensive in Gaza, the MCB reverted to its original policy, leading to renewed aspersions about a lack of commitment to the hard-won freedoms of the previous century. Over the same period, in 2006, the then communities secretary Ruth Kelly wrote to the MCB accusing it of being too passive in tackling extremism, as a prelude to announcing a diversion of funds toward local projects run by councils instead.[8] Another storm over the MCB's attitudes toward the Middle East erupted in 2009 when its deputy general secretary, Dr. Daud Abdullah, was taken to task for signing an international declaration of support for Hamas's military actions against Israel.[9] Announcing the MCB's punishment in a letter, the new communities secretary, Hazel Blears, articulated clearly the mindset that saw the MCB as incapable of serving two masters; "it would seem that Dr Abdullah's position . . . would be incompatible with his recent actions. . . . Whilst your investigation is ongoing and the matter remains unresolved I feel that it is only appropriate for us to suspend our engagement with the Muslim Council of Britain pending its outcome. It would therefore be inappropriate for the MCB to attend the upcoming faith Communities Consultative Council meeting on Monday 16th March."[10] In response to Blears's letter, the MCB declined to force Abdullah's resignation.

The paradox whereby the fate of an entire strategy of integration and outreach should hang on one man's signature, given in a personal capacity, on a controversial document may perhaps testify less to the scrupulous moral integrity of the government and more to the absurd system of patronage under which a whole community is taken to be biddable and buyable. As it turned out, the MCB's sojourn in the wilderness lasted a year, before it was welcomed back into the fold by the next incumbent of the Communities brief.[11] At the moment of writing, the MCB appears to be back in favor in government circles again. However, by the time you read this, who knows what the case will be?

Pnina Werbner has seen cause for optimism in the MCB's willingness to stand up against government pressure, suggesting that taking a visibly independent stance may garner more support from the community it serves, even in a context where many Muslim public spaces are seen as conspiratorial. She also points out that highlighting religious identity might be appealing to British Muslims precisely because it is sanctioned in law through entitlements for religious groups over matters such as places of worship and state-supported schools.[12] Such a positive pragmatic view might, however, be offset by concern about the degree to which cynicism and manipulation have come to characterize the government's dealings with its chief representative body. And to say this is not to be naïve in the face of the inevitable machinations of politics; a key feature of New Labour administrations after 1997 was their keenness to bring on board those who shared a particular consensual attitude to their priorities and to cast into the outer darkness those who did not. As Jonathan Birt puts it: "Having groomed and promoted a unified Muslim lobby for nearly a decade, the British government depicted it as part of the problem when it proved insufficiently compliant."[13]

## A Tale of Two Letters

We might profitably muse further on this preoccupation with establishing the consent of selected Muslims and what it says about the government's attitude to managing the communities that are seen to diverge from the given norm. It is not just a case of control freakery but rather an evolved top-down strategy that is authoritarian in its very impulses. It also mirrors similar strategies in other Western countries' dealings with their Muslim residents. Olivier Roy writes of how, in the United States, the Council on American-Islamic Relations is regularly castigated by anti-Islamic activists such as Daniel Pipes while at the same time being charged with placing too much emphasis on loyalty to America by some young Muslim radicals. Extrapolating from the cases of Europe and the United States, Roy describes how a "bureaucratic state logic" requires the existence of Muslim elite institutions that are inevitably at a distance from the rank and file they purport to represent: "most Western governments are usually eager to find a corporate body as interlocutor. In this sense, there is a policy of 'communitarian-ization from above,' implemented by non-Muslim states, in parallel with the quest by Muslim organizations to be recognized as legitimate partners . . . while using any such legitimacy bestowed upon them to rally a constituency around them."[14]

We have seen what happens when this strategy springs a leak. However, there is still a felt need to bring Muslims on board in some way, even if the vessel is listing. Thus, other elements are cultivated and promoted as necessity dictates. However, these often prove just as un-predictable as the officially designated partners. What happens then—when the limits of a very restrictive and one-way conversation are reached—clearly illustrates the monoglot diversity we mentioned ear-lier. Two comparable examples offer themselves, in what we might call "The Case of the Muslim Letters."

With the MCB temporarily refusing to play its expected role at the time of the Afghanistan invasion in 2001, the British government felt the need to find other authentic Muslim mediators for its views. So it came about that a number of high-profile Muslim members of Parliament were summoned by the prime minister and ordered to sign a statement supporting military action. Most of the signatories subse-quently disowned the statement, citing coercion and spin, and a num-ber of Muslim local councilors were then pressured to indicate their assent to the invasion instead. In any case, it was clear that the govern-ment was of the opinion that the intervention of a few of its own sup-posedly tame Muslim politicians would have a mitigating effect on the protests they were expecting from the broader Muslim population.[15] All this took place in an atmosphere of suspicion and recrimination that even reached as far as the House of Lords, when Lord Ahmed claimed that his telephone had been bugged and that he was being fol-lowed on government orders owing to his opposition to the invasion.[16] If things calmed down a little in the following years, the tactic of seek-ing acquiescent figures with the required cultural background has re-mained constant.

The second "Muslim Letter" came in August 2006, when a number of high-profile British Muslims, including Members of Parliament be-longing to Tony Blair's own Labour Party, took it upon themselves to write an open letter to the British government arguing that foreign policy in the Middle East and Britain's support for the "War on Terror" was fuelling fundamentalism and extremism. Crucially, this initiative was taken independent of the government and bypassed its usual internal channels for airing and resolving disagreements. Nevertheless, it still began with the premise that the signatories' cultural authenticity gave added weight to their opinion. The letter is worth quoting in its entirety:

> Prime Minister,
>     As British Muslims we urge you to do more to fight against all those who target civilians with violence, whenever and wherever that happens.
>     It is our view that current British government policy risks putting civilians at increased risk both in the United Kingdom and abroad. To combat terror the government has focused extensively on domestic legislation. While some of this will have an impact, the government must not ignore the role of its foreign policy. The debacle of Iraq and now the failure to do more to secure an immediate end to the attacks on civilians in the Middle East not only increases the risk to ordinary people in that region, it is also ammunition to extremists who threaten us all.
>     Attacking civilians is never justified. This message is a global one. We urge the Prime Minister to redouble his efforts to tackle terror and extremism and change our foreign policy to show the world that we value the lives of civilians wherever they live and whatever their religion.
>     Such a move would make us all safer.[17]

It is difficult to overstate the hostility this letter provoked in government circles and beyond. It was immediately pounced on as an error of judgment by the Home Secretary, John Reid, and his colleague Kim Howells, as no government could allow its foreign policy to be directed by terrorism.[18] Bloggers and right-wing columnists used the letter as evidence that moderate and extreme Muslims were, after all, brothers and sisters under the skin; what the extremists could not do through terror—change British foreign policy in the Middle East—

these supposedly respectable figures were seeking to do through legitimate, but ultimately seditious, argument. It appeared that the letter had backfired spectacularly on its authors.

We would argue, however, that the shortcomings of their approach relate to the representative status they were invoking and that they had for years been encouraged to assume. As such, the virulence of the reaction draws our attention to the ambivalence built into the tactics of official liberal multiculturalism with its appointed community spokespeople. Since these Muslims embodied the vaunted values of integration, reasoned argument, and democratic structures, they were taken as an illustration of the breadth and tolerance of a multicultural Britain where everyone, in a popular phrase from the early years of the Blair premiership, could be a "stakeholder." However, as the Muslim Letter Affair shows, these Muslims enjoyed this status on sufferance: any deviation from the accepted script meant that approval could be instantly withdrawn. The letter's signatories were here putting themselves forward as authoritative (authentic) spokespeople for Britain's Muslims, as the first line suggests. The effect of this opening was to draw attention to both "sides" of the hyphenated identity with which they had been branded by liberal multicultural political forms: both "British" and "Muslim." The inference was clearly *supposed* to be that the signatories personified the reconciliation of both identity positions—embodying, if you will, the fact that it was possible both to be a good Muslim and a good Briton at a time when some were suggesting those categories to be mutually exclusive. Yet the fact that the signatories did not seek to draw on representations from the wider body of dissenting public opinion—whose diversity was evident in the two-million-strong February 2003 anti–Iraq War march in London—but instead decided to put themselves forward as a kind of specifically Muslim pressure group effectively created an opportunity for the government to drive a wedge between them and other, non-Muslim citizens in order to make its evasive but wholly predictable riposte. In foregrounding their identities as Muslims, the signatories unwittingly created the conditions whereby elected officials could insidiously imply that this very "Muslimness" set them at odds with the wider community whose interests and security those officials were best placed to judge and uphold. Essentially, then, in terms of our frame, we are presented here with a peculiarly circular paradox whereby Muslim representatives were condemned for representing a body of opinion that the government did not wish to acknowledge as legitimate. In essence, they were representing incorrectly—or, in another sense, being *un*representative. The paradox was further underlined by the fact that many of the signatories had been promoted and courted by the government itself after it came to power in 1997 precisely for their supposed representativeness.

As Amir Saeed has put it, in his description of official intolerance for Muslim dissent: "British Muslims are repeatedly implored by voices in the media and by politicians of all sides to make more strenuous efforts to 'integrate' . . . and reassert their loyalty to the British state in a manner that no non-Muslim anti-war group would ever be instructed [to do]."[19] In short, the government effectively works to bind Muslims into the body of the multicultural nation but at the same time to preserve enough distance so that they can be scapegoated should the need arise. Muslims are, to that extent, seen as dispensable because they can be marginalized at any time as not really part of "us"; they are always required to perform and thereby prove their loyalty—either by statements distancing themselves from international conflicts where other Muslims are involved or, perhaps more frequently, by maintaining a tactical silence. Any statement of dissent that would be seen as a workaday expression of legitimate opinion by any other group of citizens immediately takes on the unsettling tinge of treachery when articulated by Muslims. Paul Gilroy has described this feature of the post-9/11 polity where, "authoritarian modes of belonging to the national collective supply the norm . . . anyone who objects to the conduct of their government is likely to be identified as an enemy within and bluntly advised to go and live elsewhere. . . . We are then reminded that the principle of duty must, above all, be a national one and that our dwindling rights cannot be separated from obligations that will be defined . . . by an ideal of patriotic citizenship."[20]

By way of a healthy contrast, we might suggest that not all interventions into politics from a Muslim position have been quite as naïve and gung-ho. Many Muslims became aware very early on that playing the game of standing aloof as a single, silent partner jolted into life every now and again at the behest of governmental needs was unlikely to lead to long-term goals being reached. When the planned invasion of Iraq was looming in 2003, many Muslims found themselves joining the Stop the War coalition, a nonparty, noncommunitarian alliance of groups and individuals united in many cases only by their opposition to the attack. This alliance was temporary, pluralist, and disparate but, as noted by Salma Yacoub, chair of the Birmingham Stop the War coalition, all the harder to discount for that reason: "If only the leftists had been here today, people would have said we're all lefties. If only CND had been here, they would have said it was the middle-class elite. If it was only the Muslims, they would have called us extremists. . . . Tony Blair, we are here united against this war. You cannot dismiss us all."[21] The potential for Muslims to break out of their allotted frame spaces— even while still pursuing a cause with specifically Muslim resonances— was explored at the time of the anti–Iraq War protests in a way that has not, perhaps, been followed up on since. Social justice issues may provide a space for a meeting of minds between Muslim and non-Muslim groups beyond the usual narrowly defined agendas of terrorism and integration. In any event, such coalitions represent a kind of temporary self-fashioning, in partnership with others, that refuses the terms laid out for Muslim political engagement, something that more centralized bodies such as the MCB seem to have difficulty envisioning. As Tariq Ramadan has put it: "If Muslims, in Britain and throughout the world, are to refuse to cast themselves as victims and instead . . . develop a critical political awareness, the process must begin by resisting political manoeuvres designed to lull them, to select their representatives for them, and even to make cynical use of them."[22]

The final twist in the tale and, perhaps, the unacknowledged vindication of the 2006 Muslim Letter, came three years later. It took the form of a swift retreat from the willfully blind official position of the Blair government and was orchestrated to coincide with "regime change" in the United States, as Obama took over the presidency from Bush in January 2009. As if to illustrate the continuing dependency of Britain's foreign policy on that of its bigger neighbor across the Atlantic, on

16 January the British foreign secretary, David Miliband, described the idea of a "War on Terror" as a "misleading and mistaken" doctrine, which incorrectly suggested an institutionally and ideologically unified enemy that could only be tackled militarily. More attractive now was the declared preference of the new U.S. Secretary of State, Hillary Clinton, for "smart power": "using all the levers of influence—diplomatic, economic, military, legal, political and cultural—to get what you want.[23] Less than two weeks later, the façade by which a connection between Britain's foreign policy and Muslim radicalization had been repeatedly denied also came crashing down. The counterterrorism minister, Lord West of Spithead, gifted with an earthy turn of phrase, criticized the preceding Blair administration's attitude: "we never used to accept that our foreign policy ever had any effect on terrorism. . . . Well, that was clearly bollocks."[24] However, as yet no apology has been forthcoming to the authors of the "Muslim Letter."

## The Authentic Fallacy

The fascination of politicians with securing the support of authentic Muslim representatives should give us pause at this point, since the same fascination is also characteristic of the media's dealings with minority matters. Both manifestations depend on an understanding of identity that demands a performance on the part of the viewed that will meet with recognition by the viewer. When that viewer is in authority, whether political or in terms of the power to represent in culture, the presence of supposedly authentic minority interlocutors is taken to give an inherent validity to the process. This is understandable; why should Muslims be always spoken about by others and never speak themselves? Yet, in practice, as we have already seen, the terms of their contributions are determined beforehand by the very same authorities.

Notions of authenticity, like modern conceptions of identity, in fact can be traced back to the Romantic era of the late eighteenth and early nineteenth centuries. Coinciding with ideas about the imagination, liberty and nationalism, and the revaluing of folk cultures, authenticity builds on both a strain of European post-Reformation individualism and a backlash against the mechanistic cosmology of scientific rationalism.

Nevertheless, the notion of authenticity took from the twin ideas of individualism and scientific progress the idea that if our understanding of the universe could be remade, then so, too, could our understanding of the self. Writing of authenticity, Charles Guignon describes the Romantic attempt to recover a sense of wholeness felt to have been lost with the rise of modernity, and to discover the basis of truth in one's own feelings, a quest pursued with particular vigor in the life and work of Rousseau. In *Emile,* with its rejection of socialization through formal education, and in the *Confessions,* Rousseau emphasized that the true self was to be found in feeling: "I truly *am* what I feel myself to be." However, this sense of self requires recognition by another for its validation; "it is not enough simply to be transparent to oneself. . . . There is the idea here that you can truly *be* such-and-such a person only if others see you as being that person. The look of the other is needed to confirm and stabilize one's identity."[25] This, then, leads to the urge to express oneself that is found compulsively played out in Rousseau's work and in that of the Romantic writers and artists who were inspired by him. However, as Guignon points out, in culture "every [self-] presentation is mediated by a mode of representation," thereby intruding on and distancing the ultimate goal of authenticity. This is resolved through a distinction being made between subjective truth (what I believe) and objective truth, provable by empirical or scientific means, and the Romantic preference for the former over the latter. As Guignon puts it, with this preference "we have moved from the realm of (historical) truth to that of *authenticity.*"[26]

So European Romanticism embraces in essence a record not of the facts of history but of the subject's *ongoing* search for the truth of the self. And this model of identity construction, which still exists today in the emphasis on individual freedom and the culture of self-help, runs up against the claims made by the politics of cultural identity. In short, identity politics freezes the Romantic quest for authenticity at a particular moment that is convenient for the political structures of the day. Moreover, since the raw materials of culture are drawn from an ongoing process of collective syncretism—composed of all the accommodations, crossovers, and compromises that are built through centuries of interaction with others—there is a degree of arbitrariness involved in selecting one or another feature of a particular culture as authentic. As Jean-Francois Bayart says: "Authenticity is not established by the immanent properties of the phenomenon under consideration. It results from the perspective, full of desires and judgements, that is brought to bear on the past, in the eminently contemporary context in which one is situated."[27] In supposedly reintroducing religion into what has supposedly been for three hundred years a secular Western political discourse, Muslim identity politics is sometimes seen as readmitting a kind of premodern polity—involving the ultimate authority of a God who has receded from the Western model—into a system where the nation-state is the final arbiter.

This historical perspective offers us a way of understanding the current fascination with authentic spokespersons for recognized (and bounded) identity positions. However, some such spokespeople have chafed at the limitations imposed on them by the requirement to take up "authentic representative" status. For example, the Conservative Party's own chair, Baroness Sayeeda Warsi, has suggested that the idea of representative figures for minority communities essentially contributes to their continued ghettoization. As a dutiful party politician, Warsi is perhaps too quick to denounce the representatives industry as a product of Labour's paternalistic attitude to minorities, conveniently forgetting the Conservatives' role in prompting the establishment of groups like the MCB. She says she hesitated before accepting an award from the Equality and Human Rights Commission as "Britain's Most Powerful Muslim Woman," suggesting that it ought to be taken for granted that Muslim women are powerful. She likewise recalls an encounter with the Labour minister Alan Johnson on the BBC's *Question Time* that threw into relief official attitudes to minorities: "He was asking what the 'leaders of the Muslim community' felt and I said the Muslim community do not have leaders. What is this? Are we some kind of freak nation that bows down to our leaders? And he said the Afro-Caribbean community have their leaders and so and so have their leaders and I thought, I couldn't sit in a cabinet of people who still think . . . that somehow there are these alien groups in our nation, each of them represented by a leader who talked to the government on their behalf. It's almost the kind of approach of 'we know what's best for you brown people.' I find that patronising. On *Question Time* I said where are the leaders of the white people and they all went: 'er, let's move on.' "[28]

It might be possible to dismiss Warsi's misgivings as the qualms of one who publicly deplores a system but who has personally benefited from it. Nevertheless, she raises certain valid points about the general practices employed in dealing with communities and the way white society in the West is taken as the norm and becomes the invisible part of the equation. On the one hand, such moves to find Muslim spokespeople and role models can be seen as part of a sort of uplift program, where Muslims can be encouraged to value and participate in social processes from which they are, rightly or wrongly, considered to be alienated. However, when these role models stand in for any serious attempts to consider the issues behind that alienation, they then come to serve as little more than a face-saving device or panacea, giving the illusion that Muslim concerns are being seriously addressed while allowing the normal course of ideology to flow freely as usual.

What the fascination with representativeness and authenticity has led to is a situation in which what one might almost call "professional Muslims" are touring the circuits of think tanks, select committees, and talk shows. Their input, based on personal experience and proximity to the phenomena in question, is a highly prized commodity in today's economies of power. So one has the spectacle of Irshad Manji, self-styled "refusenik" and Muslim voice of reason, making the rounds of television studios on both sides of the Atlantic and holding up every new controversy as evidence of the complicity of a mindless monolithic Muslim community that has been cowed by rampant Saudi-inspired extremism. In Britain, Ed Husain, a former Islamist with Hizb ut-Tahrir, having recanted, now helps the government with its antiradicalization policies. He has set up the Quilliam Foundation to further these aims, and it receives copious funds and a privileged seat in consultations. On the other side of the question, we can see Moazzam Begg, a former inmate at Camp Delta, becoming the poster boy of the anti-Guantanamo human rights lobby, regardless of his own rather narrow past views on the applicability of those rights. In each case, the frame that surrounds Muslims and Muslim issues can comfortably accommodate them and the immediately placeable viewpoints they offer.

## Framing Muslims in Radio Journalism

The same urge to utilize representative Muslim figures is also to be found in the world of journalism. Indeed, a marked difference of tenor and approach is evident between programs made with Muslim presenters and key participants and programs anchored by non-Muslim journalists. To an extent, then, an idea of essential cultural difference is inscribed in the very form such programs take.

Since 9/11, Muslims in the West have been repeatedly exposed to questions from various quarters about their supposed conflicting allegiances: first to the secular law of the nation-states in which they are resident, and second to "international" Islamic or sharia law. This antagonistic opposition between the secular and the religious can be historically traced back to twentieth-century anticolonial resistance movements, for example, those led by Syed Abul A'ala Maududi in India and Hasan al-Banna in Egypt, who formulated a reformist return to a pure and original Islamic faith in direct response to strategies of imperial control. Yet media coverage on Muslims tends to ignore this longer history and to frame all debates within an ahistoric binary of the "clash of civilizations." That the frame can operate to circumscribe even ostensibly sympathetic media vehicles is further evidenced by a number of recent BBC radio programs that have sought to explain certain Muslim social practices to a presumed non-Muslim audience. Even in such programs, ambivalence over the normalization and delimiting of areas of social custom were in evidence. We will argue that this frame of representation can be seen at work in a series of programs on the BBC's principal current affairs station, Radio 4, with titles such as "Inside the Harem" (2004), "Koran and Country" (2005), and "Taking the Cricket Test" (2006).

This idea of a "clash of civilizations" is often articulated in media practices as well as in their agendas. According to Elizabeth Poole, "there is always a mediating effect whereby an event is filtered through interpretive frameworks and acquires ideological significance. News, then, provides its audiences with interpretive frameworks, ways of seeing the world and defining reality."[29] In the news media this is done in two ways: first, direct news reporting, and second, indirect reportage through special issue-led programs that include a mix of styles, blending biography, travel, interviews, autobiography, and dialogue. Television relies on pictures to tell the story, and viewing audiences can expect to see some condensation of the subject matter on their screens: the reporter covering the item, the location, and so on. Radio programs, though, focus on reported speech, sound effects, and a descriptive narrative style to communicate the substance of the news story to a listening audience. As Starkey and Crisell have noted, "[radio's] words are constantly dissolving or evanescent: but unlike television's, they are wholly invisible, as are the people who utter them."[30] This quality of invisibility in radio can help us to see the constitutive practices by which liberal multiculturalism positions its authentic spokespersons within the frame described above, thereby actually reinforcing it.

As a public broadcaster, the BBC enjoys trust both nationally and internationally for its comparatively fair and impartial news reporting. However, its employment practices have at times been seen to lag behind changes in an increasingly diverse population. In 2001 the then BBC director-general, Greg Dyke, described the corporation as "hideously white," with a 98 percent white management structure.[31] He mobilized efforts within the organization toward improving ethnic diversity. The outcome of this change was the appointment in 2004 of Andrea Callendar as the BBC's head of diversity, and in 2006 Mary Fitzpatrick was hired to fill in the newly created position of editorial manager of cultural diversity. One of the principles of the BBC's diversity strategy is to address the concern of ethnic minority representation in both its programs' content and its designation of who gets to make them. However, the strategy appears to be having little effect in the way stories are flagged as "ethnic minority" issues and how such stories are represented. One such example was the widely reported case of Molly/Misbah, a twelve-year-old girl from Scotland who went to Pakistan to live with her father. In the first instance, the story was reported as one of "forced marriage," in which a domestic estrangement was inflated to become symbolic of national and cultural differences; it was assumed that Molly/Misbah had been lured away by unscrupulous relatives in Pakistan. Only later did it emerge that the girl had chosen to go to Pakistan of her own free will. The controller of *BBC News 24*, Kevin Bakhurst, admitted that assumptions had been made without appropriate facts being researched: "I think we now feel that we probably didn't show enough sophistication in covering the story on the first day. We accepted on face value the words of the girl's mother and her grandmother. I don't think in hindsight we should necessarily have accepted this so readily and we should have tried to find out more about the father as the day went on."[32]

It is against this background of rolling news, sound bites, and cultural anxieties that we need to examine specific aspects of representation in the programs "Koran and Country" and "Taking the Cricket Test," aired on Radio 4 in 2005 and 2006. At the outset, these titles reflect stereotypes of the Muslim community and qualities that are taken to set them apart from the secular nation.

"Taking the Cricket Test" is a two-part documentary: the first part focuses on the Pakistan team's tour of England in the summer of 2006 and the second part on the Manningham Mills Cricket Club in Bradford. The presenter, Sarfraz Manzoor, a well-known British-Pakistani broadcaster, commentator, and writer takes the listener on an almost ethnographic journey. His documentary has two key themes, cricket and the ethnoreligious identity of British Pakistanis. What holds the two programs together is the shadow of the 7/7 London suicide bombings of 2005. However, what makes the treatment interesting is the self-consciousness of the narrator, who at the start of the series makes known his desire to explore the accuracy of the media portrayal of young British Muslims as disaffected and disloyal to the nation. He also wants to find out what has been done since the 7/7 terror attacks to root out extremism among the young.

From the start, Manzoor confirms that in making these programs he is revisiting the Conservative MP Norman Tebbit's notorious "cricket test" from 1990. Tebbit suggested that the majority of Britain's Asian population would, if quizzed, support the cricket team from their country of origin over that of England, thereby failing what became known as the cricket test—a somewhat crude and arbitrary benchmark of integration. Manzoor finds himself looking into the reasons why sixteen years later, British Pakistanis are still being challenged over the loyalty question. In the first program he follows the Pakistani team as they visit London, Manchester, and Leeds, and on these journeys he speaks to a selection of people both inside and outside the cricket grounds to ascertain where their loyalties lie. Alongside the Tebbit test Manzoor also explores the current issue of radicalization of Muslim youth in Yorkshire and Lancashire. Other than a tenuous link confirming an eye-witness account of one of the 7/7 bombers from Beeston playing cricket the day before the bombing in their local ground, there is little else in this program that overtly links cricket with terror. Instead, what this tenuous link does quite effectively is to provide a frame for part 2 of the documentary, which focuses entirely on the predominantly Muslim team of Manningham Mills Cricket Club. As a journalist with a Muslim background, Manzoor "guarantees" a true representation for his radio listeners. Yet the key insight that emerges from part 2 is that Muslim players don't tend to congregate at the cricket club bar for a drink after play and often go straight home to their families. This is not a "normal" way for cricketers to behave and is also seen to have a negative effect on the club's finances, thus reiterating for an all-Muslim cricket club a difference based on religious identity. So when Manzoor ends the program with the question that he says is being asked of British Pakistanis today—"Which team do you want to play for?"—the answer has to some extent already been framed for them as an either/or choice between national affiliation or their own supposed religious beliefs and practices.

Another series, "Koran and Country," directly invokes stereotypes of Muslim identity in the titles of its four programs: "How Islam Got Political," "Biography of a Bomber," "Radio Ramadan," and "Inside a Muslim School." The first program, presented by Frank Gardner, the BBC's security correspondent, is a historical account of nineteenth- and twentieth-century political movements within Islam. It ends with a focus on the rise of Islamist movements. The issue that gives the program its title, "How Islam Got Political," backhandedly conjures up the long-standing Western—and in particular British—assumption of the separation of religion and state. The story of political Islam is, therefore, already read as involving some sort of leak or contamination that has occurred between private and public spheres that in Britain are presumed to have been sealed off from one another for the last three hundred years or so. Going further, Frank Gardner explains to his audience that "political Islam has two interconnected aims—they're both about reviving Muslim identity. For its adherents in Muslim countries, this can mean creating perfect Islamic states. Where Muslims live as minorities, such as in Britain, political Islam is more about solidarity with the Ummah, the global Muslim community."[33]

The program is mainly focused on the effects of this history as seen in the radicalization of young Muslims in Britain. British Muslim identity is placed within the history of migration from South Asia in the 1950s and 1960s. The program is keen to explore the shift from this originally devout seen-but-not-heard community to the current "problem" generation. What is not mentioned is the difficulty faced by different communities with regard to assimilation, alienation, and identification as minority ethnic groups in a majority white culture. Instead we have a textbook rendition of the start of the problem dating back to the admiration among British Muslims for the 1979 Islamic revolution in Iran followed by the fatwa issued against Rushdie by Ayatollah Khomeini at the behest of Kaleem Siddiqi, a British Muslim visitor to Iran at the time. The Rushdie affair is described as the "midwife of the current situation." From there the program is able to pick up the issue of antisecularism, the influential persona of Maududi, and the connecting link to the Muslim Brotherhood in Egypt.

The ostensibly more upbeat "Radio Ramadan" explains the phenomenon of temporary Muslim radio stations that are given air space for thirty days at a time by Ofcom, Britain's communications regulator.[34] These licenses are part of the Restricted Service License scheme under which a portion of the nation's broadcasting licenses are allocated to religious broadcasters. One of the key questions asked by the non-Muslim presenter of the program, Mark Whitaker, is how Ofcom regulates the Radio Ramadan stations and whether its "slimline" approach when granting licenses to mosques is encouraging certain groups to separate themselves from identification with British citizenship. For example, questions are asked about the playing of songs supporting the Palestinian struggle and the particular branch of Islam promoted through the broadcasts (Wahabism always being a more suspect and politicized branch than Sufism). Radio Ramadan emerges as an important keyhole through which wider society (including possibly the government) can look to discover what is going on in the Muslim community, an idea that, the program suggests, has as much application to national security agendas as to multicultural neighborliness.

Such implicit security concerns tend to characterize the documentaries in which non-Muslim journalists are at the helm. By comparison there is always the unspoken expectation that Muslim journalists will explain culturally specific practices and speak "on behalf" of the communities. This is emblematic of a fascination in the liberal media with the idea of the "authentic" cultural spokesperson. Whether in overseas correspondence—where in recent years the BBC has actively sought to recruit journalists with an ethnicity similar to that of those they are to report on—or, as here, in documentary reportage, there is an inherent belief that cultural insiders guarantee closer proximity to the truth. On the one hand, such an investment in authenticity is prompted by a benevolent desire to open the space of broadcasting to those outside its traditional ruling caste of white middle-class males. And no one would deny that a greater subtlety in interpretation *may* come from an intimate knowledge of customs and practices. However, at the same time, where the "Muslim issues" we have identified here are concerned, there is a tendency to use such spokespeople as native informants, as it were, reporting knowledge to "us" that will be of use to "our" white Western civil society in confronting a problem posed by the Muslim Other.[35] Such a mindset can be seen as a watered-down version of what Gayatri Spivak has identified as a modern trend on the "radical fringe" toward "uncritical enthusiasm for the Third World, [which] makes a demand upon the inhabitant of that Third World to speak up as an authentic ethnic fully representative of his or her tradition. [Yet] this demand ignores an open secret: that an ethnicity untroubled by the vicissitudes of history and neatly accessible as an object of investigation is a confection."[36] How much more pertinent is this observation in the case of avowedly hybrid subjects often born, raised, and receiving their journalistic training in Britain? Why might a Muslim reporter be expected to have a greater empathy with, for example, alienated youth? Why might he be thought to have a better understanding of the motives for terrorism? Why should she be presumed to have access to useful firsthand knowledge about polygamy or forced marriages? For the purposes of broadcasting on "Muslim issues," presenters such as those mentioned here are forced to don the mantle of expert on this or that alien practice, solely on the basis of background. It is an invidious position that results from the pigeonholing of highly versatile journalists whose fate it often is to be called on simply as commentators on what is presented as the running sore of Muslims and their "failure to integrate."

"Biography of a Bomber" is also illustrative of this situation. This program is presented by a female Muslim journalist, Nasreen Suleaman, who is positioned as a "good Muslim" foil to a "bad Muslim" bomber, Mohammad Siddique Khan, the leader of the 7/7 plotters.[37] Both Khan and Suleaman were born in Yorkshire to immigrant Pakistani parents, but other than that they have little in common. Khan is described as having been "the most English of Pakistanis" who turned out to be a "radical Islamist" terrorist, while Suleaman, by inference, serves as an example of a positive integrated Muslim. In fact Khan's lack of religious education as a child is commented on as "untypical of those times," unlike Suleaman's experience, which involved going to a local mosque to learn the Koran by rote. Another untypical characteristic of Khan is that he "never took sides" in the racial tensions that often flared up at his high school. Apparently the "slightest thing could spark off a race riot and the Uncles would join in," but Khan would stay out of it. He was also very fond of America, having visited it while he was at school, but was allegedly unable to get a visa later. Khan's return to Islam is presented as having taken place after he married his girlfriend from university, who as a Gujarati was seen to be higher up the social scale among the South Asian immigrant population. After tracing these rather involved personal patterns in Khan's life, Suleaman ends the program with the rather banal observation that "some videos, a group of like-minded friends and [a] spare front room in someone else's house was all it took." In the end we have learned little more about Mohammed

Siddique Khan than we have about Nasreen Suleaman, as the contrasts drawn between their divergent paths have conveyed little meaning beyond the impression that they embody the only two options for Muslims in British society today.

"Inside a Muslim School" is another example.[38] This program begins with an observation by the chief inspector of schools that teaching in independent Muslim faith schools is often too narrowly focused and does not equip children to live in modern Britain. This diagnosis sits uncomfortably with the Prime Minister's stated desire, after 7/7, to bring Muslim faith schools into the state sector. Jenny Cuffe, the presenter, in her case study of Al-Islah Muslim School in Blackburn, a privately run institution with approximately two hundred students, offers her listeners an opportunity to judge whether Muslim values can coexist with national affiliations. Al-Islah School comes across as an austere place, providing education to the daughters of local mill workers, laborers, and taxi drivers. Cuffe's interviews with the pupils and teachers in the school underline the importance of Islamic principles to the ethos of the school. She probes away to discover whether the school curriculum provides instruction on controversial subjects, quizzing the teachers on whether their students are allowed to develop an analytical and questioning stance. Cuffe draws on another criticism by the chief inspector: that Muslim schools fail to teach their pupils about the importance of being British citizens. The repeated reference to the chief inspector's critical comments bookends and thus shapes the documentary. It presumes that the listener's interest is likely to have been stimulated by existing popular media concerns about Muslim integration (or the lack of it). At the same time, as the title suggests, to carry out this act of penetration means also breaking through the supposed secrecy surrounding Muslim faith schools. (Cuffe makes much of the fact that Al-Islah was the only school that agreed to participate in the program, although, given the general tenor and preoccupations of such programs it is perhaps hardly surprising.)

The slightly sensationalist sense of entering forbidden territory is heightened by the suggestion that Cuffe has gained what the publicity material described as "exclusive access" to the school. Furthermore, the use of the word "inside" in this program, as in "Inside the Harem," suggests a secret space or enclave into which we are receiving an insight. These spaces are not on the postcolonial margin but inside "our nation." They are spaces "in our midst" that we know nothing about. The task of the non-Muslim journalist is, then, an anthropological one—to open up these spaces and make them known. Such Muslim spaces are resolutely nonhybrid, since the groups that inhabit them are not depicted as being interested in mixing, but instead as sealing themselves off from other cultural influences. Therefore, responses to questions of general relevance to faith schools, about their teachings about evolution or homosexuality for example, become doubly loaded when raised in relation to Muslim schools, as they are seen as the thin end of a global political wedge, namely "radical Islam" or "Islamism."

This program has similarities with "Inside the Harem," broadcast in October 2004 and presented by Shagufta Yaqub, a former editor of the British Muslim magazine Q News, and currently publications coordinator for the Birmingham charity Islamic Relief.[39] As a young Muslim woman, she speaks on behalf of her community. However, unlike Sarfraz Manzoor—who demonstrates an acute self-consciousness in his various appearances across all forms of media, recognizing that he is being positioned as an authentic spokesperson and working that knowledge ironically into his commentary—Shagufta Yaqub uses a presentational style that makes her appear oblivious to the broader media landscape in which she is situated.[40] Her role appears simply to be a reflector of a problematic Islamic phenomenon. To some extent she replicates the popular media stereotype of Pakistani Muslim women as traditional and submissive, despite her obvious professional achievements. Her self-presentation remains linked to her religion, defining her identity; in the publicity materials for the program her own hijab is much in evidence. Her understanding of religion is mediated through the Koran, Muslim male scholars, her ethnic connection to Pakistan, and her identity as a British Muslim subject. In the program—which was broadcast in two rather schematic parts, "Polygamy: The Positives" and "Polygamy: The Negatives"—Yaqub is positioned as undertaking the task of going "inside the harem" to normalize the phenomenon of Islamic polygamy for a secular society. In the first program she begins in a confessional mode, telling the listener: "polygamy is something I'd never really thought about until one day I got a phone call from a woman looking for a second wife for her husband." A few sentences later she tells us that she had to consider polygamy in a personal context when she got married in 2002 and was considering what to include in her marriage contract. She says, "I insisted on the right to continue my education and the right to initiate a divorce, but the question of polygamy was more difficult to resolve. . . . In the end I decided to leave the possibility open. If God has allowed polygamy, I thought who am I to challenge it?"

She then goes on to narrate her journey "inside the harem" in personal terms—a narrative performance that highlights the dichotomy between secular British law and religious Islamic law. As an "authentic" Muslim representative in a British context, she has the task of telling the stories of British Muslims who practice polygamous relationships in Britain, where it is illegal. At the same time, as a British Pakistani she can vouch for the Pakistani context where polygamy is legal under sharia law. The longer political history in Pakistan connected to this issue is not touched on in the program.[41] Instead, Yaqub's contemporary focus finds examples of positive polygamous relationships in Britain and Pakistan as well as spokesmen and women who speak for and against the practice. Mostly these commentators' emphasis is on men's sexual and social needs, whereas her interviews with couples project a positive female experience. She says toward the end of part 1 "whatever it is that motivates men to take more than one wife, it's clear that some women—of their own free will—choose to live in a polygamous setup. . . . Maybe it's time to accept polygamy as a lifestyle choice that some women happily make." In using the phrase "lifestyle choice" Yaqub seems to be placing polygamy in the same free market discourse as women's lifestyle magazines, which can be equally problematic in their close connections to patriarchal ideologies, purporting to give women freedom through the notion of choice while embedding them in stereotyped norms of sexuality. She does not, then, appear to appreciate the irony inherent in the program's title. Her apparent naïveté is verbalized when she confesses to her listeners toward the end of part 2: "I've learnt that far from the Orientalist's overromanticised fantasy of the harem, the reality of polygamy is quite mundane." However, having expressed her reservations on the practice of polygamy, she ends the program somewhat contradictorily by saying, "I still believe my husband has the right, in principle, to take another wife. I wouldn't want to take that right away from him because I know he would never knowingly mistreat me."

In upholding a literal interpretation of her Islamic contract of marriage Yaqub is unlikely to ruffle any feathers. Instead, her program serves to highlight the tensions between civil and sharia laws on the issue of marriage and polygamy and is a reminder of the often-repeated notion of the clash between the secular state and religious law. However, it is unclear to what extent Yaqub recognizes this central contradiction. Certainly in the documentary it takes second place to a personal narrative infused by a religious sense of duty. It also highlights her gendered position, which has to negotiate between religion, duty, and nation. The detached, slightly passive quality of her narration echoes that of the other female presenter discussed in this chapter, Nasreen Suleaman, and the unheard voices of the girls in the Muslim school. Perhaps this is because as Muslim women they are more closely identified symbolically with Islamic observance and traditional values? Unlike Manzoor, the female presenters are doubly burdened by their gender difference and seem, in these programs, unable to project a confidently critical self-consciousness that challenges stereotypical perceptions of Muslim women. Their femaleness, which guarantees their "authenticity," also guarantees their passivity as objects of patriarchal discourse.

What all these programs and others like them have in common— even those fronted by supposedly authentic Muslim voices—is the reiteration of the narrow range of issues that serve to frame all debates around Muslims in Britain. Indeed, to some extent, the representative Muslim journalists are caught in a double bind, having the task of both explaining Muslim practices to a presumed non-Muslim audience and embodying the values of fairness and balance that are taken to be indicative of successful integration. Some, like Manzoor, are able to sidestep this framing through a self-conscious narrativization, but others, like Yaqub, remain trapped in a comparatively naïve gendered expression of self that perpetuates stereotypes of Muslim womanhood. The overall problem that needs greater consideration by broadcasters is that specialist programs commissioned on Muslim topics often rely on the broader "Othering" of Muslims in the media for their sense of newsworthiness instead of developing meaningful historical connections and recognizing the links between gender, race, ethnicity, and religion: something that might be genuinely informative for a mainstream audience.

Thus, a certain set of assumptions about cultural identity and authenticity informs representative practices, both in the realm of politics and in those organs charged with the task of scrutinizing the "clash of civilizations" thesis that also takes hermetically sealed cultural difference as its core assumption. It is, therefore, no wonder that the debate often seems to be going around in circles. In terms of assumptions about inclusive practices, there is a sense in which the media not only carry the message of essentialized cultural difference, they enshrine it in the very means by which such matters are covered.

## The Illusions of Cultural Identity

An assumption that is sewn into authenticist ways of seeing is that cultural and political identities have some natural correlation. This view tends to devalue or even overlook the fact that identity is a historical construct, drawing on different raw materials at different times. For the same good historical reasons, we can see the phenomenon of Islamophobia, which has risen to an almost hysterical pitch in some quarters, as positing an essentialist (and therefore false) connection between culture and political action. This way of looking—of which the "clash of civilization" thesis is only the most prominent instance—ignores inconvenient truths such as the way identity is a *product* of conflict and contradiction, rather than being endangered by it. The politicization of identity positions relies on what Bayart has described as the belief "that a 'culture' is composed of a stable, closed corpus of representations, beliefs or symbols that is supposed to have an 'affinity' . . . with specific opinions and attitudes, or modes of behavior." This view does not allow for the ways "social actors produce their history in a conflictual manner, by defining themselves both in relation to their perception of the past *and* in relation to their perception of the future."[42]

As a result, the attempt to manufacture homogeneous political voices for communities is an artificial enterprise.

And what is true of Islamophobia must also be true of the purist Islamist positions that form the other side of the dialogue. Bayart points to the schismatic interpretations of the founding lessons of the martyrs Hassan and Hussein for Shi'ism: doctrinal disputes over the true meaning of "jihad" and "sharia"; and the "elective affinities" that characterize political Islam as they do all political identity formations. "The multiplicity of meanings of the political language of Islam governs its indefiniteness. It authorizes detours, shifts, correspondences, transitions and possibilities that culturalist assumptions ignore."[43] Islam's debts to Judaism, Christianity, and Zoroastrianism and the influences Islam has absorbed from Arabia, Turkey, and Persia are simply written out of purist accounts. Even so, they find their way in through tactical borrowings and in the very fact that the self-fashioning of "Western civilization" is thrown back as an insult in Islamist rhetoric.

The argument against identity as an organizing principle for politics is summed up when Bayart says: "there is no such thing as identity, only operational acts of identification. The identities we talk about so pompously, as if they existed independently of those who express them, are made (and unmade) only through the mediation of identificatory acts, in short, by their enunciation."[44] If this is strong fare for those more familiar with a diet in which the strategic successes of identity politics—in the United States, for example—are usually taken to point to its liberatory potential, it might nonetheless have some relevance for a situation in which religion becomes the vaunted identity marker.

In his book *Identity and Violence,* the Nobel laureate Amartya Sen has argued against the way British multiculturalism has, for him, evolved into a "plural monoculturalism," with discrete minority identities left to regulate themselves in the name of respect for cultural difference, with sometimes reactionary results. More damaging, he argues, is the tendency to elevate religious faith into the key marker of identity through which traditional differences are acknowledged and by means of which their relation to majority norms is negotiated. Need a person's identity be most authentically manifested through the culture of his or her family, or through the religion into which he or she was born?

Moreover, the privileging of religious faith is historically amnesiac since it forgets the reasons why some immigrants arrived in Britain in the first place. (For example, a large number of Bangladeshis arrived in Britain at the start of the 1970s in flight from their coreligionists as East Pakistan seceded from West Pakistan and declared independence.) Sen further warns of the danger of inviting people to participate in politics on the basis of religious ethnicities since it can lead to factionalism. As in the case of faith schools—seen as harmless when run by some religions and, as we have seen, as suspicious when set up by others—such a mode of address runs the risk of a "confusion between multiculturalism with cultural liberty, on the one side, and plural monoculturalism with faith-based separatism on the other." Sen concludes: "A nation can hardly be seen as a collection of sequestered segments, with citizens being assigned fixed places in predetermined segments. Nor can Britain be seen, explicitly or by implication, as an imagined national federation of religious ethnicities."[45]

## Multiculturalism or Multifaithism?

In a damning indictment of the left's failure to maintain its commitment to radical secular universalism, Kenan Malik pinpoints one way of understanding the rise of faith-oriented multiculturalism in Britain since the late 1980s. He distinguishes between an "old left" based on class solidarity and what he calls the "new left" that draws on the affiliations developed by third world liberation movements, feminist groups, and gay rights campaigns. In place of class, "culture" and "cultural identity" became the new watchwords of 1980s oppositional politics. Malik accounts for the rise of this new left culturism by making a connection to the struggle for black rights in the United States. What was now to be accentuated was the right to difference rather than the right to equality.[46]

Malik's account has a good deal to recommend it, not least the persuasive power of firsthand experience. However, we would argue that it is also crucial to acknowledge important differences between U.S. and British variants of identity-based politics, even if the former heavily influenced the latter. In the United States, the once-hyphenated identities—for example African-American, Irish-American, Italian-American, even Arab-American—have become cemented into the political process in the form of vote banks and lobby groups with power, prestige, and money. In Britain these vehicles of power for the most part do not exist. What one has, instead, in the rise to prominence of religious identities in the political arena is the sense of successive governments chasing rather desperately after modes of group organization and identification that always seem to be one step ahead, disappearing around the next corner before governmental representative structures can catch up. The crucial shift since the mid-1990s has been that government has stopped running after identity groups and now considers itself the arbiter of authentic representative groups, a move that depends on the lure of the largesse, in the form of grants and access to decision-making processes, that is in its gift and that it holds out to those bodies it believes it can use. (We may, of course, already be seeing the breakdown of this strategy too, as politicians attempt to bypass the rather troublesome Muslim representative groups they have been party to setting up, in favor of disarming—in both senses—appeals to local bodies and individuals.)

Veteran antiracists such as Malik and Pragna Patel from Southall Black Sisters may well have a point when they lament what Patel has termed the move away from antiracism to "multifaithism."[47] Yet they and others risk romanticizing the history of the antiracism struggle if they retrospectively downplay the fact that it also drew on identity politics and authenticity in its appeals. Malik laments the slide away from universalism: "every group . . . [in the new social movements of multiculturalism] had a specific culture, rooted in its history and experiences. That culture gave shape to an individual's identity. For an individual to be authentic, collective identity must be too."[48] This is a piercing insight as far as it goes, but he appears to see the shift from antiracism to multiculturalism as some enormous con in which old solidarities were sundered and radical energies sapped and dissipated. He becomes rather nostalgic about a time when Asian antiracism activists did not see themselves in cultural or religious terms, "preferring to call themselves 'black' which they viewed as an all-inclusive term for non-white immigrants":[49] a version that clashes with Tariq Modood's account of the discomfort such required conformity caused many Asians at the time. A stronger argument would surely be that the sundering of a politics of recognition from that of redistribution does the work of its enemies by normalizing hegemonic values and reintroducing, in the form of identity groups, the Hobbesian law of each against each and the scramble to gain government favor and resources without challenging the status quo.

Yet what critics of identity politics mainly object to is, in the end, the intrusion of religion into what was a secular antiracism landscape based on recognizable class-oriented struggles, albeit with the cultural tinge brought in by its immigrant participants. They seldom acknowledge the centrality of identity politics, in its broadest sense, to the very same struggles. In glossing over this link they miss the problems inherent in the idea of identity politics itself. Cultural identity, and the representational industry it has spawned, is flawed by its invariable insistence on authenticity. All that has happened is that the grounds for judging authenticity have shifted from those of race to those of religion. The affiliations required by identity politics are built on the shifting sands of political expediency and collective fashions. At present, the fashion is for religious cultural identities because the framing narratives of our age articulate their key concerns—both the fight against perceived international injustices and the fight against terrorism—in these terms. The consolation for old-school antiracism activists may be that when cultural identities are taken to be so expedient and malleable, they are also temporary. If one doesn't like the "authentic" choices that are available now, one can be certain that another set will be on offer in a year or two that may prove more to one's taste. Thus, cultural identities tend less to be truly organic expressions of belonging or affiliation than marriages of convenience encouraged by the political structures of the time. As such they unfortunately offer rather weak grounds for the permanent empowerment of citizens.

In conclusion, it may seem counterintuitive to support multiculturalism while expressing skepticism about the value of cultural identity. However, this need not be the case when one considers multiculturalism as the logic of practices and cultural identity as a rather clumsy graft through which matters of political representation can be addressed.

Among the criticisms made of bodies such as the MCB is that they are "self-proclaimed representatives." In fact, their representativeness is most loudly proclaimed by the government officials who see them as providing evidence of the government's own accountability, inclusiveness, and good faith. The truth—as we have seen in the case of the MCB—is often rather different. Yet this is inevitable where there is a gap between rhetoric and reality: where a nod toward the principle of group empowerment merely obscures the main concern, which turns out to be the preservation of tight governmental control on what can be said and by whom. When the two meanings of representation—political and cultural—merge, there is always some straining to fit diverse individuals and groups into a rather unshapely political garment. There is always a gap between people as they are and people as identity politics would wish them to be: always an element of self-stereotyping involved in answering the call to authenticity. In the structures of representation available in Britain today Muslims are invited, cajoled, persuaded, and browbeaten into inserting themselves in a very limiting political frame, and only rewarded if they stay there and don't rock the boat.

CHAPTER 4

# Muslims in a Media Ghetto

The Anthropological Impulse in
Realist Film and Docudrama

In the murky world of "homeland security," life sometimes imitates art. Or, more accurately, one might say that the line between life and art appears to have blurred since 9/11 and 7/7 for those policing borders, airports, and other national entry points. An instance of this confusion occurred in February 2006 when four actors who had starred in Peter Winterbottom's film *The Road to Guantanamo* were detained and questioned at Luton airport, on their return from a Berlin film festival. Rizwan Ahmed and Farhad Harun found themselves in a position frighteningly similar to that of the characters in their recent retelling of the story of three Birmingham men who went to Pakistan to organize a wedding but instead ended up spending two years at Camp Delta, Guantanamo Bay.[1] The matter was cleared up quickly, if not satisfactorily. Yet the proximity between the stereotypes of the threatening outsider seen in film and television representations and those peddled in other areas of public discourse—and acted on by security enforcement officers—suggests we might do well to consider the power of those particular nightmares to inform social relations at a deeper level than that of mere entertainment.

This chapter and the one that follows trace the recent proliferation of television dramas depicting Muslims in situations involving terrorist activity. From popular action series such as *24*, *Sleeper Cell*, and *Spooks* (shown on BBC America as *MI5*) to docudramas like *Dirty War* and *The Hamburg Cell*, and gritty realist films such as *Yasmin* and *White Girl*, these productions, whatever their ostensible sympathies, have been involved in the process of reinforcing a sense of national solidarity in the face of a threat. Most often they do so by positioning the

Muslims represented in them as *outside* the discursive boundaries of the nation. We argue that a similar process can be seen even in those representations that have a comparatively sophisticated attitude toward questions of Muslim belonging post-9/11. In the visual media this positioning predominantly takes place through *performance, metonymy,* and *framing.*

To fully grasp the significance of the recurring images of Muslims deployed in the popular media, and to understand how these map onto dominant political attitudes, we need to think about the modes of address with which television texts hail their putative audience. This is not so much a question of passive viewers being brainwashed as of a host of narrative devices being employed to produce certain discursive effects. In drama, the imperatives of storytelling are shaped by telling visual images crafted at the service of a narrative arc that leads, in most cases, to a denouement that satisfies (or occasionally challenges) audience expectations. Nevertheless, within that arc lies the possibility for numerous moments of tension and subversion. These are, of course, in part provided by the plot's twists and turns. Yet, at a deeper level, there is always the capacity for the drama—through its parade of characters and the affective mechanisms by which we are asked to judge between them and apportion our sympathies—to carry within it ambiguities that escape the overt message that might seem, on the surface, to be conveyed. In what follows, we will tease out such ambiguities as they appear and see how they often trouble the supposed agenda of a given drama. To begin with, however, it is necessary to think in more detail about how the imagined audience is constructed when it comes to post-9/11 television dramas featuring Muslims. What we will see emerging is a very specific set of recurring images being placed at the service of values that are presumed to be the central shared point of identification for the envisaged viewers—values with which, at the same time, the Muslim characters on display supposedly have a troubled relationship.

## Making Media Muslims: Performance, Metonymy and Genre

In post-9/11 dramas the stereotype tends to be articulated through an implicit distance posited between the viewer (the normalized subject) and the Muslim object of the gaze, whose difference is always in view. This process of differentiation—which is also heavily marked by racial value judgments—we have called *ethnonormativity*. The ethnonormative space is the viewing space called into being by the narrative tension between the contending groups depicted (host community versus alien wedge). Its nature is defined according to whether the viewer is empowered to recognize ambiguities and ambivalences or is merely expected to choose between predetermined ideological positions. This is the difference between the comparative banality of the "good guy/bad guy" paradigm and more sophisticated modes that evidence some degree of self-reflection about the national normalization project.

The idea of an ethnonormative space allows us to explore how certain values are constructed and projected. This activity has less to do with some inevitable or deliberate conspiracy to "manufacture consent," in Chomsky and Herman's famous phrase than with the ordinary day-to-day grammars of film and television meaning-making: the way our sympathies are drawn toward some characters rather than others, and the way some voices and messages are imbued with a greater degree of authority.[2] Ethnonormativity is, then, a by-product of nationally situated media productions and values, even when they are beamed around the world in an era of globalized media and homogenized broadcasting structures.

In this chapter we will examine these issues by means of a consideration of two different types of post-9/11 drama. We analyze the drama-documentary type, represented by *Dirty War*, which purported to explore the immediate aftermath of an imagined chemical attack on London, and *The Hamburg Cell*, which followed the terrorists who attacked the World Trade Center in the weeks and months leading up to the event. We also consider the detailed and arguably anthropological realism of the Channel 4 film *Yasmin*, which dramatizes one British Asian Muslim woman's crisis of identity after the 9/11 attacks, and of the BBC drama *White Girl*, about a disfranchised young teenager and the solace she finds in Islam. In each case problematic truth claims are made for these genres and dramas on the basis of the pigeonholing of Muslims. The productions that claim, overtly or otherwise, to have a sympathetic or even ameliorative agenda tend either to imagine a worst case scenario in which Muslims are perennial victims or to construct a compensatory fantasy in which Muslim communities can guide us back to the traditional moral moorings from which we have drifted. On the other hand, the dramas where the road to terror or its aftereffects are foregrounded seem sometimes to wander into the trap of sacrificing dramatic tension to exposition or to fall back on conventional and seemingly inadequate attempts to pathologize Islamist terrorism.

Historically, on the level of form, Muslims are most often conjured up in one of two ways. A long-standing and still much-favored mode of indicating difference is through metonymy; Muslim women wear the hijab, men appear bearded, praying, or both. In each case, dress, beards, and acts stand in for the whole person, denoting cultural orientation, religious commitment, and thus, to secular society, Otherness. Writing specifically of the Arab as depicted in Hollywood, Steven Salaita has described this tendency to impose "a specific body politic on symbolic bodies," which produces a simulated or alternative reality to stand in for the more perplexing variety of lived experience, and wherein "Arab" is at the same time a synonym of "terrorist": "in the world in which Muslims are represented . . . terrorism can be reduced to the articulation of visual symbols that signal the threatening presence of Islam . . . beards, *kuffiyehs,* prayer beads and distinguishing garb."[3] We argue that the same basic process takes place in British film and television, albeit focused more often on the country's largest Muslim minority, that of the South Asian diaspora.

Particularly in the 1990s and early 2000s, being a Muslim in film and television drama required that one perform in certain recognizable ways: those the producers deemed *significant* for the group "Muslims," according to the conventions of the form in which they are being represented. At the same time there is a visual metonymic condensation whereby the beard of the Muslim patriarch, the hijab or burqa of the Muslim woman, or the act of prayer itself perform the function of signifying "Muslimness" for the viewer while also, after 9/11, pointing up irredeemable cultural difference too.

However, in recent years Muslim characters who pose a threat to the ethnonormalized community of the nation are more likely to be depicted as "Westernized" in outward appearance. As such they are difficult to identify, thereby constituting an even more menacing "enemy within." They may be outwardly respectable, look something like "us," and hold down professions such as medicine or teaching. We would describe this particular mutation of the Muslim stereotype as a "post-Huntington stereotype," taking our cue from a passage in *The Clash of Civilizations* in which Huntington attempts to describe ostensibly culturally hybrid subjects who may nonetheless be drawn to terrorism: "somewhere in the Middle East a half dozen young men could well be dressed in jeans, drinking coke, listening to rap and between their bows to Mecca, putting together a bomb to blow up an American airliner."[4]

However, where metonymic and stereotyped elements appear as a kind of visual shorthand, their presence is never merely innocuous or incidental. In any given ethnoreligiously marked drama involving Muslims, the visual signs of Islam work in three ways: first to *establish a location* (in the manner of a cinematic establishing shot); second, to create a *milieu* (the Muslims under scrutiny will be placed in relation to a larger surrounding community figured, if only inadvertently, as "the norm"); and third and most important, to *connote cultural values that are in some way discrepant with those of the norm*. This mode can then be made to tie in with established discourses about race, nation, and gender.

Of course, a number of scholars on both sides of the Atlantic have been concerned with the matter of negative images and stereotypes of Muslims.[5] However, in much of this work the critics operate with a largely unnuanced sense of how representation and reality interact, assuming what has been called the "hypodermic model" of media influence whereby images act directly on an audience and result in the reinforcement of anti-Muslim prejudice.[6] Clearly, there is enough evidence in contemporary accounts of racist attacks and community suspicion to suggest that negative images, taken together with other modes of discourse and group identification, can contribute to a more constrained and vulnerable existence for those stereotyped. However, this does not absolve criticism of the task of examining exactly *how* such negative images and stereotypes are set up: what cultural discourses they interact with, how they might problematize as well as confirm received opinion, and how different television genres operate to confirm or reject them, in terms both of their formal qualities and of audience expectations.

Tzvetan Todorov has described genres as the "codification of discursive properties." They function as "horizons of expectation" for their audiences, who have some sense of what elements will go to make up the particular cultural package they are encountering. He describes the way "each era has its own system of genres, which is in relation with the dominant ideology. . . . Genres, like any other institution, reveal the constitutive traits of the society to which they belong."[7] To that extent, television genres carry within them traces of a consensus about the nature of reality—or, at least, the particular portion of reality contained in the particular generic form in use—and limit dissonant or peripheral perspectives.

However, precisely because genre is, in Steve Neale's terms, "an exchange through which a culture speaks to itself," television genres always enshrine at some level the ambiguity of social relations.[8] Thus, while there may be "preferred meanings"—coinciding with the perspective of dominant sections of society—they are still always confronted by other possible perspectives, resulting in what Fiske and Hartley call "active contradictions" in the television message.[9] The degree of deviation from what might be considered the "preferred" meaning of a television text will vary both from genre to genre and within generic categories themselves. However, since these different possible perspectives are always in contention by the very nature of drama itself, no program or genre can ever completely close off all alternative interpretative avenues.

### You've Been Framed: Stereotype and Performativity in *Yasmin*

We will examine these issues first through a consideration of the Channel 4 film *Yasmin,* written by Simon Beaufoy and directed by Kenneth Glenaan, which explores one young British Asian Muslim woman's experiences in a working-class town in the north of England after 9/11. The film aims to make sophisticated observations about identity crises and alienation; the central character, Yasmin (played by Archie Panjabi), coexists uneasily with the demands of her traditionalist father and the community of which they are part, while also carrying on a clandestine relationship with John, a white male fellow worker. However, her split identity must always be performed for the viewer: this is signified in the way she is frequently depicted changing from the *shalwar qamis* and *dupatta* of her domestic life to the tight jeans and crop top she favors when working and socializing with the surrounding white community, and back again. However, such performativity here collapses complex negotiations into a comparatively crude metonymic signifier of difference and serves to alert us to the fact that the film as a whole operates through an economy of Otherness—albeit sympathetically handled—wherein a representative Muslim community in extremis is visualized performing difference for the anthropological gaze of the camera. Beyond that lurks once more the question of modernity, increasingly defined in state terms, and whether these characters can be dragged into its orbit.

The plot of the film is simple, as befits its pseudodocumentary-style analysis of a community under pressure. Our focus as audience is on Yasmin's family and its immediate environment and the effects on them of the 9/11 terrorist attacks and the subsequent implementation of new antiterror laws. Yasmin herself begins by straddling the cultural divide between the British-Pakistani community of which she is a part and the surrounding white English society. But after 9/11, her fellow workers turn on her, and an unsympathetic personnel manager suggests she takes some "time off." Worse follows when Yasmin's home is violently raided by an antiterror police squad who have been alerted by some telephone calls her husband has been making to a cousin in Pakistan, who may or may not have links to Kashmiri separatists. After this watershed event, the chasm between communities is exposed and Yasmin and her brother "rediscover" their Muslim identity. He is radicalized by propagandists who distribute leaflets outside the mosque and hold recruitment meetings where photos of slaughtered Muslims from the world's war zones are shown. She experiences rejection and hostility from those she once thought of as friends, bridles at the injustice done to her husband, and finds herself temporarily detained for supposedly withholding information from an investigating officer.

In publicity interviews the filmmakers were at pains to emphasize *Yasmin*'s credentials as a piece of realism that emerged from extensive research and workshops among the Muslim communities in the mill towns of Yorkshire and Lancashire, and that mixed professional actors with performers drawn from the local population. Kenneth Glenaan insisted:

> "we haven't made anything up in the script—the poetic license is amalgamating all those stories and squeezing them into an hour and a half and into one family. Hopefully we're being as representative as we possibly can be . . . what we were trying to do is to give people a bit of dignity, really, without being too grand about it—giving people a voice. . . . I think what you get is a really interesting tone, deliberately blurring the lines between fiction and documentary"[10]

Nevertheless, as the comment about "giving people a voice" might suggest, in dealing with its object here the documentary realist form is forced repeatedly to seek out ways to make knowable the operations of a community taken to be outside the ethnonormative framework of its audience. To do so, I would argue, the film falls back most often on conventions of representation having their roots in the twin projects of colonialism and Orientalism. These, in turn, have the effect of positioning the Muslim community so that it is depicted as outside, and in conflict with, the forces of statist modernity—in effect reenacting and reinforcing the problematic colonial binary reanimated in "War on Terror" rhetoric.

Muslims, then, must appear on the screen with their "Muslimness" marked out in some way. Their existence as subjects with any other affiliations or interests is effectively voided. Yet at the same time that the Muslim "essence" is made visible, its difference from the normalized community around it is underlined. Muslims, then, exist for us on the screen as mere traces. When it comes to their representation in contemporary film and television, the tendency is for individuality and specificity to retreat behind the all-encompassing signs of "Muslimness"—clothes, skin color, ritual. And, always, the attempt to comprehend the Other simultaneously marks that Other's distance from "us." Such a system of ethnonormative Othering appears in *Yasmin* in a number of guises.

In the opening scene we are introduced to the central characters: Yasmin; her hardworking father; her wayward brother, Nasir, who deals drugs, we learn, despite dutifully issuing the call to prayer from the local mosque; and her husband, Faisal—pejoratively referred to as "Banana Boat"—fresh from Pakistan, whom she has been persuaded to marry to enable him to gain residency rights in Britain but for whom she feels no affection. As the story moves on, it becomes clear that the necessities of the pseudodocumentary form mean that Yasmin's family must carry the burden of representation for a whole community. Thus, the three main characters, father, daughter, and son, in effect operate as stereotypes. Yasmin's father is the archetypal hardworking yet disappointed first-generation immigrant from Pakistan who owns a television repair shop and holds the keys to the local mosque, whose protective shutters he carefully cleanses of racist graffiti. Yasmin is the would-be dutiful daughter who takes the place of her dead mother by cooking and cleaning for her male relatives, while covertly enjoying the "Western" lifestyle and social opportunities her workmates provide. Nasir, meanwhile, embodies the dilemmas of both masculinity and culture, with his penchant for designer trainers, bling jewelry, and the sense of power afforded by the sexual conquest of white girls.

The visual motif of Yasmin surreptitiously changing clothes, a signifier of her split identity, is foregrounded right at the start and recurs throughout the first half of the film. At the same time, in the opening scene, the introduction of the main characters is interspersed with long shots of Yasmin's anonymous Muslim neighbors, framed against the rundown streets and back-to-back houses of a Victorian town in northern England. Thus, they are "situated" but also, at the same time, "out of place." This prepares us for the idea of a group under siege from a wider host community, but it also emphasizes the objective, pseudoscientific role of the camera that can take us into the mysterious, ordinarily "closed" world of this community. Here, our relation to the object on view is that of curious outsider—why else start with the culturally performative moment of the muezzin's call to prayer, set against the fields and dry stone walls of northern England and interrupted by a shot of satellite receivers appended to the walls of houses?—and the symbolic exchange we are invited to participate in is an insight into an Other culture, in other words, essentially anthropological knowledge.

In the film, Yasmin is pulled this way and that by contending desires and obligations. Post-9/11, and after the police raid on her home, her decisions are presented as a choice between binary opposites, accepting one identity or the other, even though this type of opposition can never be brought to a resolution. Once more, her inner turmoil is metonymically signified through dress. She begins by wearing a simple, loose *dupatta,* which occasionally slips back, exposing her hair. However, near the end she is shown clad in the much more tightly fitted black Al Amira–style veil, which covers the head and is fastened around the chin, revealing only the face. She is now on the way to the local mosque, having been awoken to the other "half" of her identity by a night in the police cells and a rediscovery of the Koran.

Indeed, for both Yasmin and Nasir, their increasing alienation from valorized versions of Britishness and journey toward a renewed Islamic identification must always be performed for the anthropological gaze of the camera. Their lives are transformed to the ironic accompaniment of voiceover excerpts from the contemporary speeches of George Bush and Tony Blair, about how the United States, unlike the terrorists, values every human life, and how laws are to be changed, not to deny liberties but to prevent their abuse. Yet God, liberty, and equality—so casually invoked by the political leaders—seem to have withdrawn from what fast becomes an enclave, leaving it clear for the police cars that slowly patrol the streets around Yasmin's home, the helicopters that buzz menacingly overhead, and the plainclothes officers who try to persuade Nasir to become an informant.

The nature of Yasmin's marriage is at the heart of her gendered position as a Muslim Asian woman in the film, and gives scope for more cultural stereotyping. Not only is she required to perform the multiple roles of daughter, wife, and sympathetic older sister, she is also placed under an obligation to accept as a husband a man chosen for her by her parents but with whom she has nothing in common. She keeps her marriage secret from John and determines that as soon as Faisal has leave to remain in Britain she will divorce him. At one point she tells Faisal that while they may be married, she will never be his wife. After this, while wondering the streets, Faisal discovers a goat and takes it back home, allowing it to graze in the backyard. On one level it becomes a companion for him, and thus, as he affirms, a surrogate wife. (The goat has an ambiguous symbolic valence in the film, standing at the same time for "backwardness"—who on earth would walk around with a goat on a lead in twenty-first-century Britain?—and for those affective connections Faisal has been unable to find in the strange country to which he has been transported.)

We first see Faisal rising drowsily from the mattress on which he sleeps in Yasmin's spare room. Subsequently, he is shown cooking his meal outdoors on a makeshift stove set up in the yard. In deeds and words he is depicted as occupying a space outside the domesticity of the other characters. While their everyday experiences bring them into contact with a surrounding white English community, where they are increasingly viewed with suspicion and thinly veiled hostility, Faisal lurches through his new life, baffled at his wife's coldness. Crucially, he knows almost no English, and communicates with Yasmin in Punjabi. This disconnect of linguistic and cultural knowledge adds to the nightmarish quality surrounding his arrest. The police raid Yasmin's home in search of Faisal, the originator of the suspicious calls to Pakistan, but he is out. Instead, the rest of the family are pinned to the floor and detained. He himself is only picked up when he comes home to find the house deserted and ransacked and approaches the police to find out what has happened.

Faisal is locked up, first in the local police cells and thereafter at a detention center where the high brick wall, topped by surveillance cameras, symbolizes both the insurmountable barrier to intercommunity understanding that has now arisen and the intrusive operation of technological statist modernity of the kind that appears to have swallowed him up. He is required to "inform" on those with whom he has been communicating. When he fails to yield the information his interrogators demand, they hold Yasmin as well. In one of the most significant exchanges between Yasmin and her interrogator, the dark absurdity of the situation is brought home in a manner worthy of Kafka or Pinter:

> *Interrogator:* Under the 2001 Terrorism Act I could charge you with withholding information. You know that, don't you?
>
> *Yasmin:* What information?
>
> *Interrogator:* You tell me.
>
> *Yasmin:* I don't have any information. You don't know what information you're looking for, and I don't have any information, so I can't tell you, and you're gonna charge me with withholding that information: the information I don't have. How do I get out of that?
>
> [Silence]

The information Faisal is supposed to hold is sought precisely because it allows a consolidation of national identity by distinguishing those acts and connections that mark participants as being Other, not "one of us" in the new dispensation which insists on national loyalty and taking sides in the War on Terror. However, it can be argued that Faisal plays a part that is, in fact, radically destabilizing, both at the level of plot—his detention and treatment expose the crumbling edifice of British "fair play"—and at the level of the film's grammar, which is equally dependent on his position beyond the English-speaking characters we are being invited to identify with. On the one hand, he is expected literally to become an informant, telling his interrogators what they need to know about Kashmiri insurgents (and thus potential terrorists). On the other hand, since he does not speak English, he is kept outside the mêlée of contending voices seeking to redefine British identity and determine and delimit the position of Muslims within it. As such, he at least embodies the *idea* of a counternarrative—albeit a non-linguistic one—that might be set against the hardening attitudes of both sides.

After his release and subsequent divorce from Yasmin, Faisal wanders off with his goat, out of the movie and out of the claustrophobic world of this small Muslim community, now changed forever by its entanglement with the repressive state apparatuses of modernity. Indeed, it could be argued that it is this character, inarticulate and, in the terms of anthropological modernity, "primitive," who most effectively manages to resist the film's essentially neocolonial economy based on racial and cultural difference. Precisely because he is overdetermined as out of place, rural, and backward—a stereotype of a stereotype—he cannot be accommodated either by the British Muslim community, with its emerging political awareness, or by the enforcement agencies of national normativity, such as, the police and politicians. His awkward presence parodies the emerging orthodoxy that brands Muslims as recidivist types fatally at odds with Western modernity. He operates as a literal innocent abroad, a kind of holy fool, able to throw into relief the divergent and hardening perspectives of the newly radicalized Muslim political consciousness—represented by Nasir, who eventually goes off to a terrorist training camp in Pakistan—and the paranoid operations of the nation-state. Despite the best efforts of the police *and* the apparatus of performative anthropological realism, Faisal manages to evade capture by the binaries, wandering out of the frame near the end of the film, accompanied by his goat.

His ambiguous position and uncertain destination might make him an example of what Gayatri Spivak, drawing on Derrida, calls a "lever of intervention": a moment "of textual transgression . . . or bafflement that discloses not only limits but also possibilities to a new politics of reading."[11] While the other characters seem stranded, left to come to terms with the new ordinance that sees them as a national security threat, a man and his goat move offstage and out of the frame, headed who knows where?, in a moment of indeterminacy. (In fact, there is another incident in this film that might also work in this way. It involves an elderly white woman who wanders into a shot to comfort one of Yasmin's neighbors, who has been the object of racist abuse in a shopping mall. Although the racist attack was an intended part of the film, the shocked bystander wandering into the shot to commiserate and apologize, completely unscripted, marks another moment of textual rupture. At once, this moment registers the possible presence of a sense of white culpability for the exclusion of some northern Muslim communities, for example those that would produce the London bombers of 7/7, from wider racially inscribed notions of Britishness, and a site of individualist decency and fairness of the kind that seems to have been disallowed by the authoritarianism of the Bush and Blair governments and their rhetoric of so-called homeland security.)

Such moments are fleeting and soon disappear again over the glowering horizon toward which the Muslim characters move. One marks the limit of the film's scripting of a character who remains unknowable; the other is literally unscripted. Together, both have the potential to challenge the frame wherein ethnonormativity in political discourses and its unconscious presence in certain cultural forms work to ensure the separation of the viewing and viewed subjects, and to keep Muslims "outside" the nation and firmly in the media ghetto.

## *White Girl:* Muslims as Paragons of Virtue

If the spotlight of anthropological realism is trained on a small Muslim community in *Yasmin,* forcing its inhabitants to perform furiously to communicate their Otherness, Abi Morgan's *White Girl* (2008) reverses this approach, scrutinizing a sample of an impoverished white underclass. However, the Muslims with whom this remnant is compared arguably become such unfeasible paragons of all the homely virtues as to divest them of any flesh-and-blood quality at all. The question then becomes whether Morgan's portrayal is a corrective piece of positive representation or more a case of killing credibility with too much kindness.

*White Girl* tells the story of eleven-year-old Leah McNeill (played by Holly Kenny), her mother, Debbie (Anna Maxwell Martin), and siblings Adam and Casey, in their attempts to escape the clutches of Debbie's brutal husband, Stevie. The story opens with Leah pedaling her bicycle home to a high-rise tenement block just in time to help her mother load the van with a few meager possessions before bolting to a new home arranged for them by the council. Throughout, dim, flat lighting emphasizes the drabness of this world composed of state benefits, petty theft, and an incautious consumption of drugs and alcohol. Splashes of color do begin to appear, however, as the family arrives at its new home; to their shock, they have been relocated in a predominantly Muslim area of their unnamed northern city.

Once more the viewer is treated to anthropological glimpses of Muslim life, signified by the burqa-clad women who peer curiously at these new arrivals. However, here it is the whites who are in a minority; the camera moves in for close-up reaction shots of Debbie and Leah as they move in a swirl of Muslim street life the first time they venture outdoors. Thus, the standard anthropological shots are subtly refracted in *White Girl*, as the family find themselves in the midst of an established community, one in which they themselves constitute an alien presence, and one that reserves the right to look back at them. Indeed, the McNeill family have few qualms about making a spectacle of themselves, as their life consists of a constant round of very public battles with the pursuing Stevie, neighbors, teachers at the entirely Muslim school the children begin to attend, and arguments among themselves. In contrast to the strongly ingrained Muslim notion of decorum and shame—unstated here yet always hovering offstage as a touchstone of reasonable behavior—the McNeills are depicted as comparatively shameless: not maliciously so, but with no time, in the daily struggle for basic necessities, for the perceived luxuries of polite manners or any concern to make a good impression in a new environment they treat with suspicion.

Indeed, as in *Yasmin*, so again here a complex network of looks defines identity at the same time that partially obscured perspectives and camera angles emphasize the gap between self and other. Throughout the film we are made to look *through* things: the tassels on the edge of a bedspread behind which Leah seeks solace; a line of brightly colored shawls fluttering on a rail in the district's market; the grille in the wall separating male and female worshippers at the mosque she attends as her interest in Islam grows. This intrusive disruption of the viewer's gaze operates both to symbolize a young girl's inability to see things clearly and to replicate the idea of veiling, always a central metaphor in the depiction of women and Islam. It also serves to suggest a distance, whether between the audience and the McNeills or between Leah and her mother in the significant number of point-of-view shots we share with our young main focalizer. (Mirrors once more have a centrality to matters of identity here. Leah imagines herself as a kind of ninja the first time she sees herself in the mirror wearing a headscarf, while Debbie, as her life begins to unravel, looks in a mirror trying to locate the optimistic young woman she once was.)

As Leah's relationship with her mother comes under strain owing to her mother's inability to break free emotionally from Stevie, Leah spends more and more time with the young Muslim girl next door who is close to her own age. At one point, looking over the wall that separates their two houses, Leah remarks: "Looks dead weird seeing our house from this side." Indeed, for all Leah's culture-hopping interest in Islam, this is a film still predicated on a central irrevocable divide between white Britain and its South Asian Muslim migrant culture. If the film reverses the usual implicit prejudice by which white, Anglo-Saxon Christian culture is valorized in such a comparison, it can only do so via a straightforward contrastive approach that sets assumed cultural values in direct relief. An example appears in the two scenes that mark the halfway point of *White Girl*. In the first, with her interest in Islam growing daily, Leah participates in a prayer meeting at the mosque, where we witness her taking part in the ritual ablution (*wudu*) necessary before prayer. Her eye runs across the cool, clean interior of the communal bathroom with its colorful geometrical tiles, as she cleanses herself in the required manner. The discipline, prescribed rituals, and fellowship she finds at the mosque are a world away from the chaos of her home life, as she remarks later to her mother: "It smells nice and it's quiet. When I pray it's like everything's not bad or fucked up . . . I feel safe." This scene of comfort is immediately juxtaposed with the much cruder, more raucous ritual of a hen night in which Debbie and Debbie's mother, Sonya, are involved. We see them jostling for room in front of the mirror in a nightclub cloakroom, swigging beer from bottles and adjusting the bunny ears that seem an obligatory accessory on such occasions. Compared to the dignity of wudu, the hen party seems a debased ritual dedicated to drinking, dancing, and sexual incontinence; Debbie returns home drunk and has sex with Stevie in full view of her watching daughter. The stereotypes here, as throughout *White Girl,* are really of the white underclass whose apparently nihilistic values of instant gratification are compared directly and unfavorably with the supposed measured gravitas of the Muslim way of life. (Although, in fact, it would be misleading to suggest that the McNeills are totally shameless, since a quite acute sense of racial propriety is in evidence at the wedding reception, during which Leah horrifies the exclusively white guests by donning her hijab and kneeling to perform one of the five daily prayers; Sonya interrupts her daughter's halfhearted defense of Leah: "Debbie, she's embarrassing *us.*")

The abusive relationship between Debbie and Stevie is at the heart of Leah's disenchantment. At an age when curiosity and trepidation vie with one another, in her attempts to make sense of adult affairs, Leah finds herself drawn to a charismatic male teacher who introduces her to the basic tenets of Islam and serves as a mentor for her journey. There is no direct suggestion of any nascent sexual attraction on Leah's part, but it is certainly the case that relations between the Muslims she begins to spend more time with are much less fraught than those she has been used to. And it is here, arguably, that the difficulties with the representation of Muslims in *White Girl* become clear. All the Muslim characters Leah encounters are mouthpieces for social responsibility, eager to take every opportunity to proselytize, not so much for Islam as for a model of family life to which Leah has never been privy. At one point when she curses her feckless mother, her friend's father reprimands her, quoting a passage from the Koran about the sanctity of mothers. The hierarchy and power relations that define family life in all cultures are simply brushed aside as irrelevant to this story in which her new Muslim friends work to show Leah just what she has been missing.

The story reaches its climax when Leah reveals to Debbie that Stevie has been using she and her younger siblings as drug runners, carrying small packages of illicit substances and returning with cash hidden in the handlebars of a bicycle. Faced with this ultimate betrayal, Debbie confronts Stevie and resolves to leave him once and for all. In the film's final scene Debbie turns on her mother, whose casual parenting has ensured that she has remained practically illiterate and therefore with very limited life choices: "Why didn't you send me to school? Why don't you want more for me than you had?" She gives Stevie back his wedding ring and, in a moment showing she has learned something from her daughter's religious peregrinations, divorces Stevie, repeating the valorized form of words that can be used to annul a Muslim marriage: "I divorce you. I divorce you, I divorce you." With her mother's sins forgiven, Leah can return home. The closing shot of Leah smiling suggests that the family can now face the future together.

*White Girl* was part of the BBC's "White Season," a set of programs that claimed to look at neglected aspects of white working-class culture in a medium that often normalizes the values and perspectives of a metropolitan middle class presumed to be comfortable with Britain's urban multiculturalism. As such, one might say that the season applies an outsider's anthropological viewpoint to an unexplored section of the white population similar to that otherwise used with Muslim objects. There was certainly an element of redressing the balance in the "White Season," but it was heavily criticized in some quarters for erecting an image of a residual and beleaguered white rump, the repository of all the most reactionary entrenched political and social attitudes. While it tries to complicate this picture, *White Girl* merely ends up reinforcing it, as when Debbie launches into a despairing reflection on her own lost opportunities and their consequences for her children: "I want more for my kids. I want more for me. We're lowlife, Stevie and me, and we drag our kids down with us into all this shit, when they start out so beautiful. . . . We don't deserve to be parents." While it is ultimately more sophisticated and varied in tone than *Yasmin* and less inexorable and predictable in its trajectory, *White Girl* still operates through a rigidly defined binary schema, visually signified by dividing walls, grilles, and symbols of purdah, against which floating, dancing beautiful things like pendants, prayer beads, soap bubbles, and Eid decorations represent the lure but at the same time the impossibility of complete freedom.

We can say, however, that the entire film is structured around Islam as a repository of all the virtues of family, modesty, and charity that the white underclass is shown to have lost. As such, Islam—and the Muslim characters—are placed uniformly at the service of a white cultural and existential crisis. Unusually for post-9/11 drama, *White Girl* ventures nothing but positive images of Muslims. However, precisely because of this they exist merely as paragons, serving to remind the white central characters, in their angst, that there is a better way to live. As such, *White Girl* can finally be seen as an example of what Ella Shohat and Robert Stam call "liberal films which furnish the 'other' with a 'positive image,' appealing dialog and sporadic point-of-view shots, yet in which European or Euro-American characters remain radiating 'centers of consciousness' and 'filters' for information, the vehicles for dominant racial/ethnic discourses."[12] In keeping with this reading, our interaction with Muslims is focalized almost solely through Leah, and they serve to offer her consolation at a difficult time in her young life. Islam, then, exists not as a set of social and cultural practices in its own right but as a consolatory spiritual abstraction to serve the needs of the white girl. As a result, the drama is populated by a series of token Muslims—the teacher, the neighbor, the neighbor's father—articulating the benefits of Islam and reciting extracts from the Koran at opportune moments.

There are no antiterror raids, no rabble-rousing firebrands, no communities living in fear in *White Girl*. Asserting the right of Muslims to be depicted without such egregious branding is surely to be welcomed, particularly in view of all the negative stereotypes of Muslims circulating in the modern media. Yet this is achieved at the cost of stripping the community of at least some of its vitality. The film ends up deploying Islam and Muslims as embodiments of abstract values rather than as real people with loves, hates, sins, and (most of all) political opinions. An indication of this white liberal motor driving things along is the fact that everything builds to the moment when Debbie finally decides to leave Stevie, enabling Leah to come home and the family, divided by his oppressive presence, to be reunited as a loving, supportive unit. In the end, we wonder whether Leah's embrace of Islam has been anything more than a short-term response to the crisis engulfing her and a reaction to a lack of security at home. The audience is left to speculate about this and, in fact, a lasting commitment to Islam seems less important than that the family can look forward without fear. For all its clearly displayed valorization of the family values to be found in Islam, the fact that the real interest of *White Girl* is in its excoriating take on a kind of feral underclass behavior means that, at times, it sounds as if it has been penned by an op-ed writer on the *Daily Mail.* Though it displays a refreshing eschewal of crude stereotypical framing, *White Girl* uses its Muslims to drive through a stinging critique of a type of white working-class existence, rather than allowing them to live and breathe as something more than ciphers.

## Docudrama and the "Use-Value" Muslim: *Dirty War*

In fact, post-9/11 drama is full of Muslims positioned merely as mouthpieces, either explaining the grievances prompting Islamist extremism or operating as state agents and using their insiders' knowledge to report back information to the security services, thereby reassuring the ethnonormalized viewer that "good Muslims" do exist. Instances of what we will call these "use-value" Muslims, who operate as purveyors of "useful information" about Islam, its practices, and its adherents, can be found in the BBC's *Dirty War* (2004). The legitimacy of use-value Muslim characters is often flagged for us by the way they step out of the story, so to speak, to adopt an educative role informing us of some of the salient features of Islam. Moreover, they are seldom our main focalizers or centers of identification. Instead they exist in what we might call a state of structural subordination to the main (white) characters with whom they share screen time; they are seldom the leading figures initiating action or deciding policy at any senior level. At the same time, when juxtaposed with the Muslim villains who also populate these dramas, use-value Muslims are reassuringly like "us," albeit racially different. They are decisively distanced from their coreligionists, even if they have a more immediate, and thereby "authentic," grasp of what might motivate them. That said, when it comes to the docudrama genre, where fidelity to actual events, either real or potentially real, tempers the fictional elements, such use-value Muslims with their parroted exegeses actually work to highlight tensions between the dramatic requirements of a fast-paced narrative and the didactic impulses involved in events being recounted for historical or cautionary purposes.[13]

*Dirty War,* written by Daniel Percival and Lizzie Mickery, centers on an imagined chemical attack on London—a so-called dirty bomb—its aftermath and the pressure on the government and emergency services to contain the fallout (both chemical and political and economic). In view of its serious purpose, it is not surprising that the public information element overshadows the dramatic element, despite efforts to create a fast-paced and engaging story. In terms of its atmosphere, the film at first seems to borrow from the thriller, with sinister music playing over opening shots of ordinary people going about their business on a sunny London day, including a child with her mother and a baby in a buggy with a balloon. We are instantly aware that something terrible is going to disrupt this tranquil scene. However, the commitment to veracity, and the idea that this is a weighty intervention designed to provoke a public debate, has already been emphasized. In Britain, prior to transmission a somber continuity announcer counseled, "if you are worried about any of the issues raised in the program you can call our panel of experts who will be taking part in a studio discussion after the programme." (Similarly, when the show was bought by HBO in the United States and shown on a number of PBS channels, audience debates were also aired.) Thereafter, at the start of the program proper a stark white-on-black caption informs us—in the words of Dame Eliza Manningham-Buller, then head of MI5—that, "it will only be a matter of time before a crude chemical, biological or radiological (CBRN) attack is launched in a major western city." This is followed by the only marginally more reassuring "London is as prepared as it is possible to be," courtesy of government minister for London, Nick Raynsford. At the same time, on the specially constructed *Dirty War* page of the BBC's website, the worried viewer could find links to advice on "Preparing for a disaster," "Keeping alive under terrorist attack," and "How prepared is your area?"[14]

Yet despite its public information function and ensuing studio debate, the drama itself can be seen to make some very problematic reality claims, not least because it tends to fall back on what were already, in 2004, stereotyped imagery and roles at every available opportunity. Although it uses the visually more sophisticated post-Huntington stereotype of disaffected young Muslims who look and act "like us" yet who are involved in terrorist activity, the drama's deployment of repeated images of the skyscrapers of London's business district, and of the emergency services as our figures of affective investment recall, in a kind of secondhand way, the World Trade Center towers and the subsequent elevation of the 9/11 story to the status of emblematic national myth. At the same time, characters such as a concerned and competent government minister and a token Muslim policewoman, apparently included solely to ensure that Muslim grievances about British and American policy are aired, all feed into a fairly crude national normalization narrative that operates to redeploy and reinforce Self/Other binaries while playing on public fears.

The tussle between didacticism and drama is ongoing throughout *Dirty War*. Every now and again, clunky dialogues take place between characters so that matters of import such as the need for a balance between truth and reassurance in government information to the public, the preparedness or otherwise of emergency procedures, and the motives and *modus operandi* of terror cells can be given an airing. In the latter case, a sergeant in the antiterrorist branch at New Scotland Yard briefs his junior colleague, in a voiceover, on the favored use by terrorists of logistics and reconnaissance cells, as the screen shows us suspicious individuals dutifully manufacturing fake passports and reconnoitering their intended target.

If such separation of the audio and visual elements serves to condense information and push the story along, there are other modes of visual shorthand that are rather more insistent and less subtle. All through *Dirty War*, seemingly connecting every scene, are lingering tracking shots of the office towers of Canary Wharf, one of London's main business centers. The film opens with one of these shots and in at least eight separate following instances the viewer's attention is drawn back to these totemic buildings: a newsreader describes a civil defense exercise as the camera pans across the skyline to the towers; they serve to bring the action back to London after a scene in which the deadly chemical contents of the bomb have been loaded onto a lorry in Bulgaria; they come into view again as the terrorist mastermind drives the van containing the deadly payload to its destination; and after the attack a close-up of the towers shrouded in thick, black smoke vividly recalls the television images beamed around the world on 9/11. (Indeed, the only variation in these shots of the vulnerable London skyline is the occasional appearance of St. Paul's Cathedral, a compressed signifier of Britain's Christian heritage, its durability—as in the Blitz of 1940—and, perhaps equally important in this context, a familiar stop on the tourist trail.) The lack of dramatic logic underpinning the relentless use of the Canary Wharf towers can be appreciated when one considers that the chemical bomb has been detonated near Liverpool Street in the City of London, actually several miles away from Canary Wharf. This inconsistency appears not to bother the producers, who instead resort at every turn to the default image of modern terrorism: smoke-shrouded skyscrapers.

The film's indebtedness to the mythography of 9/11 reveals itself in other ways too. In particular, the characterization works merely to replicate established truisms about the West under attack by forces bent on its destruction. In such a scenario, it is those who deal on the ground with the impact of terrorist attacks who are the emblems of selfless dedication and our figures of affective investment. Murray Corrigan, plain-speaking and brave watch commander with the London Fire Service, offers the viewer a moral focalizing presence and a hero to root for. Corrigan (played by Alistair Galbraith) berates a government minister before the attacks for the shoddy equipment with which his crew has had to tackle a simulated chemical attack during a drill. His disgust at the hesitancy of politicians is expressed in a conversation with his wife, when he informs her that he is thinking of resigning. Yet when the real call comes, he is first on the scene and the first to volunteer to enter "Ground Zero"—another borrowing from 9/11 terminology—though he knows his antiradiation suit affords inadequate protection. Even when his commander tells him to withdraw, Corrigan continues with his job, only reluctantly obeying as his air supply runs out and he tears off his protective helmet to round up his team, ensuring a huge dose of radiation, which brings him, in the last scene, to an isolation ward and almost certainly a protracted and painful death. As a good man battling in his own way both the evil of terrorism and the sound-bite culture of politicians, Corrigan knows what must be done and at what cost. He thus becomes the British answer to the fire crews and emergency workers who were fêted for being first on the scene on September 11 and for embodying bravery and dedication.

In the show's advance publicity, the producers of *Dirty War* claimed that they had "consulted the Muslim community about the representation of the terrorists": a backhanded compliment if ever there was one![15] In truth, they need not have bothered, since the terrorists on display here merely embody a menacing, instantaneous threat and an irrevocable Otherness. This particularly applies to Rashid (played by Raza Jaffrey, a couple of years before he jumped the fence to star as MI5 officer Zafar Younis in *Spooks*). A figure of motiveless malignity, Rashid is a folk devil who springs fully formed into the London of *Dirty War*. When we first meet him, dressed in a smart business suit, he is arranging to rent a flat above an East London takeaway as the cell's operating base. Yet once he is captured by antiterrorist officers he reverts to type, refusing to yield information even under brutal interrogation, instead cursing and spitting as his captors look on helplessly at television images of a poisonous cloud mushrooming over London. Rashid takes his place in a long line of sullen, expectorating fanatics—"nutters," as the sergeant calls them—whose soul motivation in life is to cause mayhem and kill as many people as possible.

Yet Muslim grievances *are* articulated in *Dirty War*. This takes place through the deployment of a use-value Muslim character, Detective Constable Sameena Habibullah. She is seen at the start arriving at her new job with the antiterrorist squad. She has been drafted for this service because of her presumed insider's knowledge of Muslim communities and command of Urdu and Arabic. Habibullah exists to show us that not all Muslims are fulminating "nutters," and patiently explains to her sergeant the idea of the Ummah, the root of not only extremist disaffection but also the alternative she embodies: "If you're Muslim you're part of a much wider family. . . . These fanatics are just a tiny minority and people think we're all like that. I take my faith seriously. I care about what's happening in the world, but you don't see me strapping explosives to myself, do you?" So the viewer is to be reassured: not every Muslim is a threat, and some even hold values similar to ours. Habibullah is as good as her word, working late into the night tracing the terrorists' entry points, going on a raid and placing herself at considerable risk. Yet she never shakes off the faintly patronizing mantle of Muslim expositor. Late on—too late to prevent the attack—the police find the ringleader, and Habibullah is part of the team sent to interrogate him. Ahmed Ibrahim Abbassi, Lebanese immigrant and terrorist mastermind, sneers at his inquisitors. He sees himself as defending Muslims who are suffering at the hands of the infidel in Ramallah, Kabul, and Baghdad. Yet Habibullah draws him into a partial consideration of his actions when she claims that what he has done is a crime against Islam, not a defense of it. The West will retaliate, more Muslims will suffer, so what has been achieved? The standoff between the "good Muslim" and the "bad Muslim" ends inconclusively, but with the promise of more strife to come, when Abbassi proclaims: "We expect your retaliation. It is what unites us and divides you."

Thus, the message of *Dirty War* is that continued vigilance is necessary. It presents a world in which all the developments in surveillance that have provoked heated debate between the government and civil liberties groups are vindicated by the necessities of the times we live in. The emergency coordinating team is able to supervise the response to the dirty bomb via a suite of monitors linked up to the capital's omnipresent CCTV cameras. The cameras, regularly perched on every street corner, allow the authorities to witness the explosion, foil a follow-up attack, coordinate crowd control and decontamination, and track down Abbassi as well as he tries to make his escape. A controversial form of technology with Orwellian potential is here presented as a key tool in antiterror operations. Many responses to *Dirty War* are possible, and some of them are anticipated in the drama and its peritexts. In the end, however—as the credits roll over scenes of devastation and an exclusion zone of three and a quarter square miles that will remain uninhabitable for thirty years—having been disquieted by the images on our television screens, viewers might at least sleep a little easier in their beds knowing that a benevolent Big Brother is watching them.

*Dirty War* was one of a spate of dramadocs commissioned in the opening years of the twenty-first century that imagined the consequences of a number of millennial disasters, for example the flooding of London as a result of climate change; the exhaustion of oil supplies; and—in the immediate aftermath of the 2001 anthrax scare in the United States—a smallpox terror attack on the United Kingdom. In each case the integrity and coherence of the drama came a distant second to the topicality and shock value of the events depicted. One could, therefore, object that a docudrama like *Dirty War* resists such a reading as that given above, with its emphasis on awkward expository elements, on account of its priority to inform rather than entertain. Indeed, because of this split register, incorporating a civil defense imperative alongside a human interest storyline, the presence of any kind of dramatic tension is to be welcomed. However, it is in the secondhand and somewhat questionable borrowing of the iconography of 9/11—the ubiquitous towers, the emergency services as heroes, street-level chaos and panic—that *Dirty War* finally reveals a lack of imagination as it reaches to push the nearest available buttons of white Western paranoia. Interestingly, the then Home Secretary, David Blunkett, took the BBC to task for screening what he considered a sensationalist program that would fuel public anxieties, particularly through its use of realistic news broadcasts to "cover" the attack.[16] Blunkett's intervention seems more likely to have been prompted by the timing of transmission, while opposition to the Iraq war was still at its height, since *Dirty War* is hardly a modern equivalent of Orson Welles's *War of the Worlds* broadcast: certainly not sufficiently disturbing to induce mass panic, not least because the elements of drama and didacticism are never properly balanced or brought together. The binary foundations of its visual and narrative politics are such that, for all DC Habibullah's reasonableness and dedication to duty, *Dirty War* ends up underlining the notion of white Westerners under threat from faceless alien hordes who can sneak across their borders, bringing their death-obsessed ideologies and devices of mass destruction with them. A stronger case against immigration and for surveillance and ethnic profiling can seldom have been made on British television.

## *The Hamburg Cell:* Crises of Masculinity

If *Dirty War* suffers from an essentially derivative relationship to the imagery and iconography of 9/11, *The Hamburg Cell*—dealing with actual events leading up to the attacks themselves—eschews, until its very final scenes, an overdetermining visual reliance on the shock value of the events of that sunny September morning. Instead, *The Hamburg Cell* offers a much more dramatically sophisticated narrative that builds in intensity to the inevitable denouement. We are already aware of the handiwork of the hijackers and their puppet masters, and such foreknowledge adds to a feeling of claustrophobia and impending apocalypse. There are no "tame" Muslims here, no heroes to root for—only a tale of monomania and mass murder. Rather than being hamstrung by their dependence on matters of historical record, writers Ronan Bennett and Alice Perman and director Antonia Bird turn the inexorable path to wholesale slaughter into a gripping and comparatively nuanced analysis of the radicalization process. They do so through a technique that might be called parallelism, which is not without stereotyped elements but also is shaded by more complex character exploration. The 9/11 hijackers exist within, but also at a tangent to, Western society; and in the two figures with whom we are most engaged, Mohammed Atta and Ziad Jarrah, we see, respectively, an awkward ascetic longing for martyrdom and a confused young man who has been goaded and cajoled to give up everything for a calcified version of faith. What unites them is a perceived crisis of masculinity in the Muslim male—a reading common to some of the more simplistic attempts to pathologize Islamic extremism—that leads these two very different characters toward the same horrifying conflagration.

Formally, *The Hamburg Cell* is a circular narrative. The drama opens with a prefiguring of what will also be the final scene, albeit played sequentially in reverse, as though in a forlorn attempt to rewind time—if not to change history then at least to give us a better understanding of its causes and agents. Atta and his accomplices hurry down the covered gangway and on to United Flight 11 at Boston's Logan Airport, while Ziad Jarrah takes a final bus ride to Newark's LaGuardia Airport to catch United Flight 93, passing on the way the distant landmarks of the city his friends' actions are about to scar forever. We then track back five years to explore the process of indoctrination that has now reached its culmination. Providing a thread through the story are insistent captions, forming a timeline of the years and months leading up to the attacks. Augmented by voiceover segments, they chart the formation and movements of the Hamburg cell and Osama Bin Laden's 1997 fatwa against "Jews and crusaders." They also record the lengthy trail of intelligence information that accumulated in the months before 9/11, including increasingly urgent surveillance reports about a planned "spectacular" attack on the United States, all of which were ignored by the authorities.

The single most striking and controversial aspect of *The Hamburg Cell,* and what makes it different from the other dramas in our survey, is that it operates entirely from within the worldview of the conspirators. There is no normalized majority community to offer us a cozy fallback position, to combat or even to reflect critically on the action. Instead of a Muslim enclave at odds with the world around it, Bird's film shows us a slippery and apparently cosmopolitan group—not least in terms of the frequent easy international comings and goings through which the plan is put together. Instead of the inside/outside models seen in *Yasmin* or *White Girl,* we have a physical juxtaposition of worlds, a parallelism between the spaces occupied by the terrorists and their host nations, if not in their views of that world. Thus Mohammad Atta walks past the sex shops and fleshpots of nighttime Hamburg on his way to a prayer meeting at the Al Quds mosque, to the accompaniment of his own excoriation of the materialism and worldly ills of modernity. The two things, fleshly cupidity and the austerity of faith, exist side by side without ever really meeting. Indeed, the punctilious brand of Islam espoused by recruiters such as Abu Mohammed and Ramzi Bin al Shibh requires that these two worlds have as little to do with each other as possible.

This message is strikingly embodied in the character of Mohammed Atta, played by Kamel Boutros. Part of the drama's interest being to understand how jihadis are created, an attempt is made at psychological probing for the underlying causes of extreme actions. However, in the case of Atta this tends to resolve itself by means of fairly standard diagnoses of sexual repression and the stifling influence of a tyrannical father. Atta becomes a walking bundle of complexes. The most powerful of these is a deep aversion to the opposite sex and any manifestations of sexuality. As well as traversing Hamburg's Red Light district with his eyes fixed firmly on the ground and his coat buttoned up to the neck, Atta scowlingly reverses an art poster featuring a reclining nude that adorns the kitchen of his student digs, turning its offensive nakedness to the wall. Later, in Florida, he picks his way uneasily through a gaggle of bikini babes lounging by a swimming pool as he goes to meet his coconspirators, and even the promise of beautiful virgins to keep him company in paradise fails to rouse his interest. Underscoring this reading of Atta, we are given his now infamous last will and testament, in which he insists: "The person who will wash my body near my genitals must wear gloves on his hand so he will not touch my genitals. I don't want any women to go to my grave at all."

Atta's portrayal, or at least the writers' attempt to psychoanalyze him, recalls the aforementioned readings of the Muslim male as suffering from unresolved issues around sexuality and masculinity, for example the crude caricatures in Martin Amis's volume *The Second Plane*.[17] In a central scene of *The Hamburg Cell*, Atta makes a final journey home to see his parents, having recently gained his master's degree. Instead of celebrating his son's achievement, his father badgers him aggressively to push on and take a Ph.D., comparing him unfavorably with other relatives and reminding him: "We are successful people," before leaving him with the stern injunction "Do not disappoint me." After this, Atta enjoys a tearful farewell embrace with his doting mother. The same issues of parental pressure and expectation, which are also shown to operate for Ziad Jarrah, take on an almost parodic excessiveness in the case of Atta. We are being invited to make familiar associations between extreme patriarchal oppression and an equally extreme response that aims ambivalently both at filial tribute and symbolic patricide on a grand scale. Essentially, Atta-the-monster can be understood, like his history-changing precursor Adolf Hitler, as an example of an "authoritarian personality" produced by an excessive exposure to the Law of the Father.[18]

However, despite the demands of piety, the attractions of life are always battling with the impulse to martyrdom, especially in the character of Ziad Jarrah. He is an altogether more complex case than the
repressed, pious Atta. Although it is similarly suggested that internal-
ized parental pressure to be a success has a warped outcome, Ziad has
a much more ambivalent relationship to worldly pleasures. When he
meets his future wife at a student hostel in Greifswald, Germany, at the
start, his seduction lines include a list of his interests: "cars, planes and
pretty Turkish girls"; and even as he begins to fall under the sway of
Abu Mohammed, he is still more interested in the hadith's pronouncements on lovemaking than on jihad. Indeed, one of the interesting features of *The Hamburg Cell* is that it fails to offer a persuasive rationale
for Ziad's attraction to extremism. One gets no real sense of why this
well-to-do young man would be attracted by the hyperbole of the
Islamist vision, or what curiosity drives him to attend Abu Mohammed's
meetings. At most, his transformation appears to be the result of shy-
ness, lack of self-esteem, and a susceptibility to peer pressure, combined with a competitive instinct and threatened machismo. At one of
the prayer meetings Ziad, who is Lebanese, is confronted by a Palestinian
firebrand who accuses Lebanon, and thereby Ziad too, of siding with
Israel in recent conflicts. Their argument quickly escalates, ending only
with Abu Mohammed's intervention and Ziad's exasperated yet earnest
question "Do you want me to blow myself up?"

For whatever reason, Ziad's radicalization proceeds at a rapid pace.
Typically, however—and despite a mesmeric performance from Karim
Saleh as Jarrah—the character still externally *performs* his journey
to jihadism: swearing off alcohol; raising a hand to his new wife for
answering back and not dressing more modestly; and going off to an
training camp in Afghanistan where he works harder than anyone else.
Yet even as the fateful date approaches, he seems still to feel the lure of
the sensory stimuli and delights he is preparing to forsake. Part of the
plan depends on the plotters gaining entry to the United States to train
as pilots. Ordered to blend in, Ziad, in T-shirt and shorts, jogs along a
palm-fringed Florida beach flirting with pretty girls before joining his
flight school tutor at a barbecue, where he scoffs a hamburger and

downs a pint of beer. His wife later joins him, and they enjoy a last holiday together, cruising the streets in a shiny new convertible, strolling on the beach, and sharing an ice cream. In all this there is a strong sense of Ziad savoring, for a final time, the sensual pleasures he once took as his right; toward the end he rues having been sometimes "too in love with this life." In a fascinating, uninterpreted scene set in the early hours of September 9 2001, Ziad is pulled over by a traffic cop for speeding. As played in *The Hamburg Cell* this moment is pregnant with possibility. Ziad seems to court arrest, stepping on the accelerator even as he sees the police car's swirling lights in his rear mirror; is he hoping to be detained so as to avoid his aerial consummation, trying to leave a trail to embellish the myth, or just experiencing the exhilaration of speed one last time?

In the end, for all its difficulty in following the 9/11 terrorists' tortuous mental pathways to jihad, *The Hamburg Cell* at least has the virtue of not making Mohammed Atta, Ziad Jarrah, and Co. fanatical dummies or cartoon villains. Surely our understanding of political or religious extremism of any kind can only be served by attempts, documentary, fictional, or otherwise, to explore seriously character and motivation. Of course, on a purely hypothetical level it could be questioned whether the Hamburg cell plotters can actually be stereotypes at all, in that word's original sense of a "rigid trace," since in the post-9/11 world they have become the "original" terrorists to which all subsequent traces, all depictions, such as those studied in this chapter, make inevitable reference. Alternatively, haven't they stereotyped themselves almost *avant la lettre*, so to speak, through their dogmatism and the scale of their act? Setting such considerations aside, the paradigmatic "Muslim threat" embodied by the 9/11 hijackers has served to provide fertile ground for film and television producers whose interests often have more to do with the cut and thrust of intrigue and high-octane action than with serious attempts at historical or cultural understanding. Such dramas provide the focus for the next chapter.

# CHAPTER 5

# Troubling Strangers

## Race, Nation, and the "War on Terror" in Television Thrillers

In a pertinent intervention in 2004, the documentary maker Adam Curtis criticized television's obsession with Islamic terrorism, claiming that programs such as *Dirty War* and *Spooks* take "the path of least resistance" and fall too easily "into line with the concerns expressed by the government"; "The opportunity to tell thrilling stories about sleeper cells in every major city has drawn networks into a 'complicity' with Tony Blair and George Bush."[1] If official rhetoric has since become less combative and more conciliatory as President Obama and Prime Ministers Brown and Cameron have sought to engage more with Muslim communities and nations, the thrill of the antiterror chase still serves as staple fare for film and television producers. As a result, the depiction of Muslim characters tends still toward nefarious fanatics, innocent victims, or, in occasional well-meaning reversals, exemplary embodiments of moral rectitude. Names and situations change, but the stereotypes persist. Moreover, in these dramatizations of encounters between the security services and their quarry, all the world becomes a stage for a battle that is really about policing aberrant elements who can never really be part of "our" civil societies. Different thriller series have dramatized these tensions in different ways. However, we would argue that for all their efforts to tell an exciting yet ultimately reassuring story about rescuing the nation, the ideological messages such productions inevitably contain are always challenged and exposed, not so much by the alien value system that directly contests them as by internal contradictions that expose nations as fluid entities constructed out of shifting alliances and unstable inclusions and exclusions.

We will examine some of the most popular and lauded post-9/11 television thrillers to see this process at work. In Fox's hugely successful *24*, a highly ideological narrative nonetheless has to work hard to reconcile the discrepant identity positions it would call on and bind together against a threat from without. In doing so, those racial coordinates that have historically shaped U.S. culture and politics are brought to the surface again, and even in the process of spinning them for the status quo, old antagonisms are recalled and overlooked alliances momentarily spring back into view. *The Grid*, by contrast, appears to offer a more pragmatic, watered-down account of the war on terror. The focus is more on the individual relationships of the main characters, alongside which the terrorists remain largely undeveloped and unexplored. However, the apparent sympathy the show demonstrates for the Muslim CIA agent who plays a key role in defeating the international conspiracy is actually undercut by a narrative arc that unequivocally forecloses the possibility of any such hybrid identity as "Muslim-American." The BBC's long-running spy series *Spooks*, has received much criticism from the Muslim community for egregious stereotyping. However, in its most controversial episode, it can be seen to be deliberately juxtaposing fairly crude stereotypes with more complex characterization that serves to encode metaphorically the position of all Western Muslim communities after 9/11 as outsiders treated with suspicion and always required to demonstrate their loyalty. Showtime's *Sleeper Cell* goes a stage further. While still placing Muslims firmly within a framing agenda to do with terrorism and treachery, this series actually uses the unnerving ability of a terrorist cell to pass unnoticed on the streets of Los Angeles to raise probing questions about Americanness itself, and to call into question the unequivocal difference claimed between "American" and "terrorist" by advocates of "clash of civilizations" binary simplifications. As we explore each of these cases, we will do well to keep in mind Tim Jon Semmerling's observation about the comforting utility of our film and television villains and how they sometimes offer a reassuring distraction from the harder questions we might ask ourselves: "our filmic villains are narrative tools used for self-presentation and self-identity to enhance our own stature, our own meaning and our own self-esteem in times of our own diffidence."[2]

## Getting Your Hands Dirty: Race, Nation, and Realpolitik in *24*

By sheer coincidence, Fox's drama *24* first aired in November 2001, just two months after 9/11 and less than one month after President Bush had signed into law the Patriot Act, designed as a response to the New York attacks. The Act—its title an acronym for its aims: Providing Appropriate Tools Required to Intercept and Obstruct Terrorism— allowed law enforcement agencies to intercept telephone and electronic communications, view financial, medical, and other records, and gave additional powers to identify, detain, and subsequently deport immigrants suspected of terrorist-related activities. It also made provision for U.S. authorities' use of foreign intelligence information with no regard to how it may have been obtained. All these powers have been invoked, and their attendant issues debated, in the topical world of terror plots and political intrigue that *24* presents. Eight series and numerous spin-offs were made in the years between 2001 and 2010, during which time *24* became one of the longest running espionage-based thriller series in television history, regularly scoring average viewing figures of between 11 and 13 million in the United States alone. The series has proved one of Fox's most popular exports, too; it has been aired in Europe, Africa, Latin America, Australia, and even the Middle East.

Although *24* became more interrogative in later series, exploring issues such as the ethics of torture, extraordinary rendition, and the moral compromises that might be necessary to save lives, in fact *24* remained one of the most shamelessly gung ho of post-9/11 dramas. Characteristically, the most frequent recurring threat to America in the series came from Muslims—mainly Arabs and susceptible Arab Americans. Looking specifically at series 2, in which agent Jack Bauer (played by Kiefer Sutherland) is sent on the trail of Islamist terrorists and their coconspirators who have planted a nuclear bomb somewhere in Los Angeles, we wish to suggest that true "Americanness" and American values are distinguished from those of the villains via a process of racialization wherein all threatening elements become, in a sense, "Muslimized"—expelled from the bosom of the nation, which is here conceived as an extension of the white, blond, Protestant family.

The persistent theme of families and fathering, and the failings of father figures, likewise indicates that the structure of normalization in 24 depends on a deeply conservative reiteration of family values. The ultimate "Otherness" of Muslims and Muslimized characters in relation to this discourse is guaranteed by their disregard for families and the consequences of their actions for wives and children. However, as a twist in the apparently simple white hegemonic trajectory on display, in the character of the black president, David Palmer, 24 takes its place in a line of terrorist dramas stretching back to the late 1990s in which African-American characters take the lead. In these often nationalistic films, such characters operate to imaginatively resolve historical racial tensions in the United States and facilitate a realignment against the true racial enemy, the Muslim Arab. Paradoxically, Palmer's role is to be the benevolent patriarch to an unruly extended family of 300 million Americans, conceived as a totality in Anglo-Saxon terms.

Applying the insights from the previous chapter about ideology and genre to the terrorist thriller genre, and 24 in particular, one can trace the lineaments of a crude, conservative message, operating on the basis of a post-9/11 notion of America in peril, where the failure to sustain patriarchal hegemony has opened the door to a veritable deluge of threats from disaffected interlopers of various kinds. However, the very rigidity of this attempted reentrenchment makes it prone to disturbing moments of self-revelation, where the antimiscegenatory and racist coordinates of the project loom into view, and the central concern to ward off infiltration and "contamination" takes such brutal functionalist forms that it erases the moral distinction on which the "War on Terror" depends.

In this regard, and as a barometer of ideological shifts and political anxieties, 24 allows itself to be read in a similar way to that suggested by Bennett and Woollacott in their analysis of the James Bond novels and movies. They suggest that James Bond works to "reconstruct 'Englishness' as Britain slips from world power status after the Second World War:" 'The Bond films operated . . . both to shift and stabilize subject identities at a time when existing ideological constructions had been placed in doubt and jeopardy, when . . . the articulating principles of hegemony were in disarray and alternatives had not been successfully established.'"³ The same kind of refraction of geopolitical realignment can be said to be present in some of the distinguishing features of *24*. Its famous split-screen technique, for instance, manages to indicate simultaneity of action and viewer proximity—drawing us in and closer to the action—while also emphasizing relative inertia; we see plotters preparing or villains closing in while one of the agents cogitates or takes a phone call, losing valuable seconds in the show's characteristic desperate race against time, measured always by its insistent ticking clock. At the same time, the different points of view enabled by split screen mimic the panoptic perspective of modern surveillance technology.⁴ All this is indicative of a sense of a culture under threat from enemies seen and unseen, with imminent dangers that must be countered by any means necessary.

However, it is on the level of realpolitik that the post-9/11 context makes itself felt most acutely: in the extent to which previous rules of engagement are deemed no longer to apply. For example, the first episode of series 2 opens with South Korean interrogators in Seoul torturing a prisoner to gain information about the nuclear bomb plot. Having extracted what was required, they pass immediately to the next room, where U.S. agents anxiously await the result. Here, at the start of the series, a key incident gestures toward two of the most controversial methods in the current U.S. military intelligence armory: rendition—where a suspect is handed over to those (conveniently non-American) hands who can in their own contexts torture with impunity; and the act of torture itself, once regarded as the heinous marker of those with less civilized and enlightened values but now a supposedly "legitimate" counterterrorism weapon. (Joel Surnow, *24*'s creator, in happily conceding the show's conservative animus, mused: "If there's a bomb about to hit a major US city and you have a person with information . . . if you don't torture that person, that would be one of the most immoral acts you could imagine."⁵) Neoconservative instrumentalism is further enshrined during the episode when Jack Bauer shoots dead and decapitates a prisoner order to gain the trust of a key conspirator against whom the detainee was to testify. The new political realities he embodies are articulated when he berates a more cautious senior officer: "You want results but you never want to get your hands dirty. I'd start rolling your sleeves up."

In fact, torture has "come home" in *24*. Bauer is more than willing to employ it when the situation demands. Later in series 2, physical and psychological interrogation techniques are pushed to the limit when Bauer questions a linchpin in the nuclear bomb plot, the Arab terrorist Syed Ali. With his beard indicating both villainy and, here, cultural unreliability, Ali is part of a long line of two-dimensional Hollywood Oriental bad guys described by Jack Shaheen and, more recently, by Ziauddin Sardar.[6] He wears black, speaks mainly in Arabic, and frequently spits when raised to anger. Ali is captured during a raid on a Los Angeles mosque but resists even the most brutal interrogation techniques. When Jack warns that he can inflict more pain than Ali ever imagined possible, the prisoner contemptuously replies, "Then I will have much more pleasure in paradise."

Toward the end of the extended torture scenes that take place in episode 12, the cartoonish malevolence and simplistic zealotry of Syed Ali is brought up against the perceived key organizing principle of the society Bauer is out to defend—the family. Earlier we have seen how family is aggressively propounded as a space of nurturing and the site of our supposed affective investment as viewers. (One thinks of President Bush's advice to Americans in the days after 9/11 to "live your lives and hug your children.")[7] Family also becomes that which distinguishes "us" from "them," in a way not found in comparable British terrorism thrillers, which tend, when they feature affective relationships, to focus more on the shifting sexual liaisons of the central characters. The series begins with Jack Bauer's attempts to patch up his relationship with his daughter, Kim, who still blames him for the death of her mother. Kim is working as an au pair for a couple with a young daughter. As in almost all the family units in this drama, the womenfolk are identikit blondes with similar levels of emotional frailty. The father of Kim's host family turns out to be a sexual predator and psychotic, leading to an extended subplot in which Kim tries to save the child from her sadistic father and weak-willed mother. With his flashy convertible and mysterious business associates, he finds a double in the "true outsider," Reza

Nair, a Westernized Muslim who is to marry another ubiquitous blonde, Marie Warner, the daughter of an inadequate father figure, businessman Bob Warner. Although Reza turns out to be an unwitting dupe, the suspicions that we are invited to entertain about him serve not so much to expose racial prejudice as to confirm the message, elsewhere expressed much more overtly, that the mixing of Western and Arabic cultures is a mistake to be avoided at all costs.

Fathers fail in their protective duties in *24* inasmuch as the enemy is seen to be already *within*. Just as Bob Warner has been too detached a father—allowing Marie to fall under the spell of jihadists while a student in London and countenancing her engagement to a Muslim—so there are concerns about infiltration, contamination, and a lack of necessary measures to combat miscreants on the national political level. Society and the nation are viewed as an extension of the family and, in the good and bad parenting motif that runs through the series, delinquent elements must be punished and malevolent outside forces repelled. It is significant that the threatening figures are either Arabs or have been educated in Europe, where they are presumably immune from the benevolent patriotism of the American education system and thereby more prone to radicalization. A chastened Warner tells how Marie went missing for several weeks in London after the death of her mother, emerging more subdued and with her old spirit of political activism apparently extinguished. His CTU (Counter Terrorism Unit) inquisitor comments sagely, "That's precisely what happens when you're radicalized. Handlers train you to stop talking about anything. . . . You're better able to blend into the background." The superior knowledge of the security services is similarly demonstrated when the unfortunate Reza objects to being hauled in as a suspect: "I grew up in London. I'm marrying an American girl, a Protestant. So, if you're going to racially profile me you should at least get it right." The reply is immediate and describes a variant of the post-Huntington stereotype mentioned earlier: "Our main targets are European Muslims with Western educations, passports and the potential to blend into Western society. So tell me, Reza, how's my racial profiling now?" Although Reza's willingness to become "like us" takes the form of a desire to replicate the family values of marriage and hard work, he remains always marked by Otherness in the dyadic narrative of the "War on Terror."

In the same way, President Palmer's vulnerability derives from admitting a viper into the bosom of the family. He is beset by plotting and intrigues emanating from within the U.S. military and intelligence communities and even from within his own administration. But all these threats are symbolically condensed in the duplicitous form of his estranged wife, Sherry. His gullibility and helplessness in the face of her machinations can be read as an indicator of the ineffectuality of his brand of tolerant liberalism. In the post-9/11 climate of crisis that *24* records and plays out, the fractious state of his own political family— his administration—bleeds relentlessly into an image of the wider family of Americans now under constant threat. As the softer, more diplomatic face of the nation, Palmer acts as a dramatic foil whose predicament permits the necessary excesses of agents such as Jack Bauer. This failure to protect the family forms the most visible symptom of a crisis of masculinity—similarly linked to the indulgences of liberal politics—which necessitates the reassertion of an extreme hypermasculinity in the actions of Bauer.

Significantly, it is frequently the case in *24* that threats to patriarchal law and order come from women. To the scheming first lady, Sherry Palmer, we can add the fanatical conspirator Marie Warner and Nina Myers, the original treacherous female from series 1 who, as the killer of Jack's wife, is the show's preeminent destroyer of the family. The women who work against the ideological settlement represented in their different ways by Palmer and Bauer join an assorted cast of malcontents and dissidents, all self-interestedly involved in the loose affiliations of an extended conspiracy. Nondomesticated, nonfamily-oriented women join radical anarchists, frustrated politicians, and Islamist terrorists as the enemies of the nation. In one way or another they are all "Muslimized," shuffled in the same pack as the trump card of Arabic religious malevolence, since they aim at the same thing: the destruction of liberal democracy in America.

Back in the torture room, gentle persuasion is getting nowhere. Clearly, stronger measures are necessary. With brute force too having failed, Bauer shows Syed Ali a live video feed of his family being bound by masked men in their home country. The family will be slaughtered in front of him, one by one, if Ali does not reveal the whereabouts of the bomb. Jack laments, "I despise you for making me do this." There are many ways in which the early series of *24* seem to tap into the zeitgeist, something reflected in imagery and incident. When it comes to the video link, we have almost a case of what Simon Cottle, quoting Michael Ignatieff, has called "the torturer as video artist." Like the grim images of mediated violence—the beheading of hostages on video by Islamist insurgents— or the casual "souvenir" violence of torture at Abu Ghraib, Bauer's tactics are an example of how the "digital image, moving or still, has become an instrument of coercive interrogation."[8]

Meanwhile, back at crisis HQ, President Palmer learns of Jack's tactics. Characteristically, he hesitates, allowing his chief of staff to administer a sobering dose of pragmatism about the numbers game the two sides are now engaged in: "a few people may have to die to save millions." Despite Palmer's humanistic intervention, Bauer ratchets up the pressure, but Syed Ali only froths and fumes. So Bauer gives the order for Ali's eldest son to be shot. Only after this, with the prospect of losing his second son too, does Ali relent and give up the location of the bomb. Of course, we soon discover that the assassination was staged and the child is physically unharmed. In the process we have learned that Jack effectively cares more for Ali's family than Ali does himself, since Ali was prepared to sacrifice his own flesh and blood in his fanaticism. (We are reminded constantly of Bauer's anguish at having been forced to watch his own wife die in the previous series.) Ali is the most zealous and misguided of the children of Abraham. It takes God, in the guise of Jack Bauer, to step in and prevent this particular filial sacrifice.

The scene reveals Bauer to be the realist and Palmer the naïve idealist. It is not so much that Palmer's blackness prevents him from being an effective leader as that in many respects he represents the "better self" of an America forced by circumstances to take unpalatable decisions and act against its true nature. Dennis Haysbert as Palmer is a kind of latter-day Gregory Peck figure, embodying tolerance and decency, but transposed to an era when these values are no longer adequate to the demands of the situation. The situation requires, in part, the screening off of Americans from nefarious outside influences, all of which have a hub in Saudi Arabia and the Middle East.

In this respect it is possible to read the President Palmer character as the ultimate fulfilment of the racial rapprochement through which African Americans have been imaginally brought into the bosom of power and made symbolically central to their country's fight against the real racial adversary, the Arab. As such, he is only the most recent in a line of black American film heroes pitted against unscrupulous and brutal Arabs, who embody national values and thereby suggest that all the struggles dating back from Civil Rights to slavery can finally be laid to rest, sealed off as the history of another time before America came to discover a crossracial self, defined by those who stand against it.

Hishaam Aidi has recently traced the long history of what he describes as "black internationalism" in relation to the Orient. Taking their cue from the Bandung Conference of 1955, with its focus on self-determination and anticolonial politics, black internationalists such as Malcolm X championed Black-Arab relations as a means to oppose white supremacism and colonial power structures. Aidi shows how, Cairo in the 1950s and 1960s was seen by Malcolm and many other black activists and writers as a place where all races could meet and mix on a comparatively equal footing. Further anticolonial solidarity can be seen in relations between the Civil Rights movement and the FLN in Algeria. However, according to Aidi, a shift took place in the 1970s, with revisionist historians now seeing Arabs as having overrun black Africa and actively participated in the slave trade. At the same time, Arab nationalism was seen as having turned its back on the greater dream of Pan-Africanism, articulated at decolonization by Kwame Nkrumah and others. Slowly, the idea took hold that Arabs were hostile interlopers on the African continent: a notion that appeared to be supported by the 1998 bombings of U.S. embassies in Dar Es Salaam and Nairobi, and the Darfur crisis.[9]

Debates continue around the exact reasons for this change in the relationship between black and Arab; Aidi speculates that it may be partly attributable to the rise of a black American middle class who no longer identified with anticolonial solidarity. Taking up this idea, Moustafa

Bayoumi has recently argued that traditional racial discourses—which historically placed black Americans in the space of suspicious, marginalized pseudocriminality—have been tweaked since 9/11. The introduction of racial profiling quickly evolved from an unpopular blunt instrument to an ethnically specific means of identifying potential terrorists, transforming the previous position of treating Arabs as effectively invisible, or at most as an afterthought in the discourses of racial difference. However, according to Bayoumi, not only do Arabs now endure the stigmatization previously the preserve of black communities but also ideologically interpellated "blackness" is now used to guarantee the values of democracy, decency, and, of course, family for which the U.S. is said to stand.[10] One may, perhaps, see a trace of this change in the popular media of cinema and television. In the movies *The Siege* (1998) and *The Kingdom* (2006), American values are embodied by African-American leading characters played by Denzel Washington and Jamie Foxx. President Palmer performs a similar binding role in *24* as the nation's father figure, albeit underpinned by the necessary violence he would never personally condone. In Bayoumi's reading of such constructions, the African American man knows better than the white man how to talk to Arabs. At the same time, the moral preeminence of such black characters suggests that the United States can be understood to have overcome the blinkered racism of the past. Such a narrative has the effect of evacuating any possibility of racism in the present: since anti-black prejudice, the default signifier of historical race inequality, has supposedly ended, the current suspicions of Arabs in general must be well founded—some of them *do* attack "us" after all—and cannot therefore be racism. Bayoumi shares with Aidi a sense that the historical African-American commitment to cross-racial solidarity and anti-colonialism of the early and mid-twentieth centuries is occluded in contemporary accounts. Recent film and television constructions, such as, those cited here, work to ignore or even erase this history, which is now the uncomfortable, inconvenient part of the legacies of Edward Blyden, W.E.B. Du Bois, and Malcolm X.

Anticipating Barack Obama by some seven years, *24*'s President Palmer may have risen to the highest office in the land, thereby supporting the idea of black Americans fully integrated and thriving in a rainbow nation, but his beleaguered administration struggles to cope with the machinations of those, both within and without, who challenge values that were set in place long before this rapprochement, the threat to which can only really be addressed by brute force and right-wing pragmatism. Ethics have no place in this world, although morals, in the sense of ideological convictions elevated to a quasi-religious status and defended with similar zeal, can be used to mobilize characters (and, it is suggested, viewers) through the rallying cry of the family under threat.

During the Crusades, the Knights Templar carried before them into battle a banner divided horizontally, the upper half black and the lower half white, "because they were fair and favorable to the friends of Christ but black and terrible to his enemies."[11] In 24, and other dramas like it, black characters are overlaid on plots whose colonial trajectory involves restating the rightness of white Western hegemony in the face of those who would contest it. Whether in the "Holy Land" or the "Land of the Free," the basic ethnic coordinates of the struggle remain the same, and President Palmer finds himself occupying the White House on sufferance, the figurehead for a system that can only assert itself by betraying its own self-defining principles.

### *The Grid:* Squeezing Out the Hyphenated Subject

If even so rigidly conservative a series as 24 suggests that the thriller genre does not simply act as a conveyor belt for the dominant ideology, we may expect some degree of subtlety in the way contending discourses are organized in other dramas. While the Muslim counter-discourse in 24 is a travesty composed of psychopathic plotters and duplicitous diplomats, most other vehicles attempt some sort of presentation of Muslim grievances. However, even where this is the case one often finds a clearly displayed hierarchy of credibility, having to do with the way our sympathies are directed. In televisual contexts further removed from the corridors of political power in Washington and when more of the target audience are perhaps skeptical about the "War on Terror," different strategies and tones are in play. When we move to transatlantic dramas, such as, another Fox terror drama, *The Grid* (2004), it is useful to bear in mind Peter Golding and Graham Murdock's remarks on the constraints on form imposed by international coproduction: "partners search for subject matter and narrative styles they can sell in their home markets. The resulting bargain may produce an Americanized product which is fast-moving, based on simple characterizations, works with a tried and tested action format, and offers an ambiguous ending." In reality, however, the compromises inherent in such hybrid arrangements "inhibit a full engagement with the complexities and ambiguities of the national condition."[12]

Similar themes of racial purity and the dangers of miscegenation to those found in *24* are also played out in *The Grid*, which in its title sequence and general production values strongly resembles *24*. But this is a softer version with the rough edges of its politics smoothed over for a transatlantic audience. A coproduction with the BBC, directed by Mikael Salomon, *The Grid* follows a group of British and American intelligence agents pursuing an al-Qaeda offshoot across four continents, facing misinformation and diversionary tactics along the way as they race against time to foil a series of linked plots. The show starts with that most ubiquitous of visual clichés: the veiled woman. At the start, a woman in a full-length burqa receives a vial of the nerve agent Sarin from a scientist somewhere in Kazakhstan. Immediately afterward she unveils to reveal an attractive, carefully made-up face, the kind that—along with more "Western attire"—will allow her to pass unsuspected through a customs checkpoint, en route to deliver her deadly burden to its destination in London. Thus begins the series of international movements that literally and metaphorically mark the coordinates of the grid within which this latest episode in the War on Terror will be waged.

Likewise, the more international cast of characters in *The Grid* leads to insistent differences in the way, for example, the U.S. and British agents are depicted. Distinctions based on perceived national characteristics pale into insignificance, however, when set against the otherness of their shared quarry, Islamist activists recruited from various parts of the globe, including the metropolitan centers themselves.

While we are, as usual, invited to identify with the Western agents, our particular focalizers and centers of affective investment are the two American agents, Max Canary (played by Dylan McDermott) and Maren Jackson (Julianna Margulies). Alongside them the main British agents, Derek Jennings (Bernard Hill) and Emily Tuthill (Jemma Redgrave), are dogged, more pragmatic, and ultimately less glamorous. Canary and Jackson are tough and professional, but their emotional lives are laid out before us, too. Canary had a friend who was killed in the Twin Towers attacks and now enjoys a complex relationship with the dead man's wife. Jackson embodies the successful and determined Western career woman, while remaining recognizably "feminine," with her headstrong reactions and smouldering sensuality; we first see her in the throes of passion with her businessman lover.

The Islamist terrorists, on the other hand, are an unusually diverse crew for this type of show. In addition to utterly flat characters, for example their principal funder—introduced, in a spectacular compression of time-honored Oriental types, above stop-frame subtitles, as a "Fundamentalist Saudi Oil Billionaire"—we have an assortment of post-Huntington stereotypes seemingly culled from contemporary newspaper accounts of terror suspects' profiles. There is the economically disadvantaged British Muslim: the seemingly integrated but actually disaffected second-generation Chechen-American student (embodying the threat from within like a sort of souped-up, culturally distanced version of John Walker-Lind, the "American Taliban"). And there is the Muslim medic from Egypt, torn between his vocation to save lives and the murderous cause he comes to espouse.

The point here is that the Muslim characters, in contrast to their Western counterparts, are mediated to us via externals, by social circumstances and actions, *not* through any kind of emotional life we are invited to identify with. As in so much of the fiction and film about contemporary terrorism, the Americans, and to a lesser extent the British, are *psychologized*: for example, Canary's adopted son is still traumatized by images of 9/11, and Canary encourages him to work through his feelings. The Muslims are, in contrast, *pathologized;* they and their religious, social, and political systems are seen as inherently predisposed to violence, be it terrorism or brutal law enforcement.

Inasmuch as there is any psychological prompting here, it is a kind of heedless sadomasochism, a perverted and repressed offshoot of the kind of intimate relations the Western characters are free to enjoy. The terrorist mastermind and former al-Qaeda commander Youssef Nassariah (aka Muhammad) articulates a credo of sorts when he observes, "Pain, real pain, obliterates everything: memory, love—even faith."

Moreover, since it is assumed that we, the viewers, need an emotional connection with the characters with whom we are being invited to identify, pathos is always experienced at the individual level—in the personal travails and relationships of the Americans—rather than in, for example, the killing of scores of Africans in the Lagos bombings near the end of the first episode. The spectacular explosions and ensuing chaos make a suitably apocalyptic ending point, but the episode actually finishes with us alone in an elevator with Jackson, who—having been duped into expecting an attack on the New York Subway system—breaks down in tears. As well as ensuring that her core femininity is once again emphasized—with the clichéd message on the compromises necessary for a woman to make it in a man's world—this diminuendo finale, following the crescendo of the bombing, ensures that the individual's anguished response to personal and professional failure is made more affecting than the carnage that claims countless anonymous Africans.

In fact, the most interesting character in *The Grid* is the obligatory good Muslim, the Middle East analyst Raza Michaels, played by Piter Fattouche. Once again, part of the function of the good Muslim is to explain aspects of Muslim history and culture to Western interlocutors. He is used early on to articulate some of the positive aspects of Islamic civilization and culture. We also find that his questioning of the different aspects of his own identity, as a Muslim but also as an American, is an ongoing process; at one point he suggests that being an American makes him a better Muslim, although he does not say why. Yet despite the predictable ideological utility of this character, he is not easily or comfortably incorporated in the unfolding clash of civilizations that the show tirelessly adumbrates; he is never really trusted by the more hawkish elements in the CIA.

The parallel fates of the young Chechen American, Kaz Moore—

killed trying to detonate a bomb on a chemical tanker in Chicago Harbor—and Michaels, point to the conclusions we are being invited to draw. Michaels's heroic death—he dies trying to dissuade a young suicide bomber from blowing himself up—appears to allow the character to be fully recuperated as a misunderstood individual exonerated in the manner of his death from all suspicion as to his loyalty. Yet within the broader tide of a story in which matters are resolved through the simplistic confirmation of binaries (agents versus terrorists, us versus them) his demise also works to cancel out the possibility of any middle ground, any hybrid identity. Unlike the Chechen American, whose apparent predilection for such Western pleasures as beer and cars is simply a veneer behind which lurks a more sinister, alien animus, Michaels's "in-betweenness" is presented sympathetically, but in the end still represents a kind of utopianism potentially distracting from the War on Terror, which requires for its paranoid effects the rigid observation of difference. The hyphenated identities so often celebrated by postcolonialism are here the object of deep and justified suspicion.[13] Michaels's death is, in fact, the natural culmination of a storyline whose later stages have him drawn into an emotional and ultimately sexual relationship with the British agent, Emily Tuthill. On the night before his death, Raza has sex with Emily. The coy fade-out on this scene is immediately followed by a shot of Raza in an attitude of prayer next morning. Emily wakes up and, in one of those jarring didactic moments that abound in this drama, says that she understands that Raza's culture forbids sex outside marriage. In reply, he confesses that he is falling in love with her, presumably legitimizing their liaison for a normalized audience conversant with and sympathetic to the conventions of voluntary romantic love (as opposed to the unreasonable, repressive injunctions of Islam). Soon after this Raza is killed.

Thus, Raza Michaels's apotheosis is highly ambiguous. He is allowed a hero's death and a consummation with the white Western female, but the antimiscegenation antinomies that shape the drama's ideology mean that his reward can only be brief, and his belated consecration as a true defender of civilization comes at the cost of his own life; "we" know who "we" are because we are not "them." For all its surface rhetoric of tolerance and its nods toward the complexity of modern terrorism, *The Grid*—unlike *24*—is ultimately evasive about the true exigencies of a global "War on Terror." In the final scene, with the plot foiled and the terrorists successfully disposed of, the camera pulls slowly away from the captured Nassariah/Muhammad, who is shown behind receding rows of fences, in a dressing gown, bending to relight the stub of a cigarette. He is detained, presumably indefinitely, at some unspecified location, snowbound and patrolled by military guards. Yet the obvious location for an "enemy combatant" of Muhammad's stature would surely be Camp Delta. Instead, the main perpetrator of evil can live out his days, sans shackles and orange jumpsuit, with as many creature comforts as he can persuade the authorities to grant him. There is no torture, extraordinary rendition, or detention without trial in the world of *The Grid*. And "our" civilized values are enshrined in the very fact that Nassariah/Muhammad is not the recipient of the kinds of brutality he has often meted out to others. We can therefore feel reassured about the legitimacy of such spaces outside the jurisdiction of national and international law. There are worse fates after all.

### Passing Strangers: Playing with Stereotypes in *Spooks*

With its right-wing patriotism and instrumental violence, *24* has long been in the sights of the Council on American-Islamic Relations, which accuses it of fomenting anti-Muslim prejudice. Its closest equivalent in Britain is the BBC's popular thriller series *Spooks*, which focuses on MI5. Similar accusations of stirring up Islamophobia have been leveled at *Spooks*, never more vociferously than in the controversy surrounding "Nest of Angels," an episode in series 2, aired in 2003. The terms of that particular debate are instructive for the attempt to map the construction, perception, and circulation of stereotypes, so it is worth recapping it briefly here. "Nest of Angels" portrays young Muslims being groomed as suicide bombers at the fictional Parkmount Mosque in Birmingham. The mosque has fallen under the sway of a heavily bearded and transparently malevolent Afghani radical cleric, Mohammed Rashid (played by Quarie Marshall), who has links with al-Qaeda. Neither the efforts of the "good Muslim" patriarch, Fazl Azam (Roshan Seth), nor of the young Asian MI5 agent, "Johnny," sent to infiltrate the mosque, are of any avail in dislodging the turbulent priest.

"Nest of Angels" was broadcast first on one of the BBC digital channels and thereafter on the BBC's flagship station, BBC1, where it attracted 7.8 million viewers. It also attracted the attention of the Muslim Council of Britain, the most high-profile of the plethora of bodies set up to "represent" the interests of Britain's widely divergent Muslim communities. A letter from the MCB's Inayat Bunglawala to the then controller of BBC1, Lorraine Heggessey, accused the corporation of inciting religious hatred and distorting the reality of Muslim life in Britain.[14] Reports sought to connect transmission of the *Spooks* episode to an attack on a Muslim student in Birmingham and graffiti about suicide bombers outside a mosque. The barrage of over a thousand complaints that followed was mainly due to an e-mail campaign coordinated among Muslim groups set up to monitor media representations of their communities. The existence and activities of such groups ought to act as a caution against any notion that Muslims are merely passive victims of stereotyping, lacking the ability or motivation to challenge framing. What is of more interest here is the way the MCB missive recognized the general outline of stereotyping in character and plot but entirely missed the more complex narrative trajectory of the episode and, more significantly, the representational politics of which *Spooks* is a part.

Bunglawala's letter accused the BBC of reinforcing negative stereotypes and offering "grossly offensive and Islamophobic caricatures of Imams, Muslim students and mosques." Suggesting a rather simplistic relationship between fiction and reality—one challenged in Heggessey's response—the MCB letter expressed the fear that "Nest of Angels" would "lead many of your viewers to suspect that mosques are criminally dangerous places indeed, full of brainwashed and violent individuals." Interestingly, Bunglawala also picked up on two of those metonymic signifiers of Muslimness discussed in the previous chapter: "The 'bad Imam,' Muhammad Rashid[,] was shown with a flowing beard, whereas the 'good Imam' Fazl Azam was shown as being clean-shaven, thereby buttressing the impression that bearded Muslims are to be feared. In fact, you will find that most 'good' Imams are actually bearded in line with the example of the Prophet Muhammad (peace be upon him). . . . The mosque is a place where Muslims gather for their five daily prayers. Yet in the entire program, not a single Muslim was shown actually performing the salah, the Muslim ritual prayer."[15]

What is striking here, however, is the determined assertion that the real religious and cultural significance of beards has been misrepresented and that the *salah* would offer an unproblematic corrective via the performativity of Muslim ritual, in turn indicating religious devotion, sincerity, and goodness. Even in 2003, at what this study would suggest was a cruder moment than today in the framing of Muslims, such a claim seems oblivious to the broader politics of representation everywhere apparent, in which both beards *and* the Muslim act of prayer were already construed as markers of Otherness and threat. While it may have a valid concern to raise about a rising tide of Islamophobia, Bunglawala's call from "within" the community to recuperate a positive representation through the use of performative elements already tainted with suspicion in the popular consciousness seems well-intentioned but vain. As it turned out, Lorraine Heggessey was able to counter the MCB's charges on their own terms—those of good and bad Muslims—by emphasizing that the show's balance was firmly tilted in favor of the good Muslim characters. In fact, the MCB's pleas from a position assuming the existence of a standard of common representational fairness momentarily mislaid, seriously underestimates the depth to which a "clash of civilizations" mindset had impregnated the society of which the spooks were fictional outriders. It was left to the more militant fringe group Hizb ut-Tahrir, reflecting on the affair, to assert: "It is not sufficient to limit ourselves to complaining about the broadcast of such programs or calling for the BBC to change her policy, since Western media outlets will continue to air such programs in the name of freedom of speech. Rather it is necessary, indeed an obligation, to challenge the ideas that underpin Western societies such as their freedoms that create immoral and perverse societies."[16] Let it never be said that stereotyping is one-way traffic.

Bunglawala and Heggessey might be forgiven for reducing the matter to questions of good and bad Muslims, since that is often the starting point (and sometimes the end point too) of discussions about media representations. However, they might also have taken encouragement from the way the show set out the characters in its pretitles opening scene, in which the bad Muslim Rashid's interrogation of "Johnny" is interrupted by the sympathetic but powerless Fazl Azam. Outside the mosque, the regular team of MI5 agents sit in a surveillance van and fret about the loss of audio contact with their vulnerable colleague. Having discovered Johnny's transmitter, the glinty-eyed Rashid confirms his evil nature by having his burly henchmen beat and torture the rookie spy before hurling him from a window, sending him crashing onto the roof of the surveillance van below.

In this instance, good and evil seem delineated very distinctly, not to say crudely. However, in keeping with the moral ambiguity and ethical questions that follow the agents through every case they undertake, as the drama unfolds more complex types of affiliation are raised, and a note of ambiguity is struck that not only goes beyond to the rather one-dimensional MCB understanding but in fact can be said to reproduce the ambivalent position of Muslims as a whole in relation to the sanctioned (and narrowed) demands of Western national identification. As it develops, "Nest of Angels" achieves a level of complexity one might expect from the pen of the episode's writer, Howard Brenton, one of the most respected British dramatists of the last forty years. In fact, if in shows such as *24* and *The Grid* the security services are the nation in miniature, then *Spooks* shows a nation that is inclusive and multicultural and at the same time torn by anxieties and doubts, the demands of expediency, political intrigue, and a mistrustful relationship with its allies. An ostensive setup involving agents safeguarding British national security against a range of threats is, in fact, only one aspect of a drama that is also keen to explore the psychological cost to the secret agents of a life of danger, double-dealing, and subterfuge.

As MI5 stands helplessly by, not knowing enough about Rashid's plans to intervene, he grooms a young boy, Abu Hassan, channeling his unfocused disaffection and secondhand anti-Americanism into a commitment to building the House of Islam in England, something that can only be achieved by the shedding of the "blood of martyrs." Indeed, as always in the espionage-based thriller, a contest takes place throughout "Nest of Angels" around knowledge. MI5 needs an agent with the right cultural background, and more experience this time, to again infiltrate the mosque and discover Rashid's plot, but has none available. At this point we are introduced to a character who will destabilize the certainties set in place in the basic plot scenario and lead the agents—and the viewer—on a dance of uncertainty that lasts until almost the final scene.

A freight train emerges from a tunnel at night. In the flickering light shed by the trackside lamps a disheveled, bearded character can be seen clinging precariously to the end of one of the wagons. Dawn breaks, and the stranger makes his escape from the goods yard and finds his way to London. There, in an iconic shot, he is seen with a wandering mendicant's staff in hand, like some kind of pilgrim, making his way across the Millennium footbridge toward that ubiquitous symbol of Britishness, St. Paul's Cathedral. Presenting himself at police headquarters, New Scotland Yard, he informs the officer on guard, "I am an agent from North Africa. I can be of great use to your country."

This man, Ibn Khaldun—a name Brenton takes from the renowned fourteenth-century Muslim polymath and traveler—has come from Algeria via France (and that permanent conduit of right-wing anxiety about illegal immigrants, the Channel Tunnel). All that is known about him is that he was a university lecturer, was arrested by the Algerian secret service, and was forced to work for them, penetrating a jihadist terror group. But his cover was blown, and a car bomb meant for him blew up his wife and family instead. Agent Tom Quinn goes to see him in the cell where he is detained and negotiates his release, even though, as he admits, "we don't know what he is." A tense cat-and-mouse game follows between Khaldun and the spies who believe, or rather hope, they have enlisted him to go undercover and expose Rashid. Uncertainties remain over Khaldun's motivations. Is he truly an Anglophile wishing to serve the country he has idolized from afar in the form of cozy cultural narratives such as *Peter Pan,* or is he, as he claims on meeting Rashid, a double agent sent to infiltrate British intelligence? Fears are raised when Khaldun begins to miss his regular rendezvous with Tom, and when he discards the "ridiculous James Bondery" of sophisticated tracking equipment provided for him, tossing it into a canal. In his dealings with both sides he seems entirely plausible and, for that reason, potentially duplicitous.

In his transience and his apparently shifting affiliations, Khaldun could be seen as an embodiment of Zygmunt Bauman's "stranger," that paradigmatic yet disturbing figure of the margins created by the modern nation in its desperate but always unfulfillable craving for order. The stranger flourishes beyond the ordering categories of insider/outsider, friend/enemy, with their totalizing drives: "Against this cozy antagonism . . . the stranger rebels, . . . He calls the bluff of the opposition between friends and enemies as the *compleat mappa mundi*. . . . And all this because the stranger is neither friend nor enemy; and because he may be both. And because we do not know, and have no way of knowing which is the case."[17] The "undecidability" of the stranger makes for doubt. It creates an ever-present gap in the project of total knowledge that lies at the heart of both the modern nation and, by definition, its intelligence agencies. Bauman elaborates on the unsettling tension between involvement and indifference, detachment and participation that presents itself in the stranger: "The commitment the stranger declares, the loyalty he promises, the dedication he demonstrates cannot be trusted."[18] This is certainly the case with Khaldun in *Spooks,* as Tom complains when his unreliable charge fails once again to appear for a briefing.

Yet Khaldun's status as a stranger does more than simply confound the binary opposition set up at the start. In fact, we would argue, it becomes emblematic of the position of all Muslims within Western nations post-9/11. This is especially true in the early days after the attacks, when Muslims were called on directly to distance themselves from the actions and beliefs of the 9/11 terrorists, under pain of expulsion from the bosom of national membership. If those Muslims-beyond-our-borders were transformed fairly indiscriminately into an all-purpose enemy by the clumsy twin rhetoric of Bush and al-Qaeda, then communities in the West—whether in London or New York, Dearborn or Bradford—suddenly found themselves transformed into unsettled and unsettling strangers by the same forces. Spied on, viewed with suspicion, and in some cases detained or transported, the Muslim in the West reignited fears about the unassimilated stranger whose presence troubles the utopian voyage of the governable nation into a postmodern future in which friends and enemies will be able to be easily identified and neutralized. (Had the MCB taken the time to consider the narrative arc of "Nest of Angels," they might have seen that beyond the initial caricatures the drama operates as a kind of allegory for the position of Muslims: doubted by the majority communities around them and having always to prove their fidelity.)

In essence the problem is one of reading. Bauman speaks of "the acute discomfort we feel when we are unable to read the situation properly and to choose between alternative actions."[19] In a moment of exasperation, Tom Quinn echoes this perplexity: "What if Khaldun's not what he says he is? What if he's been an extremist all along? What if he's here to co-ordinate the attack? The trouble is I don't know, I just can't read him." He is forced to reevaluate his own reactions when Khaldun gives up his life, pursuing the young would-be martyr into a children's playground and trying unsuccessfully to persuade him not to pull the cord on his bomb belt. "I misread Khaldun. . . . Actually he was a hero." Shortly before, in his last rendezvous with Quinn, Khaldun has described how Rashid requires him to accompany the *shahid* or 'martyr' on his final mission. It is a test for him to prove his commitment to the cause. "And it's an old trick," he remarks ruefully. "Get the stranger to do the filthy thing." Only in his death can the stranger prove, once and for all, to either side, where his loyalties lie. Read in the way we suggest here, "Nest of Angels" dramatizes the impossibility, in the aftermath of 9/11, for Muslims to satisfactorily demonstrate their allegiance to the nation—at least in this life. In thrillers such as *Spooks* and *The Grid*, vindication can only come through a rite of blood. In truth, both sides try to "get the stranger to do the filthy thing."

Brenton thus gives a decisive twist to what appears at first to be a standard thriller set-up involving good Westerners fighting swarthy evildoers. In fact, *Spooks* has always had a fairly sophisticated vision of Britain and its place in the world, and what the values might be that are actually worth defending. Brenton's achievement in "Nest of Angels" is to throw back an image of British society's own exclusionary and judgmental tactics regarding Muslims; Khaldun's unconventional arrival and itinerant habits make him emblematic of the "illegal immigrants" and "asylum seekers" who are the enduring objects of tabloid vilification. As the hero of the piece, however, he confounds such judgments and suggests that the Muslim can occupy a space other than those of villain or victim, even if acceptance requires another type of martyrdom. We ought also to take extremely seriously the cries from Muslims who see representations such as those that are regularly displayed in *Spooks* as one more derogatory brick in a now very big wall of Islamophobia and prejudice. Even so, that *Spooks* can and does raise questions about how vigorously literal and ideological borders ought to be policed should turn our attention once more to the raw materials of cultural representation—genre, narrative arc, characterization, and so on—which are never deployed in quite the same way twice.

## *Sleeper Cell:* Turning America Inside Out

Similar generic flexibility is on display in Showtime's Emmy-nominated series *Sleeper Cell*, first aired in 2005. This show's main claim to fame was that it featured the first Muslim action thriller protagonist in Darwyn Al-Sayeed (played by Michael Ealy). Executive producers Cyrus Voris and Ethan Reiff deliberately set out to challenge simplistic stereotypes in the creation of Darwyn, a character "inspired by the fact that there are Muslim Americans in the US military and law enforcement who are faithful followers of their religion whilst being loyal, patriotic Americans."[20] In fact, *Sleeper Cell* does employ a number of familiar negative Muslim stereotypes while weaving its tale of a Muslim FBI agent who goes undercover to penetrate a sleeper cell planning an atrocity on U.S. soil. The series is, however, distinctive in setting those images alongside other, more complex, characterizations and in interrogating the ideological and social landscape of modern America so as to call into question certain commonplace, supposedly civilizational assumptions by which "we" are distinguished from "them."

Part of the challenge to facile cultural judgments comes in the form of a didactic agenda pursued throughout the series. So the ethnonormalized non-Muslim viewer learns of the difference between Muslims and Sikhs (both communities having been targeted in the post-9/11 backlash) doctrinal variations within Islam; dietary restrictions; and attitudes to sex and marriage. Also significant is the marked break with the predominant depiction of mosques as places of moral, and therefore usually also literal, darkness. In contrast to the dimly lit, suspicious mosque interiors of 24 and *Spooks,* Darwyn proceeds straight from prison, where he has been planted to learn more about the extremists' plans, to an open, brightly lit mosque, where women and smiling children mingle with male worshippers and a strong, positive sense of community clearly exists. Significantly, the series also ends there, after the defeat of the terrorists, with a closing shot of Darwyn reverently kneeling alone in the streaming sunlight. Not only is the conventional visual icon of the dangerous mosque overturned, but in the final scene the fact that Darwyn can pray alone—rather than as one of a menacingly homogenous set of prostrating figures—gestures toward the keen personal sense of faith that motivates our hero throughout.

Another change from conventional modes of representation appears in the composition of the sleeper cell Darwyn is sent to infiltrate. If we accept that the preeminent figure of Muslim otherness in U.S. film and television drama is the Arab, *Sleeper Cell* is immediately striking for the cultural diversity of the cell members. As well as Darwyn the African-American covert agent, the group includes a Bosnian, a French former skinhead, and a blond, all-American Californian boy. Each has a backstory that is revealed as the series progresses; Ilya the Bosnian, for example, watched the slaughter of his family by Christian Serbs, waited in vain for America to come to their rescue, and has harbored a deep-rooted hatred of the United States ever since. Such grievances are here articulated by characters embedded in the story, rather than by the token use-value Muslim characters that tend elsewhere to be deployed for the purpose. The multinational, multiethnic makeup of the cell effectively undercuts the stereotype of the inevitably Arab, always bearded fanatic. However, as if to link this diverse cast of plotters back to the geographical home of the ideology they serve, their leader, Faris Al-Farik (Oded Fehr), is himself an Arab and receives his instruction from shadowy masters in Saudi Arabia.

The eclectic personnel of the sleeper cell confounds easy recognition by the outward markers of Muslim Otherness; none of them sport full beards or wear kurtas, for instance; all prefer the regulation American uniform of jeans and sneakers. Indeed a criticism of America's melting-pot version of multiculturalism could be read in the ease with which the cell members move among the rest of the population going about their daily business. Has America's inclusiveness become its undoing, as writers such as Steven Emerson have famously suggested?[21] However, the matter is more complicated than one of foreign arrivants bringing their degenerate ways with them. Why, for example, has Tommy, the young Californian, turned to a violent political Islam, whereas Darwyn—a member of a community with a rather more serious experience of historical victimization—opted to join the FBI to fight both for the United States and for the peaceful brand of Islam he believes in? In answering such questions, Sleeper Cell takes us on a journey of twists and turns where expectations are challenged and judgments—even about the supposedly inherent qualities of America itself—are subject to scrutiny.

This journey begins, in episode 1, with Darwyn's release from prison, first contact with Farik, and initiation into the cell. Just as Darwyn must blend in with the group led by Farik, so, of course, the sleeper cell must merge with its surroundings. So Darwyn first meets his new confederates at an outdoor birthday party for the daughter of a coconspirator, at which children of all creeds and races enjoy a sunny day in the park. The group bonds over an impromptu game of football that takes place to a pounding hip-hop soundtrack, and their apparent unobtrusive "Americanness" is further confirmed when Darwyn and the other men go bowling.

In most post-9/11 thrillers the boundary between those who are inside the nation, and thus to be defended, and those who seek to come from outside to disrupt civil society is soon fairly obvious. In Sleeper Cell, however, the signifiers are more scrambled and unclear. As has been suggested, 24 tends ultimately to work at the exalted level of governmental ideology, confirming the rightness of what is identified as the national interest through its domestic visual correlative, the sacred American family. Yet, whereas the threat there—for all that it may creep up the manicured lawns of middle-class America—always comes from without, in Sleeper Cell the strapline warns us that "they" are already here, hold down jobs, and are indistinguishable from "us": "Friends, Neighbours. Husbands. Terrorists." In Darwyn we have an American who is also a practicing (read performing) Muslim. Yet we are also confronted with a situation such that the Muslim terrorists also "perform" like regular Americans; at one point Farik gives two of his charges a few days off, encouraging them to "have a Big Mac. Go watch a movie in your multiplex cinemas. Just spend the weekend like a couple of average Americans." Indeed, throughout the series, and especially in the first episode, we see the constant reiteration of heavy, yet somewhat ambivalent signifiers of Americanness. Football, bowling, rap music, and casual sex figure in an idiosyncratic list and take the place of the straightforward paragons of family, faith, and freedom more usually deployed. The Los Angeles in which the action takes place is a townscape often traversed at night and made up of bars, lap dancing clubs, adult bookshops, prostitutes, and cheap convenience stores. These terrorists are parasitic and flourish on the squalid underbelly of LA, exploiting its potential for anonymity to secure chemicals and explosives through black market trading, coercing the vulnerable, and ruthlessly disposing of enemies. Similarly, in this drama there are no agents with an array of untiring technical geniuses providing backup from a state-of-the-art base. Unlike Jack Bauer, with his twenty-four-hour hotline to the president, Darwyn Al-Sayeed inhabits a much more unstable hinterland as a covert agent planted among the enemy, always deniable, forever expendable.

At the end of episode 1, having embedded himself successfully inside the cell, Darwyn is forced to take an oath of allegiance that seems designed specifically to mimic the pledge repeated by all Americans from early childhood. Yet, instead of the familiar formulation: "I pledge allegiance to the Flag of the United States of America . . . ," Darwyn must affirm a completely different affiliation: "I pledge my absolute fealty to a life of struggle, a life of jihad . . ." This direct challenge to what is sometimes seen as a sacred incantation ensuring Americanness appears to posit a binary contest between two sets of values, beliefs and, thus actions. However, the very fact that the cell manages to operate unsuspected—except by the authorities, who have decided to let the plot run in order to glean information about a wider conspiracy—problematizes this essential difference. In a way, the power of Farik's group lies not in its Otherness but in its proximity, its faithful shadowing of all things American. Farik acknowledges this directly at his first meeting with Darwyn. The Saudi has lured our hero to a synagogue he has been attending, pretending to be a Jew, the better, he says, to know your enemy. Divulging his real identity in a nearby diner, Farik makes an announcement that can be seen as the key to the unsettling power of *Sleeper Cell:* "Most people in the Middle East look alike, sometimes even to each other. I've passed as Persian, Turkish, Coptic Christian as well as Sephardic Jew. Don't African-Americans have a long history of trying to pass for white?"

Here, the idea of "passing"—more often applied to the troubled racial politics of the United States—is shifted by Farik onto the level of culture. In the absence of clear-cut, definitive markers of racial difference, it can only be through the strict observance of distinguishing cultural practices, be they dress, diet, or religious ritual, that the Other can be recognized. In choosing to dispense with such signifiers, the mixed group of terrorists can effectively re-create themselves as whatever their interlocutors wish to see at any given time. This is especially true of Farik himself, who works as a security consultant and in his spare time coaches a children's softball team. Arguing against the conventional view of race passing as a betrayal of an authentic identity, Kathleen Pfeiffer has argued that passing can, in fact, be seen as a manifestation of American individualism itself: part of "the mythology that animates American notions of autonomy, self-determination and free choice."[22] Quoting Werner Sollers, Pfeiffer suggests that the American celebration of self-improvement and unlimited possibility challenges both conventional categorization *and* the assumptions on which much identity politics is based; a "widely shared public bias . . . has strongly favoured achieved rather than ascribed identity, and supported 'self-determination' and 'independence' from ancestral, parental and external definitions.'"[23] In their different ways, each member of the sleeper cell has forged a new identity for himself, not simply through conversion to Islam but also through a deliberate rejection of foundational aspects of his old self. What unites these acts of transformation is, in the end, nothing more than the desire to sow destruction at the heart of the world's new imperial power. Their re-creations offer a dark parody of American self-reinvention.

If matters are complicated by good Americans performing Muslimness and bad Muslims performing Americanness, an extra turn of the screw comes from the fact that a number of the Muslims on show are not very good at actually performing their Muslimness anyway. Christian (Alex Nesic) is an inveterate womanizer who maintains a sort of emotional fidelity to his estranged Moroccan wife even while he sleeps his way through most of the available women he encounters. Similarly, when Farik's Saudi contacts turn up in Las Vegas to finalize plans for the attack, one of the first things they do is avail themselves of the services of two local call girls. Stripped, in these moments, of any semblance of a morally demanding spirituality, who are they? In what does their Muslimness actually inhere? Don't they cease to manifest any recognizably Muslim characteristics at all? Do they, in fact, deconstruct the necessary televisual coordinates of Muslimness, expose and break the frame, as it were? On another level, this can be seen as part of the show's controversial determination to humanize, rather than demonize, the terrorists, not so as to exonerate or sympathize with them but so as to present them as flawed subjects, often hypocritical, and wholly unable to live up to the standards they would impose on others.

What is more, the same temptations and failings beset Darwyn. Early on he finds himself drawn to a young single mother, Gayle. With somewhat implausible haste they jump into bed together. At the end of a softly lit scene of undulating bodies and tangled limbs, Darwyn admits to "feeling a little weird": "Muslims aren't even supposed to have sex outside marriage." Gayle replies, "No kidding? Same with Catholics." We would argue that one of the reasons Darwyn works as a hero for the non-Muslim viewer is precisely because of these moments of recognizable and flawed humanity, when the high demands of his moral code occasionally prove too much to support. (They also, of course, reveal him to be a red-blooded male.) Taken together with the Sufi-inflected brand of Islam to which he subscribes, where the sexes pray together and music is a sanctioned part of the worship, one might suggest that for the American viewer Darwyn represents "Islam Lite": Islam with all the alien and uncomfortable bits taken out. These can then be projected onto the other Muslim characters, all terrorists, whose premodern pathology is always bubbling to the surface in bouts of pitiless violence and who, with their involvement in honor killings, stoning, and cruelty to animals, participate in a freak show of perceived Muslim barbarism. By contrast, as a flawed hero, Darwyn nonetheless speaks up for the "real" Islam that has been misrepresented by thugs like Farik and therefore misunderstood by America at large. On a visit to Gayle's sister and her husband, Darwyn is confronted about his refusal to eat bacon. He patiently explains both the reason for the original sanction—trichinosis in the time of the Prophet—and that it has become a tradition, but his host accuses him of religious fanaticism and brackets him with the Taliban. In response, Darwyn's exasperated question reveals his sincerity while also suggesting a certain absence at the heart of a secular way of life: "There's got to be something in your life that you do or don't do just because you believe in it." In a land where 78 percent of people say they believe in God, Darwyn here has the comparative virtue of a real religious faith. Moreover, as is shown when he encourages a young Afghani fugitive to read the Koran for himself rather than rely on the word of priests, Darwyn's religion is articulated in terms recognizable to the historically shaping U.S. ideology of Protestant individualism. Despite his Muslimness, Darwyn is a man for all seasons, for all true faiths.

Indeed, the honorable nature of Darwyn's beliefs and the way they inform his actions work to suggest that, unlike his, the faith of the other conspirators is really religion as compensation for various flaws. All members of the cell are compensating for types of personal lack, and these center most frequently on their failures regarding that most American institution of all, the family. Just as Christian's casual treatment of women seems linked to his failure to hold onto the affection of his wife, the person who brought him to Islam, so too Tommy's jihadi sentiments seem merely the latest phase of an ongoing attempt to antagonize his mother—Lynne, a liberal professor at Berkeley—that has previously included a disastrous stint in the army. The level of self-awareness in these characters is hard to gauge, yet Tommy (played by

Blake Shields) recognizes that his utility to the cell stems from his ordi-nariness: "just another American idiot cruising the mall." He admits to always having had problems with authority: "I think that's why I be-came a Muslim, because in Islam you don't answer to other human beings. You surrender only to your Creator." Yet he is always seeking the approval of his comrades in arms, and he sees the planned bombing of the Dodgers stadium as his chance to amount to something, and, perversely, prove himself to his busy and neglectful mother. If we have the nation-as-family in *24*, here families are absent, dysfunctional, or dead. As Gayle remarks to Darwyn—himself the product of a broken home—in the early stages of their relationship: "An ex-con and a single mom. It's not exactly a winning combo."

Along with psychological complexity comes a degree of moral ambi-guity. Farik is instrumental in closing down a child prostitution ring run by his principal funder in Mexico, but only at Darwyn's urging and after Darwyn has saved his life. More often, ambivalence appears through internal doctrinal and tactical discussions, and conversations with outsiders. So, for instance, the group encounter a white American Muslim mercenary who is perfectly happy to train insurgents to fight U.S. forces in Iraq but flatly refuses to participate in targeting civilians. Such equivocation is accompanied by the suggestion of a moral and terminological double standard: as when Tommy debates with a cap-tured hostage, "Do you know what percentage of your tax dollars goes to waging war on innocent Muslim men, women and children all over the world? You use a $100 million jet to drop bombs on civilians and you're a hero. You take 'em out by blowing yourself up on the street corner, you're a terrorist."

In such exchanges as this—which works to raise questions about ter-rorism and state violence normally overlooked in the genre—we are witnessing ambivalence rather than relativism or moral equivalence. This is because *Sleeper Cell* is fully dialogic in a way most other thrillers are not. Sometimes such dialogues are direct, as when a reformist preacher from Yemen whose mission is to deprogram militants debates the legitimacy of violence and the true meaning of jihad. For the most part, however, different voices and political positions jostle within the narrative and, in fact, give it its distinctive texture and tension. For example, Lynne uses her position as a history professor to lecture on how 9/11 forcibly reconnected America to a history it had hitherto chosen to ignore. "For every action there is a reaction," she declares. "We now need to make those connections between America's foreign policy past and the disturbing present in which we find ourselves." Her oration is interspersed by scenes of her son and his French coreligionist brutally beating a Christian evangelist who has had the temerity to approach them. Yet this juxtaposition is so obvious as to be banal, and undercuts the simplistic pseudohistoricization, based purely on rhetoric, that Lynne is offering. (In fact, she remains a clanking stereotype of the liberal academic—even at the end refusing to take responsibility for her son's violent fate, despite his direct indictment of her, preferring as always to blame the government.) The fabric of *Sleeper Cell* is composed of such partial but contending viewpoints. A sanctimonious liberal view rubs up against inherently conservative state security discourse. Blinkered jihadist dogma is confronted by peaceful, reformist brands of Islam. And the fragile idea of a homeland worth defending is called into question by directionless working-class figures such as Gayle, and Ernie, a broke chemical worker who is bribed to smuggle out phosgene for the terrorists' use, for both of whom the American dream has turned sour. Such careful vignettes point to the fact that unlike *24*, which is based almost entirely around the twists and turns of a frenetic plot, *Sleeper Cell* is, in the end, a character-driven drama wherein actions are motivated and explained by reference to a number of contending worldviews, not just the one-eyed perspective of heroes and villains.

From all this it will be seen that, even though Muslims and Islam are still placed in the frame of terrorist issues, *Sleeper Cell* is not interested in simple solutions that reinforce binary oppositions. While one might expect as much from a drama that employs a Pakistan-born writer (Kamran Pasha) and an "Islamic Consultant" (Omar Haroon), this comparative complexity of approach is in fact implied as early as the opening credit sequence. The image of a hand-drawn map of the Middle East, with Syria and Iran featured prominently, is replaced by a shot of the horse-head pumps of an oil field. These, in turn, give way to newsreel footage of tracer fire flying over the buildings of Kuwait City, which merges into the nighttime skyline of downtown Los Angeles. A child flying a toy plane segues into a fighter jet taking off from an aircraft carrier. And a group of schoolchildren reverently raising the Stars and Stripes becomes an angry mob on a Middle Eastern street burning the same flag. The rapid cutting together of these images indicates association, not binary difference. It gestures toward proximity, connectedness, and consequences rather than distance and irreconcilability. As such the credits, and *Sleeper Cell* as a whole, return us to the Semmerling quotation with which this chapter began, suggesting that the filmic creation of "the enemy" is always also a process by which "we" seek to make "our" selves more securely distinct. The hesitant, damaged America of *Sleeper Cell* seems, at some level, to have lost the cultural confidence to insist on such firm distinctions. The picture the drama paints seems to be one of decay and lost moorings. Continuing his argument, and employing the insights of Jack Shaheen and Homi K. Bhabha, Semmerling notes the "anxious repetition" of the image of the evil Muslim in American visual culture, suggesting that such Othering is really a cover for "our" own sense of lack. This lack, he says, is "why we [American viewers] are more likely to see the first image . . . of the 'evil' Arab rather than accepting the second image. [But] once the second image of our lacking Self is discernible . . . the perceptual slide . . . between the two images is very slippery."[24] The unsettling viewing experience of following the sleeper cell through its machinations is due, at least in part, to that perceptual slippage, which the drama deliberately sets in place and toys with. In the end, it is as much about what is (and is not) America as about terrorism.

In essence, then, there appear to be two types of post-9/11 thriller dealing with the presumed threat from Muslims: the first offers a fairly instrumental and unquestioning recapitulation of national discourses and psychosocial boundaries; the second begins by deploying the usual set of stereotypes only to unsettle them and even use them to reflect back at the viewer some of the more unthinking prejudices and smug attitudes the West has been encouraged to indulge in as civilizations supposedly clash. We have suggested that even the more overtly conservative productions cannot help but betray the inconsistencies and double standards required to keep the rhetoric of cultural irreconcilability afloat. Yet in the end, it could equally well be suggested that the deployment of stereotypes in the more liberal productions, by its very nature, serves to confirm, by repetition, the traduced version of Muslim being. What all these shows have in common is that "Muslimness" exists for us largely through performance and is only guaranteed by its juxtaposition with surrounding cultural values that are different, more familiar, more "Western."

# CHAPTER 6

# Performing beyond the Frame

## Gender, Comedy, and Subversion

On 22 June 2009, in the glittering surroundings of the Versailles Palace, President Nicolas Sarkozy, in his first state of the nation speech, turned his and the French nation's attention to the matter of Muslim women's dress. He singled out the burka as a symbol of Islamic repression: "the problem of the burka is not a religious problem, it's a problem of liberty and women's dignity. It's not a religious symbol, but a sign of subservience and debasement. I want to say solemnly, the burka is not welcome in France. In our country, we can't accept women prisoners behind a screen, cut off from all social life, deprived of all identity. That's not our idea of freedom."[1] His speech redraws borders between what are seen as irreconcilable differences of dress culture in a multicultural society and reignites a civilizational discourse among Western imperial nations, which have historically represented Islam as a backward religion. This backwardness is exemplified in their treatment of women and control over their sexuality. Historically the veil and women's bodies have come to acquire definitive significance in the representation of "normal" cultural values and are often upheld as visible examples of an Islamic conservatism that is directly at odds with Western values of progressivism.[2] In Sarkozy's state of the nation speech, the burqa is projected as a direct threat to the French tradition of *laicité* and women's dignity and seen as a symptom of "subservience and debasement." This restriction of Muslim women's bodies can be contrasted with the freedom of their French counterparts, whose bodies are subject to a commodification directly responding to the needs and desires of a heteronormative culture. And, it almost goes without saying, the most immediately recognizable French example of this gaze is Sarkozy's own third wife, Carla Bruni-Sarkozy, a model turned singer, whose career in fashion encapsulates that industry's manipulation of a fantasy of visual perfection for women. Bruni's self-projection as a glamorous object to be looked at in a society that places a high price on sexual attractiveness has undoubtedly raised her profile in her newer role as first lady of France, as fawning headlines accompany her on state trips around the world, and she regularly steals the limelight from her less prepossessing husband. For instance, she became the subject of media speculation in Britain about her motives for not wearing a bra under her tight Roland Mouret dress while hosting a state banquet. Such speculation is symptomatic of British tabloid journalism's penchant for gossip and rumor, but was soon superseded by further allegations related to infidelity in the Bruni-Sarkozy household, based on information gathering from Internet sources such as Twitter. While Bruni's body image confirms a particular stereotype for French women, in contrast Muslim women in representations by the Western media seem stuck in a binary division as either passive victims of fundamentalist Islamic practices or heroic icons such as Mukhtar Mai, a gang-rape victim from a village in Pakistan whose case received worldwide coverage, highlighting the fault lines of the Pakistani legal system and her determined attempts to fight back.[3] Since the seventeenth century, the two most well known stereotypes of Muslim women have been those of the harem and the veil. They have succeeded in normalizing a particular perception of "Muslim" cultural practices with reference to women in Western societies.[4]

In the United States and the UK since 9/11, the issue of saving Muslim women has been taken up by the wives of prominent politicians, for example Laura Bush and Cherie Blair, who have taken it upon themselves to speak out on behalf of the women of the Muslim world—especially Afghanistan, whose womenfolk have been seen as the silent victims of an oppressive Taliban regime and whose suffering has been used to justify the moral dimension of the "War on Terror." In their respective attitudes both Laura Bush and Cherie Blair inadvertently recall an earlier colonial agenda that was at the heart of arguments for the "mental and moral development" of women.[5] More generally, the desire among liberal feminists to speak out on behalf of the freedom of Muslim women and against those seen as their oppressors repeats a well-worn pattern in which the voice of the "Third World" woman herself is effectively silenced, evacuated from an argument that is about her but in which she is seldom invited to participate.[6] If the women of the countries that the West has identified as exhibiting reactionary gender politics are not being spoken for by self-proclaimed champions of women's rights, they are having their supposed best interests interpreted for them as part of a reactive nationalism among Islamists. These two positions tend to squeeze out other possibilities for self-directed expression by Muslim women in certain parts of the world. As such they are another element in that all-encompassing frame that is the subject of this book. Further afield, Muslim religious conservatives' retrogressive enforcement of oppressive strictures and reduced opportunities for women has fed off the active promotion of a Muslim reformation led by Western governments that targets diasporic Muslim citizens, requiring them to be beacons of civilization and take up positions in relation to Western interventionism that are supportive, or at the very least quiescent.

### Muslim Cosmopolitanism and the Ummah

In this book we have been interested in exploring the dialogic process that takes place between the media's representation of Muslims as stereotypes and Muslim groups' deployment of some of these stereotypes in order to re-present themselves. We would argue that in adopting these stereotypes, such Muslims not only reinforce the limited images imposed on them by the West but also construct their own stereotype of a secular liberal West through which a finite, bounded notion of Muslimness can be delineated. To counter the dominant discourse of secularism, which perceives religion as deviance, some Muslim groups have initiated a counteroffensive to normalize aspects of Muslim practice on behalf of a transnational Ummah.

We wish now to broaden the scope of our argument and include the context in which the Muslim Ummah is imagined in the West and the way it conceptualizes itself in turn. The Islamic Ummah is understood to be a "global Muslim community" and has historically operated within the milieu of trade and travel networks. As a general code of practice, the Ummah privileges the Koran and Sunnah or sayings of the Prophet Mohammad and regulates conduct in accordance with the principles of Islam. It is not a national construct, but in the past it has had sympathetic overlaps with the territorial struggles of Arab nationalism.[7] In recent times, the rise of globalization in the modern world has had an impact on the traditional networking patterns of the Muslim Ummah, and many Muslim communities who now live as minorities under non-Muslim rule have had to contend with a different idea of the Ummah, which according to Olivier Roy can no longer link itself to specific Islamic cultural values associated with a particular region.[8] Instead there are group formations that revolve around universalizing ideas of Islamic culture. Historically, philosophical interventions by intellectuals, such as the renowned poet Muhammad Iqbal, have brought to light ethical considerations and humanist ideals within the religious sphere, projecting a cosmopolitan idea of Islam. Therefore, when speaking of an Islamic cosmopolitanism among the Ummah, we have to take into account the current Muslim condition, which is not a utopia consisting of "citizens of the world," as cosmopolitanism was first defined by the Socratically inspired Cynic philosopher Diogenes in the fourth century BCE, but rather a politics of an Ummah with a finite, bounded notion of Muslimness in contemporary history. While the collective impulse of the Ummah has similarities to the cosmopolitan idea of belonging to a single world community, that impulse shares the same confusion about where the loyalty of the citizen lies.

Scholarly studies of Islamic cosmopolitanism represent different models of thinking about the subject. The idea of Islamic cosmopolitanism can be traced back to the Ottoman period, which fostered an "internationalist" atmosphere with its open borders and a culturally cosmopolitan "attitude," notably in the cities of Alexandria, Istanbul, and Beirut.[9] Amartya Sen acknowledges both the eleventh century polymath Ahmad Raihan al-Biruni and the sixteenth-century Mughal dynast Akbar as key examples of Muslim cosmopolitan thinking in

South Asia.[10] However, in contemporary times, with the rise of global-ization and the dominance of a free market economy in the developed world, a new global Islamic cosmopolitanism is surfacing, mediated through a diversity of ethnic identities among a diasporic Muslim pop-ulation settled in the West. This Islamic cosmopolitanism plays out through material culture and manifests itself in the marketing and branding of Islamic goods such as Ummah chocolate, Islamic fash-ion, lifestyle magazines such as *Emel, Q News,* and Islamic comedy, films, and music. It is a dialogically constructed cosmopolitanism at ease with the norms of capitalist societies in which diasporic Muslims are located.

In recent times cyberspace has become the most popular space for establishing and maintaining transnational and/or cosmopolitan Muslim networks. Miriam Cooke and Bruce Lawrence argue that the Internet "reveals a paradoxical aspect of the metaphorical function of networks: they are de-territorialized and gender inclusive even while remaining socially restricted in other ways."[11] Thus the Internet offers an ideal space for such an imagining of the Ummah and the individual-ized expression of diasporic Muslim subjectivities. The Internet can also be read as a site of global multiculture where "(a)lternative circuits are appealing when mainstream circuits are alienating."[12] Websites that promote Muslim business and engage with ethical concerns participate in the creation of a new space for the operation of Islamic cosmopoli-tanism. Muslim Internet companies linked to such sites tend to repli-cate current trends with regard to the graphic design of their websites, thus visually normalizing their image and products for a capitalist con-sumer base. However, they are distinctive in their approach toward a global cosmopolitanism, in that they brand their business with an Islamic ethical consciousness. This is clearly divergent from the more supposedly "value-neutral" global marketing structures of an imperial cosmopolitanism favored by multinational companies. This branding also represents a cosmopolitanism that is sometimes at odds with the universal representation of the United States as the definitive plural so-ciety desired by all across the globe and an ideal home for the cosmo-politan individual.[13]

## The "Islamic Barbie": Marketing Muslim Children's Dolls

We can usefully explore the tension between a more conventional, globalized cosmopolitan marketing phenomenon and its differentiated Islamic equivalent in the branding of lifestyle dolls for young children across the world. Since our examples are marketing phenomena aimed at young girls, they also tell us much about respective ideologies that operate to define the available spaces for Western and Muslim femininities. As we will see, however, the inherent dialogicality in the way such constructions are formed means that the two proffered identities are mutually shaping.

The two dolls in question are the all-American classic Barbie, manufactured by Mattel and first produced in 1959, and the more recent Islamic dolls Razanne and Fulla, manufactured by Noorart and New Boy Studio, respectively. The dolls contribute toward the formation of globally recognized paradigms for female youth, offering role models for young girls as they make their first, hesitant attempts at self-fashioning in the world. The Muslim doll Razanne, who is presented as an alternative to "hedonistic" Barbie, nevertheless bears a striking resemblance to her pleasure-loving counterpart and participates in the same consumer culture. Yet in contrast to Barbie, Razanne's sexuality is downplayed, and she has a hijab and a *jilbab* (full-length coat) for outdoor use, which are designed to encourage modesty and emphasize her Muslim identity while at the same time allowing space for following the latest fashions for indoor wear. The doll participates in the creation of a normative visual stereotype of the Muslim woman, which has emerged both out of Western stereotypes of Muslims and the self-stereotyping that occurs among Muslims living in Western societies.

To understand why Muslims feel the need for the affirmation of such visual stereotypes, we have to look toward the diversity of ethnicities that make up the Muslim diaspora and the complexity of their identifications within minority contexts. In order to gain recognition and to counter rejection of their faith-based identities in secular nations, some Muslims feel obliged to perform their religious identity through dress and other actions. The complexity of the conflation between ethnic and religious identifications can be understood by means of the way Arab identity in America is itself subject to stereotyping and monologic representation by the mainstream media. Sally Howell has noted the way Arabs in America "feel bruised by a media that seems interested only in portraying them as terrorists, oil-sheiks, sexpots or lechers." She also argues that Arabs in Detroit try to construct their own subjectivity by expressing "individual and group identities that lie beyond mainstream television channels, art galleries, and publishing houses."[14] Razanne was designed by a Muslim couple from Detroit who are now based in Texas. She can be read as part of an attempt to restate a positive identity for Muslim children of Arab ethnicity growing up in the United States. However, perhaps *because* she represents an answer to what is felt to be an undesirable model of femininity, Razanne is, we would argue, actually a stereotype of a stereotype. She participates both in the homogenization of a transnational Islamic identity and the conceptualization of a global cosmopolitan Ummah taking shape over the Internet, but she does so in terms dictated by pre-existing cultural tensions and views of the Other.

The Razanne doll is sold primarily through the Internet website called Noorart, representing a Muslim company, whose marketing strategy around Razanne relies on toned-down mimicry of a recognizable branded product: Mattel's Barbie. Razanne embodies the modest Muslim woman who retains her cultural values while living in the West. With an estimated potential market of eight million Muslims existing in North America, the consumer ethic of brand buying has been utilized to capture a niche market of both ethnic minority and Muslim buyers. Companies such as Noorart have received an unexpected boost since the events of 9/11 from buyers who find themselves increasingly at odds with American foreign policy and wish to dissociate themselves economically from the imperial retribution that has followed in the wake of the events of 9/11. A report by the Chicago bureau of Reuters has argued that Muslim Americans feeling the pressures of a renewed nationalism in the United States, hinged around the notion of a "clash of civilizations" between Islam and the West, have turned toward Muslim-branded products as a way of asserting their identity in the face of a narrowing white majority view of their community.[15]

The popularity of Muslim-branded products is not limited to North

American consumers; similar trends are taking place across the Middle East and Europe. Significantly, a variety of Muslim dolls have been marketed in the Middle East , ranging from the national Iranian duo Dara and Sara to the Syrian Fulla. Dara and Sara were introduced to the Iranian market in 2002 as an attempt to curtail the popularity of Barbie and Ken. Developed and marketed by the Institute for the Intellectual Development of Children and Young Adults in consultation with the Iran's Ministry of Education, the dolls are supposed to be eight-year-old siblings. They wear modest clothes representing traditional values, and Sara has a white scarf covering her hair. According to the Iranian toy seller Masoumeh Rahimi, the dolls are an important addition to the market, as they are representative of Iranian values and a much-needed intervention against the "wanton" Barbie, who she believes to be "more harmful than an American missile."[16] In 2008 Iran's prosecutor general, Ghorban Ali Dori Najafabadi, voiced his concerns in a letter to the vice president, Parvis Davoudi, regarding the increasing popularity of Western culture in Iran through the importation of such toys as Barbie and Batman and Harry Potter figures, signifying a "social danger" and the destruction of indigenous cultural values.[17] Similarly, the Iranian police force held a fashion show in 2007 to promote a more varied selection of approved Islamic dress and to educate the nation's fashion designers about what its women should be wearing instead of getting their ideas from satellite television. This drive was particularly aimed at women who wore tight overcoats, high-heeled shoes, and token scarves, mimicking what the authorities called a "Western doll" effect.[18] Once again, the control of women's bodies and deportment was depicted as central to national well-being. Yet these are not simply anticolonial statements by the authorities but a predictable attempt to control women's sexuality under the guise of nationalism. The very existence of a literal "fashion police," as opposed to the style gurus supposed to stalk the streets of Western cities issuing diktats about this season's trends, not only indicates a lack of irony but an attempt to stamp national power on the areas that most in the West would class as private.

In contrast to the comparative lack of consumer interest in the Dara and Sara dolls is the greater success of the marketing of Fulla, whose svelte body type resembles Barbie's, but is less curvaceous, and whose wardrobe is equally expansive. The most noticeable differences between Barbie and Fulla are in clothing, lifestyle, and hair color. The sleek, dark-haired Fulla wears a full-length black *abaya*, which covers her from head to toe when she is outdoors, owns a wide selection of head-scarves, has fashionable clothes for wearing indoors, and most signifi-cantly does not have a boyfriend. For the manager of a toy outlet in Damascus, Mohammed Sabbagh, "Fulla is one of us. She's my sister, she's my mother, she's my wife. She's all the traditional things of Syria and the Middle East."[19] Fulla also has her own website, *Fulla—Live the Dream*, which offers her blog, diary, songs, videos, and tour guide (www.fulla.com). According to the website, accessible in both Arabic and English, Fulla is sixteen years old, Arab, loves and respects her family and friends, and is "the spirit of any girl who strives toward ex-cellence, creativity, renewal, and peace." In contrast to Barbie, her pur-suits in life are not determined by how much fun she can have but are dedicated to making "the world a better place for everyone." Her web-site is designed to educate young Muslim girls about morality, family values, and Islamic history; she embodies all that is goodness and vir-tue in a young Muslim girl. She is also a recognizable brand associated with food items, luggage, stationery, and so on, all available for pur-chase on her website. In those respects she is not dissimilar to Barbie.

The British press has taken a considerable degree of interest in the transnational Razanne and Fulla dolls since their arrival on the market. They have been reported on in both the national broadsheets and the tabloids, with articles ranging from the *Guardian*'s "Islamic Barbie" to the *Daily Star*'s "Burkha Barbie." Both Razanne and Fulla feed into the public imagination of Muslim stereotypes, reconfirming the popular perception that Muslim values cannot be integrated with the demands of secular modernity. The matter of Muslim women's dress itself has been a topic of public controversy in England since 2002, when Shabina Begum, a thirteen-year-old British Muslim girl, was suspended from Denbigh High School for ignoring the school uniform code and con-tinuing to wear a jilbab. She initiated legal proceedings, supported by her legal guardian and brother and advised by the Islamist group Hizb ut-Tahrir. She was initially turned down by the High Court in 2004 but won her case in the Court of Appeal in 2005. In 2006 the House of Lords overruled the Court of Appeal and restored the High Court decision in favor of the school because she had contravened the school uniform policy.[20] According to Emma Tarlo, the political activism around the hijab/jilbab debate deployed by Hizb ut-Tahrir has allowed for a sartorial means of "rejecting and resisting 'the West' from within the West."[21] The legal tussle around Shabina Begum's right to wear the jilbab and hijab underlines a national debate between advocates of freedom of choice in what to wear and those who object to these garments as a perceived marker of separation and difference. This politicization of the veil was also evident in MP Jack Straw's later stand that Muslim women needed to take off their niqabs during one-to-one consultations with him in his Blackburn constituency. Thus Muslim girls' and by extension Muslim women's visible identity has become inextricably linked to the politics of what they wear in a multicultural society. The ins and outs of the Shabina Begum case highlight the problems Britain has in tolerating certain minority religious practices, and while the hijab has not been banned, national debates on matters of Muslim women's clothing have become extremely heated as both sides invoke the preservation of women's freedom to justify their positions.

The prescription of a suitable dress culture for young Muslim girls has long been on the agenda in Muslim societies. This is particularly evident in the voiced concern about the exposure of young impressionable girls to the supposed loose morality of cosmopolitan dolls such as Barbie. The debate about Barbie's unsuitability for a Muslim audience in particular was ignited in 2003 when the Saudi religious police declared "Barbie dolls a threat to morality, complaining that the revealing clothes of the 'Jewish' toy already banned in the kingdom—are offensive to Islam."[22] Even more interesting was the appearance of the Fulla doll in Kuwait as a veiled version of Barbie. Most significant, Fulla has become a bestseller in Egypt and other Muslim countries. Since her launch, her rise to fame has been faithfully recorded by publications in the United States and the United Kingdom, often with a predictably barbed headline. In one of the UK tabloids, the *Daily Star*, the front-page headline "Burka Barbie: She Puts Fun into Fundamentalism" was accompanied by a close-up of Fulla's face in full black hijab.[23] The story itself is continued on page 3, where juxtaposed against the un-covered breasts of "Annie the Page 3 Girl," we see the demure and fully covered Fulla dolls with the accompanying caption "Burka Barbie Can't See Ken." The underlying message to the readers is that of the incompatibility of liberal Western values with the Arab values that embrace what Muslim traditionalists term "modesty" for young women.

Razanne has not enjoyed the same kind of tabloid publicity. She has been in existence longer; she was first introduced to the children's market via the Internet in 1996. Her publicity campaign in the Middle East and the UK was launched in 2004. Prior to that she had only been marketed in the United States, Canada, Singapore, and Germany. Razanne is the brainchild of an American couple, Noor (Sherrie) and Ammar Saadeh. According to Noor, Razanne provides an alternative to the "overly sophisticated and skimpily dressed Barbie doll." She is, as Jo Tatchell of the *Guardian* called her, the "Islamic Barbie," and comes with a heavy dose of ideology.[24] The website advertising Razanne includes the usual informative descriptions as well as a text box highlighting the educational and play benefits that girls who own her will gain. Other than the universalizing attribute of shaping interactive play, it is said that Razanne "builds Muslim identity and self-esteem," "provides [an] Islamic role model," and "promotes Islamic behavior." She comes in various guises. There is an "in and out" Razanne, who dresses in the latest fashions, including above-the-knee skirts, while at home but dons the jilbab and hijab when going out to signify her modesty. She is, to quote her creators, "more than just a fashion statement." She comes with her distinctive coloring book, which gives us a day in the life of Razanne from daybreak to sunset. Another outfit, Playday Razanne, demonstrates that Muslim girls can have fun in the playground as long as they dress modestly in a loose-fitting jumper and scarf. Another role she can adopt is that of a Muslim Girl Scout. Although Razanne's body is prepubescent, unlike the caricatured "adult" body of Barbie, continuing the range is a group of adult professional outfits, including Dr. Razanne and Teacher Razanne; according to Ammar Saadeh, these versions of Razanne reinforce the importance of education and religious piety in Islamic society as well as shattering the stereotype that Muslim women can't have careers. The most recent addition to the range is a new ethnic category in the Playday Razanne collection: Razanne dolls wearing "light and breezy two-piece sets" or the shalwar qamis worn by Asian Muslim women. The information included with the doll explains that the shalwar qamis is a modest dress that combats conditions of extreme heat. The three ethnic variations are "Caucasian," "Pakistani Indian," and "Black," as well as three "racial" colorings: fair skin/fair hair, olive skin/dark hair, and dark skin/dark hair. Questions have been raised about the possibility of a future "Ahmad" doll, but so far the creative team have no plans of mimicking Barbie's celebrated relationship with Ken by introducing a male Muslim doll. In the words of the Razanne story maker and creator, Noor, "it wouldn't fit with Razanne to have a boyfriend."

Not only Muslims admire the virtues personified by Razanne. Numerous messages of support have been posted on the website's message board from non-Muslim friends and supporters, mainly commenting on the pleasing modesty of Razanne in contrast to Barbie's nakedness and immorality. Saadeh says: "The main message we try to put forward through the doll is that what matters is what's inside you, not how you look."[25] But the dilemma for the Islamic Barbie is that it *does* matter how she looks, because she has to personify Islamic identity through role play and religio-performativity as her life story unfolds. In response to Mattel's ethnic representations Moroccan Barbie and Leyla (a slave in the court of a Turkish sultan), Saadeh sighs: "It's no surprise that they'd try to portray a Middle Eastern Barbie either as a belly dancer or a concubine." Saadeh acknowledges that Razanne is a critical response to these kinds of stereotypes.

Noorart thus attempts to blend the values of an American lifestyle with those of a variety of Muslim ethnicities, in order to reach a new set of consumers generated by Internet communications. In another context, Inderpal Grewal suggests that the multiple human subjects of transnational consumerism are not "in opposition to either globalization or nationalism." Writing about economic liberalization in India and the phenomenon of the "traveling Barbie," as exported by Mattel, Grewal points out that Barbie in a sari is "not an Indian or South Asian

Barbie" but "what Mattel calls the traditional Barbie"; she is essentially American in body but plays at being Indian through dress and performativity. "The doll suggests that difference, as homogenized national stereotype, could be recovered by multinational corporations, that the national could exist in this global economy."[26] However, one can question exactly which nation is being privileged; in other words, whether ideas of a central, normalized Western female identity are being subtly reiterated via the stereotype of exotic ethnicity. Radha Hegde has looked at the ethnic element in the multicultural packaging of Barbie and concluded: "Barbie as ethnic spectacle demonstrates how a certain type of 'Indianness' is created and promoted through the white female body of a plastic Barbie. Indianness is packaged as a newly improved product and sold as the Orientalist fantasy of white femininity."[27] We might want to consider whether the same is true of Muslim versions of the doll; there are enough stereotypes of Muslim femininity, and all of them seem to play out through matters of dress. This commodification of stereotypes via dolls has also been discussed by Ann Ducille in relation to debates on multiculturalism and Mattel's failure to accommodate racial difference despite the promise of cultural diversity. Her critical reading is in response to Mattel's targeting of the ethnic market in the early 1990s, when Mattel addressed racial difference in the form of the "brown skinned" Shani, "honey colored" Asha, and "deep mahogany" Nichelle. Ducille sees these as a mere symptom of the fashion industry's commodification of a style known as Afro-chic.[28]

Of course, Barbie is a problematic icon for women, as critics such as Mary Rogers have pointed out.[29] As an iconic doll she represents fantasy, and the gendered female identity of a young white adult. However, as a fictional character, her biography is constructed in the interests of marketing and sales. She has no parents nor does she have any children. Her family consists mainly of siblings, and the rest of the characters in her biography are friends, except for her boyfriend, Ken. Thus Barbie is a hegemonic global brand that packages an imperial cosmopolitan agenda through aggressive marketing and legal representation. We as consumers are tied not simply to Barbie the doll but also to her lifestyle.

Mary Rogers locates Barbie within the fashion industry as a mimetic construct that allows women to imagine themselves as "perpetually young and ephemerally ageless" and essentially views Barbie's identity as performative, despite her fixed body plastic. She argues that Barbie's assemblage of accessories points "to a self continuously in the making under shifting circumstances"; "Barbie represents the sort of contemporary selfhood some see as embattled and others see as liberated. . . . [She] represents the sort of interaction as well as the sort of selfhood ascendant in postindustrial societies with their commodity cultures . . . her identity hovers between two cultures, the modern and the postmodern."[30]

## Performing Muslim Femaleness

Judith Butler's work on gender and performativity can help us understand Razanne. Butler offers a "performative theory of gender" in which gender identity is not predetermined but is enacted repetitively according to cultural practices.[31] We wish to engage with this idea of gender performativity, which proves useful in our understanding of a number of phenomena in the relations between those two supposedly monolithic entities "Islam" and "the West." In this idea's most direct application—to areas of gender and sexuality—there are immediate implications for our understanding of Barbie and Razanne. Barbie creates the stereotype of a white, blue-eyed, blonde American beauty that is the object of desire (for both sexes). She has a voluptuous body, her accessories are in tune with modern fashions, and she consumes a number of the luxurious comforts on offer in material society. She even has her own bubble bath. Barbie is marked with desire. Razanne on the other hand has been described as possessing a preteen body and a sensible and modest attitude in contrast to Barbie's frivolity. She too has accessories, but they are predetermined by religious conformity or professional obligations. So Praying Razanne has a prayer rug, Razanne the schoolgirl has a backpack and books, Teacher Razanne a cell phone, laptop, briefcase, and sunglasses, and so on. Razanne's responsibilities begin at sunrise, when she gets up to say her Fajr prayers, and during the day she observes a sensible and modest dress code, wearing her jilbab and hijab whenever she goes out. Her creators state: "Razanne helps Muslim girls understand that in the home they can be the ultimate fashion statement" on the condition that they dress modestly outside. In other words, Razanne is marked with the loss of the very desire that is cultivated by Barbie. By appropriating a modest universalizing Muslim identity for children who grow up in Western societies, she offers a parodic response to the excesses of Barbie. In a moment that brilliantly encapsulated the doublethink around female freedom and desire, a CNN report about Razanne plainly stated: "the new girl on the block doesn't give Barbie much of a run for her money. After all, Barbie is everything Razanne is not—curvaceous, flashy and loaded with sex appeal."[32] This desexualization of Razanne, in contrast to the highly sexualized Barbie, is epitomized by the fact that Razanne comes equipped with sensible white knickers that cover her reproductive organs, whereas Barbie's sexuality is fetishized through her amply proportioned breasts. We would argue that Razanne's performative behavior is, correspondingly, an attempt to stabilize the meaning of "Muslim woman" and set it firmly within the foundational discourse of Islam. An important link is also to be made here with anticolonial sentiment and nationalist movements.

Various scholars working on nationalism have illustrated the ways women are appropriated as symbols of identity and differentiation in the struggle toward liberation. For example, Valerie Moghadam in her overview of the gender dynamics of nationalism, revolution, and Islamization has remarked that nationalist struggles tend to make motherhood sacred and to categorize cultural identity as an expression of women's role and status. In Islamist movements gender politics take a central role, and women become the carriers of tradition and a supposedly authentic Islamic identity. Women are made to represent the structures of the family, the home, and the movement's religious ideals.[33]

It can be argued that Razanne presents a counterhegemonic move against multinational brands such as Mattel's Barbie. Similar trends have been growing in recent years, and there is now a burgeoning market for Islamic products such as Mecca Cola, Qibla Cola, and Ummah chocolate, which compete alongside Coca-Cola and Cadbury's. In addition, the popularity of Islamic banking is rising, with consumers choosing both Muslim banks and the financial packages respecting Islamic ethics that the multinationals now regularly offer. This suggests an absorption of what was once a niche market into the practices of the mainstream.

Noorart represents a key moment in the shifting of attitudes among the migrant Muslim community settled in America. They are no longer content to sit back and be stereotyped and marginalized. Instead they have embarked on their own project of self-representation, with the aim of universalizing an Islamic code of behavior among young Muslim children.[34] Historically, Islam has been highly differentiated according to the cultural codes of different regions. What is interesting about Noorart is that they have used the medium of the Internet to spread a globalizing image of young Muslim girls that is in direct response to the dress codes of the dominant self in Western countries. This Muslim self participates in a liberal lifestyle but does so by means of an obedient ring-fencing a "modest" and Islamic lifestyle beginning with early-years education. The hijab and the jilbab are thus normalized as key components of Muslim identity for girls from the age of three years.[35]

Razanne is marketed as a fashion trend, which competes alongside Barbie and Bratz dolls. In sporting the latest fashions at home in the domestic sphere and donning her outerwear for public life, Razanne conforms to the public/private dichotomy, but the ambiguity in her private sphere comes from her appropriation of the latest Western fashion trends alongside the performativity of her ritual obligations as a Muslim. Noorart thus offers an alternative conceptualization of Muslim identity by engaging with current market trends and a centralized cosmopolitan culture of commodification. However, it is arguable whether Noorart, by positioning Razanne in response to the discourse of Western secular femininity, actually manages to break out of the frame of stereotyped representation, or whether the stereotype is merely reinforced through the universalizing of a female Muslim subject. Women as always are made to carry the burden for an entire culture.

## Hyperperformativity, Stereotypes, and Recognition: The Case of Shazia Mirza

The ideas of parodic performance (or hyperperformativity) that we have suggested characterize the construction of the various "Islamic Barbie" dolls mentioned above also have a resonance when applied to more general matters of crosscultural signs and their recognition. In Chapter 3 we saw how the makers of the film *Yasmin* found that the easiest way to symbolize Yasmin's awkward crosscultural position before 9/11 was to have the character change costume according to the context in which she operated. Although the binary coordinates indicated by this visual performance were in the end rather simplistic, it is nevertheless true that the visual still dominates our cultural value judgments. For example, when Mattel announced plans to bring out limited edition Barbie dolls "from around the world" to mark its fiftieth birthday, the news that their number would include dolls in hijab and burqa evoked cries of feminist outrage from New York's National Organization of Women, which objected that "selling a doll that is clearly wearing a symbol of violence is not acceptable."[36] The organization had simply decided that the burqa, in all contexts and at all times, was a symbol of violence against women—its rather halfhearted attendant caveats about a woman's right to free choice notwithstanding. This view takes no account of different types of veiling, or how these emerge from specific cultural contexts at certain points in history and reflect particular gender power relations and views of women that are not all the same. Equally, the sheer number of female testimonies that Western governments' belligerent responses to 9/11 drove many who had never veiled themselves before to don the hijab as a symbol of their threatened cultural identity ought to indicate that reciprocity is at work. Might we not interpret some contemporary expressions of Muslim identity—the upsurge in veiling, the sudden popularity of traditional dress among Muslim men living in the West, and so on—as a kind of hyperperformativity whereby Muslim communities and individuals interpolate themselves into the framing narrative of irreconcilable difference? In other words, are such actions simply about a sense of religious duty or do they sometimes serve to frame a sense of cultural obligation to push back against perceived antagonists? The question then becomes whether such hyperperformativity—and more especially the strategic assimilation and deliberate transgression of stereotypes—offers a way to explode fixed essential discourses of difference or ultimately can only result in complicity in one's marginalization.

These issues are played out in the career of Britain's most prominent "Muslim comedian," Shazia Mirza. Mirza rose to prominence in the weeks after the 9/11 attacks owing to her stage costume, topped by an austere black hijab, and her willingness to squeeze humor out of uncomfortable topics and confront audience expectations head on. (Her notorious opening line, instrumental in catapulting her into the public consciousness, was, "Hello. I'm Shazia Mirza—at least, that's what it says on my pilot's license.") Her feisty persona immediately challenged the stereotype of the passive, browbeaten Muslim woman, while her deadpan delivery hinted at and travestied the idea of Muslims as humorless automata. A British Pakistani from Birmingham, Mirza represents a shift in the center of gravity of "ethnic" comedy in Britain, after the Golden Age of the late 1990s with its Indo-chic and celebration of all things ethnic. Preeminent among the numerous television shows capturing this multicultural moment was the BBC's *Goodness Gracious Me*, featuring a quartet of British-Indian comedians, which set out to expose some of the attitudes toward South Asians still prevalent in mainstream white society in a series of sketches that often involved a reversal of stereotypes or an exposure of their vacuity. At the same time, the program acknowledged the existence of stereotyping and prejudice within and between diasporic communities themselves. With its subtle, multivalent humor, the show was quickly coopted as an example of successful multicultural Britain; the triumph of integration could be read in the fact that the various ethnicities that made up Britain could unite over a good joke.

After 9/11, and during the emergence of a less tractable brand of assertive ethnoreligious identity, negative stereotypes closed in, mainly around Britain's Muslims but also, by implication, around the South Asian population more generally, or anyone who might "look Muslim." In response to these changed conditions the more assertive presentational style of someone like Shazia Mirza operated on the margins of "good taste," provoking and unsettling. Tarlo describes Mirza as employing "the art of sartorial provocation" and shows how her subversion operates on several levels: "By donning a hijab, she was at one level simply claiming the right to speak about Muslims 'as a Muslim.' But in doing so, she was of course picking up on one of the most sacred and semiotically saturated contemporary symbols of our times and taking it into the very spaces it was least expected to frequent—the tainted macho beer-swilling world of London's pubs and clubs from which 'Good Muslims' were by definition self-excluded. . . . In effect, Shazia used the hijab as a powerful means of exposing and reflecting back to her predominantly white male audiences 'Western' stereotypes of Muslims at a time of extreme political tension and sensitivity."[37]

Once more, the idea of a heightened, parodic hyperperformance is a useful way to think about how Mirza's intervention troubled existing categories and dividing lines. By donning the hijab, and introducing it into an arena from which it (and Muslims in general) had been traditionally excluded, Mirza forced one to consider the gap between "Muslimness"—however that might actually be defined—and its outward signs. This action immediately challenged viewers who might conflate the one (a piece of cloth covering the head) with the other (the essence of the faith): it drove a wedge between them, as it were. We can here apply Judith Butler's insights, originally related to issues of gender, about the potentially subversive quality of masquerade. Arguing against any such thing as an "essence" of femininity, Butler famously contends that femaleness is brought into being through the act of performing roles in a certain, sanctioned, "feminine" way. This performance, or masquerade, can be "troubled" by its "subversive repetition" and "parodic recontextualisation"—Butler cites the exaggerated performances involved in drag and camp as examples. We would suggest that in a similar way, Mirza's stage performance in the years after 9/11 operated as masquerade—raising questions about whether "Muslimness" could be finally identified and pinned down or in fact was always being confused with its outward signifiers—especially in the case of women. We quote Butler but insert the word "Muslimness" in place of "femininity" used in the original: "the question here is whether masquerade conceals a [Muslimness] that might be understood as genuine or authentic, or whether masquerade is the means by which [Muslimness] and contests over its 'authenticity' are produced."[38] Effectively, Mirza was encoding the cultural identity of Muslimness *as it was perceived* by the viewer; in other words, she was subverting a stereotype by employing, repeating, and exaggerating it. In a postmodern sense, it might be claimed that this kind of act is what Butler calls a "parodic recontextualisation" of a dominant stereotype about Muslim women, an imitation that effectively calls into question any idea of an "original" truth behind the image. Mirza's work—and that of her American counterpart, Tissa Hami, who employs a similar stage strategy to confront ideas of Muslim women as weak and voiceless—has a double target. What are being challenged are both the racist naturalization of the "host" culture and the misogynistic naturalization of some conservative Islamic gender codes. (Mirza has encountered much criticism and some actual physical opposition from conservative Muslims who object to her supposed sacrilegious performance of Muslim femininity.)

The key here is that what is under attack is the locus of misrecognition—the viewer doing the stereotyping—not religious faith or notions of piety as such. Mirza's brand of hyperperformativity challenges binary stereotypes by creating, momentarily at least, a third location that registers the fluidity of linguistic and cultural codes making up modern Britishness. What are we expecting in the moment between the emergence onto the stage of this slight, soberly dressed, hijab-wearing Muslim woman and the moment when she opens her mouth and begins her routine? The mismatch between the small, gaunt figure and the sharp patter that emerges from her, enacts a moment of what one might call cultural estrangement, alienating the audience from its preconceptions: something that will be equally true for a white Western viewer familiar with supposed truisms about Muslim womanhood and a Muslim viewer who might not expect such great incongruity between outward signs and the reality beneath. At first sight there is an undecidability about Mirza's stage presence, something that challenges the audience to venture out from their cultural comfort zones and, perhaps, to recognize that there is a much greater degree of borrowing and plurality in cultural identities than official rhetoric often allows.[39] Shazia Mirza's response to the pressures facing Muslims living in the West, then, is a far cry from the Islamic answers to Barbie doll, that blandly reflect back fixed and idealized images of a "modern" Muslim femininity. Her deliberately overdetermined performance works, in a sense, to unpick the stitching of ethnic and cultural essentialist readings of religion and gender.

However, it could be that the performer herself will inevitably become, in the end, trapped by the persona she has created. Mirza, for example, stopped wearing her hijab-topped outfit after a few years, complaining that she had begun to feel trapped by it and by the burden of "representing Muslims."[40] Perhaps the tactic of confronting a stereotype through the deployment of one of its main constituent parts is only a beginning. The danger of typecasting—the performer's version of stereotyping—is never far away. Nonetheless, the mismatch between visual image and articulating subject does work to deny pigeonholing demands, from culturalists of one side or another, for what Bakirathi Mani has called "perfect reproductions of nation and culture"— demands that always seem to focus on female attire.[41] The undecidability of strategies of self-presentation that emphasize hybridity, or that play around with the expectations of the interlocutor, confuse and frustrate the simple operation of stereotyping, which always works through neat demarcations and closed off identities.

### Comedy against Stereotypes

Mirza's success owes something to the recently trumpeted phenomenon of "visibly Muslim" subjects: those who choose, through dress, beards, and so on, to outwardly display their faith and cultural orientation. Of course, in other ethnicities, this self-fashioning has been embraced as one of the birthrights of a multicultural society. However, as we have seen throughout this book, when it comes to Muslims, the meanings attached to such decisions by non-Muslim onlookers are almost entirely negative. Once more, perhaps comedy can play a part in confronting such a response, which is after all simply one of prejudice.

The debate around the Danish cartoon controversy of 2006 quickly degenerated into an exchange of clichés about Western freedom of speech versus Muslim intolerance or blasphemy versus sanctity. The more interesting question of conflicting notions of the role of humor was quickly buried beneath more apocalyptic interpretations of the affair. Whether something is funny or not is, in the end, a matter of personal preference. However, it is revealing that it was around the issue of humor that the cultural battle lines were drawn. Azhar Usman, the burly, bearded, and "visibly Muslim" third of the U.S. comedy trio *Allah Made Me Funny,* observed: "The cartoons are the single flashpoint that has defined the Islam and comedy debate and I think that it's a result of the fact that Islam has become politicized. Some people think that being a Muslim is about going out on to the streets and waving placards about rather than connecting with God and their faith on a personal level. . . . I don't go shouting in the street, I get up on stage and make jokes about it."[42]

*Allah Made Me Funny* is a group composed of three U.S. Muslims with different ethnic and cultural backgrounds: Usman is Indian American, Mohammed Amer is Palestinian American, and the founder of the company, Preacher Moss, is African American. They thereby represent three of the variety of backgrounds that go to make up the Muslim diaspora in the United States, and each brings the resulting cultural inflections to bear in his stand-up comedy routine. For instance, Preacher Moss is quick to draw analogies between being black in the United States and being Muslim. What links these identities, through Moss's wry delivery, is an experience of exclusion and victimization— although he never insists on such terms—and the rueful, sideways view of the world that results and that makes for humor. Indeed, the trio move between what one might call Muslim in-jokes—about the paradoxes and peculiarities of Muslim life and practices—and material that might have a wider appeal, having to do with the inherent absurdity of airport security checks, policing, and "homeland security" policies.

In a sense, *Allah Made Me Funny*'s broad joviality is a less disturbing, perhaps less radical comedy vehicle than Shazia Mirza's or Tissa Hami's deliberate transgression of expected gender norms. Nevertheless, there is always a knowing awareness in their comedy of the proximity of material that is *halal* (acceptable) and that which might be considered *haram* (forbidden) by Muslim sections of their audience. In fact, the comedians play around with the (always subjective) distinction between the two, playfully putting a toe across the line and threatening to bring up something that could be offensive but then coyly retreating or moving off on another tangent. They are comfortable with discomfort, however, and these moments often constitute the high point of their shows: the moment when, instead of laughter, there is momentary silence or a slight intake of breath among the audience, wary of what may be coming next. In this way, they do, after all, acknowledge that boundaries are there to be pushed. Unfortunately, this cagey irony is sometimes lost on reporters who have covered the troupe's international tours and who seem more interested in what the comedians' faith means they cannot say rather than what they actually include. The hackneyed question "What *won't* you joke about?" seems to follow the comedians wherever they go, and they invariably answer cheerfully that blasphemy and cruelty have no place in what they do. Although it is a legitimate question, it is one that is clearly framed by the stereotypes of Muslims as po-faced malcontents with no feeling for the lighter side of life and an inability to laugh at themselves that were reanimated by the cartoon controversy. (Context is all-important here; consider, for example, the absurdity of asking a family entertainer why he doesn't use profanity in his act, or a holiday camp comedian why he doesn't employ cutting-edge satire.) To suggest that all comedy *should* offend, push boundaries, and unsettle is in itself a culturally loaded judgment, and one that doesn't even apply to all Western comedy, let alone that with its roots in other cultures.

Nevertheless, a sharp answering awareness of the power of stereotyping is in evidence in some recent films that deal head-on, but humorously, with the world remade by 9/11. One thinks of how prejudice and stereotyping work to cripple hope and break apart lives in Nicole Ballivian's remarkable *Driving to Zigzigland* (2006), which tells the story of an aspiring Palestinian actor (played by Bashar Da'as) who comes to America hoping to further his career. He is only ever offered terrorist roles and has to take a job as a taxi driver to make ends meet.

The negative and hostile reactions he gets from his passengers when he tells them he is from Palestine causes him to invent a different country of origin for himself; he tells people he is from Zigzigland—either "South of South America" or "between Spain and China," depending on his mood—thereby mocking Americans' frequent ignorance about the world in which their nation exercises such great power. However, behind the offbeat comedy, the human tragedy of Bashar's position is never far away; he cannot land his dream acting role, is visited by the FBI, gets a letter from Homeland Security, and is eventually deported when he cannot pay off his debts.

More direct and combative is Jackie Salloum's short film *Planet of the Arabs* (2005), which, following Jack Shaheen's lead, looks at how Arabs are portrayed in Hollywood. In this case, Salloum employs a montage technique, piling one outrageous caricature on top of another, from a variety of Hollywood mainstream fare, to create an increasingly ludicrous and grotesque mountain of prejudice and propaganda. Although it was made three years earlier, *Planet of the Arabs* could almost be seen as providing an effective riposte to another montage film, *Fitna,* by the Dutch right-wing demagogue Geert Wilders. Wilders notoriously intersperses decontextualized excerpts from the Koran with scenes of violence and bloodshed perpetrated by those claiming a Muslim faith, in an attempt to suggest that the strictures of the one lead to the excesses of the other. It is beside the point to observe that *Fitna* is a piece of crude propaganda entirely devoid of any artistic merit. It is, rather, intriguing to set its pompous and apocalyptic scaremongering alongside Salloum's much cooler and ironic tapestry of stereotypes, many of which predate by years the supposed recent increase in Islamist violence around the world.

Different genres of comedy will obviously have different relationships to the ways society recognizes its foibles and peculiarities. For the most part, the generic forms that have dominated television comedy have been domestic sitcoms, coming-of-age narratives, and comedies involving mismatched buddies. In recent years, these venerable forms have found themselves playing host to the trials and tribulations of Muslim experience—as least as productions have emerged through the filtration systems of the North American television commissioning process.

*Aliens in America* (2007), a short-lived series on the CW television network, centered on the Tolchuk family in Wisconsin and, in particular, their awkward sixteen-year-old son Justin and his attempts to gain popularity among his peers at school. To help their gawky son, the Tolchuk parents agree to host an international student, expecting a blond Scandinavian who will instantly raise their son's popularity rating. What they get, however, is Raja, a Muslim orphan from Pakistan. The series follows the developing friendship between these two teenagers, their adventures and misadventures, and the dawning realization that what they have in common is more important than the cultural and religious differences that appear to divide them. Along the way, the show is able to poke fun at the small-town insularity that reveals itself in the wariness and horrified disbelief with which the inhabitants, and Justin's schoolfellows, greet their new arrival. To underline his "difference," Raja continues to wear a shalwar kamis and skullcap, despite having plenty of time to assemble a new wardrobe. However, his costume is merely there to remind viewers of his exotic provenance and raises few unsettling questions—male attire always being read more transparently than the semiotically loaded clothes of the Muslim female.

*Aliens in America* does tackle directly post-9/11 ignorance and fear of the cultural Other. Yet, in the end, the viewer's point of interest and identification is really with the growing pains of the teenage misfit, Justin, rather than with any cultural dislocation or alienation felt by Raja. Indeed, Raja is quickly shown to share the same tastes as his young friend, in music, girls, and socializing, and his respectful good humor reveals that the real difference lies only in how such character traits are displayed. For these reasons, the program belongs very firmly to the coming-of-age and buddy traditions; elements such as the central character's intrusive voiceovers recall *The Wonder Years,* while the comedy engendered by the stranger who ends up in a foreign land holds echoes of *Relative Strangers* and (the definitive alien-in-America show) *Mork and Mindy.* In this respect, *Aliens in America* has in its sights the tribulations of small-town teen America rather than a more ambitious exploration of what lies behind cultural difference. In the end, the funny Pakistani comes among "us" and exposes "our" prejudices but in the end turns out to be just like "us." There is certainly something to be said in favor of the show's message of humanist tolerance, but perhaps it misses a chance to go deeper into the labyrinth of modern cultural tensions.

More ambitious is the CBC sitcom *Little Mosque on the Prairie*, created by Zarqa Nawaz. The title plays on viewers' memories of the 1970s NBC adaptation of Laura Ingalls Wilder's memoir of frontier life *Little House on the Prairie*. Yet *Little Mosque* forgoes the twee moralizing that sometimes marked the older series and instead takes an incisive approach to tackling community relations and stereotyping. If Charles Ingalls and his family were nineteenth-century pioneers forging a new life in the untamed Midwest, in *Little Mosque* the extended Muslim "family" of Mercy, Saskatchewan, blazes its own trail by establishing a place of worship in the local church hall, facing fearsome rednecks and hostile "natives" along the way.

Importantly, our sympathetic identification is with the harassed, beleaguered yet undaunted Muslim group. We are taken inside their daily lives, loves, and dilemmas—they are normalized, shall we say?—and our engagement with the non-Muslim community surrounding them is less detailed. In the course of the first series, for example, we meet Yasir Hamoudi, a construction company owner, his convert wife, Sarah, and his daughter, Rayyan, who wears the hijab and is a doctor by profession. The family reflects middle-class aspirational values shared by immigrants; they are all outsiders trying to fit in while retaining their religious faith. However, it is this very faith, which signifies suspicious and possibly violent tendencies to white society, that disrupts the customary narrative of social advancement. In the first episode, for instance, the Muslim community's attempts to set up their mosque on church premises leads to a panic when their conversations about burying the dead are overheard by a local farmer. At the same time the congregation's new imam, Amaar, is detained by security officers at the Toronto airport when an innocent cell phone conversation about how his journey will lead him to his destiny is misinterpreted by worried fellow passengers. Other characters embody different Islamic ethnicities, attitudes, and degrees of orthodoxy: they include an African-Muslim coffee shop owner, Fatima, and Babur, the conservative single father of a rebellious teenage girl. The issues that exercise them all week by week include dilemmas about when to start fasting for Ramadan, how to curb the enthusiasm of an over-zealous new convert, and the difficulty of extricating Yasir from a second marriage engineered for him by his formidable mother. All of this takes place against a background of suspicion, articulated most forcefully by the right-wing local radio talk show host Fred Tupper, who takes every opportunity to castigate the interlopers and their nefarious Eastern ways.

If it were just a case of embattled Muslims and bigoted white people, *Little Mosque* would probably offer little of note. However, the show foregrounds stereotypes and kinds of misrecognition as central to its interpretation of Self/Other identity formation at a personal level too. Everyone in the show seemingly misreads everyone else. The talk show host misreads the Muslims, but the Muslims also misread each other, not least because of the comparative three-dimensionality of their characters: Yasir's business instincts mean that his motives are always mixed; his wife struggles to be a better Muslim against the ever-present temptations of her Western lifestyle and tastes; Babur is constantly baffled by his daughter's refusal to behave like a "good Muslim girl"; and the smouldering tension in the relationship between Amaar and Rayyan always threatens to break out into something more romantic but never quite does. Misreading and miscommunication take place on account of age, gender, ethnicity and background. The result is a comedy that, while deploying its fair share of clichéd situations and stock figures, also presents Muslim life in the round and not set against a more "normal" majority population from which Muslims represent some kind of deviation.

Each of these comedy shows and performers works from a recognition of the stifling presence, but also the comedic potential, of crude stereotypes. The best of them realize that it is not enough simply to reverse the stereotype and that one needs to challenge the conventional wisdom on which stereotypes depend, either through parody, pointing out inconsistencies and absurdities, or employing a shift of focus that forces the ethnonormalized viewer to take a look at things from the "Other" side. Thus, comedy can be an important tool in combating framing depictions of Muslims and Muslimness. We are not proposing here that all Muslims should suddenly take to the stage, start parodying themselves, or take their religion less seriously. Rather, we are suggesting that since stereotypes exist nowhere but in the eye of the beholder, challenges that work ironically with a knowledge of likely prejudices and then directly frustrate or confound them might have a role to play in loosening the grip of reductive images. It could well be that the inherent irreverence of comedy itself always offers a space to blow apart narrow, dour constructions of cultural separation and a hostile and defensive emphasis on uniqueness. In this way, we might begin to find new ways of seeing, and being, beyond the frame.

## Crossing Boundaries, Breaking the Frame

Throughout this book we have seen government officials and news and television producers frantically pursuing that elusive thing called Muslim life, with a view to pinning it down and taming it, in the interests of either administrative policy or the generic requirements of a particular medium. Their efforts tend, perhaps inevitably, to result in stereotyping at some level. They have to fix and deal with a certain set of dominant characteristics from all the variety of experiences, beliefs, and positions that make up Muslim subjectivity. Our contention has been that too often this urge has resulted in a chronically narrowed flow of ideas and images that have the effect of bringing Muslims into being as radically different entities on whom all the forces of discipline must be brought to bear.

While cultural forms sometimes participate in this narrowing, it can also be the case that more ambitious productions may have a greater success in revealing something valuable about the depth and complexity of actual Muslim experience. And in doing, they will surely bring us back to the *encounter,* rather than the clash, of cultures, which has always enriched and enlivened both the Muslim and the non-Muslim worlds. This encounter is there in the forms of comedy discussed above, in which performers and writers draw on the experience not of East versus West but of the East *in the* West—that is, if those categories have a meaning any more. In the realm of visual art, for example we can see painters, calligraphers, and installation and performance artists drawing on a global legacy that rejects the inaccurate (we might say, imperial) view of cultures as sealed off from one another. For example, the work of Vaseem Mohammed, from the East End of London, blends European modernist and Islamic styles to produce works in which skylines from Muslim cities emerge through the angular broken lens of cubism, or tiny examples of Islamic calligraphy appear on the blistered surfaces of irregularly shaped canvases, or a mosque shimmers through a haze of textured blue paint. Rashid Rana, from Lahore, explores stereotypes of masculinity and femininity. His best known and most widely exhibited work is *Three Veils,* in which images of shrouded female forms are revealed in a visual effect akin to Seurat's pointillism; on closer inspection we see that the image is made up of thousands of tiny pornographic pictures. In this way, Rana is able to juxtapose the Western stereotype of the Muslim woman whose individuality has been obliterated by the burqa with the Muslim stereotype of Western women as defined by and only valued through their sexual availability. (Rana's other work in a similar vein includes an image of Bollywood icon Shahrukh Khan composed of small images of other, anonymous men, thereby raising questions about ideals of masculinity.) Also interested in exploring the fusion of Eastern and Western styles is Imran Qureshi, who reproduces the tradition of the Mughal miniature but transvalues it by populating its minilandscapes with modern-looking figures carrying shopping bags, wearing combat trousers, and so on.

This hybridity of form is not merely an artistic conceit; it reflects back on contemporary identities as they are experienced. What is being mapped is the modern world in which subjects, whether they move freely around the globe or are contained in one place, cannot escape the profound influence of others. Why did the Taliban choose to ban television when they took over in Afghanistan? And why did American forces target the Al Jazeera offices in Kabul in 2001 and Baghdad in 2003? In both instances what was feared was another message, an alternative perspective, that might fire the imagination and shatter the stereotypes of "us" and "them." Fortunately, such retrograde efforts are too little, too late. That cat is well and truly out of the bag. Pnina Werbner has usefully distinguished between the cosmopolitans who are able to zip around the world freely, partaking of global culture at will, and those whom she terms "transnationals," whose "hybridity is unconscious, organic and collectively negotiated in practice . . . they think globally, but their loyalties are anchored in translocal social networks and cultural diasporas rather than the global ecumene. . . . [They] have to contend with incredible social and economic hardships, and they draw on culturally constituted resources of solidarity and mutual aid for survival."[43]

In the realm of Muslim political activism, as we have seen, there is a dawning awareness that the goal of social justice and inclusion for Muslims is entirely reliant on the forging of shared campaigns with non-Muslims. This goal simply cannot be achieved alone, since the structures of cultural identity politics allows groups to be isolated and picked off in a policy of divide and rule. Instead, we can look to temporary, shifting political alliances, such as, the organizations that sprang up in opposition to the Iraq war, and the new forms of community media and cultural practices that are born out of the overlap between South Asian and Arab cultures and those of the West. In particular, Muslims' use of new media forms, such as, the Internet, is already carving out a space beyond the stereotype—even if this book has placed its own emphases elsewhere. Such initiatives create hybrid identities through fusion. They may not be permanent, and they are certainly not static, but they have a better chance of making real interventions in modern political and cultural life than do older forms of fixed identity politics.

It is for this reason that we are skeptical of claims for "positive" representation as such. It could well be argued that more favorable views are important to counter the enormous volume of negative portrayals of Muslims that we have traced in this book. "Positive" representations are taken to boost self-esteem, provide role models, and so on, thereby incrementally pushing forward the agenda of equality. The importance of positive depictions has been at the forefront of other campaigns around identity—in particular, regarding the African-American experience in the United States. However, an understanding of Muslim connectedness, both to other Muslims and to the wider world, is potentially of more value in this case because it reminds both sides in the "clash of civilizations" that the separateness that is advanced as a reason for shoring up "our" culture against the barbarians at the gate—from whichever hemisphere they come—is a complete fallacy. It always was and it always will be.[44] It is no longer a matter of a "positive images approach" or of who gets to produce the stereotypes. Rather what is needed is a recognition of the ubiquitous cultural interpenetration that has always marked relations between Islam and the West, and an attempt to work this realization into the mainstream representational landscape, and into both cultural and political views of Muslims as something more than just a strategic problem. There *are* ways beyond the frame, as we have seen, but it will take effort, openness, and a new vision of what politics can be to make these meaningful.

# Conclusion

The framing of Muslims, with which this book has been concerned, is a serious and ongoing feature of contemporary life. We have attempted to show the origins, durability, and psychosocial utility of contemporary and durable stereotypes. Finally, then, it is not as if the increased awareness of Muslim culture and practices since 9/11 has acted as a purgative of the tendency to stereotype the Muslim Other. Indeed, in some respects suspicion and hostility toward Muslims has increased with the steady drip of negative images and the coincidence of other political issues and agendas. Two instances prove the tenacity of Muslim framing.

On 4 January 2010, Anjem Choudary, leader of Islam4UK, a local derivative of the outlawed extreme Islamist political body Al Muhajiroun, announced his group's intention to stage a march commemorating the Muslim dead of the war in Afghanistan. The group intended to process, carrying symbolic coffins, through the small Wiltshire town of Wootton Bassett, until then the gathering place of mourners wishing to pay their respects to the remains of British servicemen killed in the conflict as they made their way through the town on the way from the nearby military airport where they had been repatriated. The plan was greeted by the British press with howls of outrage at the sacrilegious disrespect shown to the grieving families of the servicemen who were honored by the crowds that regularly lined the streets for each somber vigil. Every major national newspaper featured the story prominently with appropriately disgusted headlines, apoplectic op-eds, and a steady stream of obligatory token Muslim columnists wheeled out to heap their own opprobrium on Choudary and his group.

Coming quite soon after another Islamist rump had barracked a returning parade of British troops in Luton, Islam4UK's plans made dispiriting reading for many Muslims, who must have felt their collective loyalty fall once again under scrutiny. However, one feels it must have set eyes a-gleaming among the editoriat of the British dailies, for whom honoring the military dead ultimately trumps whatever reservations their newspapers might otherwise ordinarily express about the Afghan and Iraqi conflicts, and who know the value of a Muslim scare story when they see one. Choudary subsequently made the rounds of television and radio news studios and appeared to equivocate about whether the publicized march would, in fact, take place at all. When pressed, he pointed out that the object of the exercise had been to gain publicity for the otherwise unheralded deaths of civilians in Afghanistan, and, no doubt, for his own fringe group. And, as he gleefully pointed out, that day's headlines were ample evidence of the success of this tactic already. In a sense, any actual parade would now be, to an extent, beside the point: mission already accomplished.

Most journalists and correspondents were too busy indulging their righteous indignation, and eliciting furious splutterings from a competing gaggle of similarly outraged politicians, to consider whether or not they may have been ever so slightly outwitted by Choudary: manipulated into giving him exactly the oxygen of publicity that he craved. Only Tom Sutcliffe in the *Independent* paused to consider whether all the brouhaha might be exactly what Mr. Choudary was after.[1] And, in truth, this is not really a story of a wily Muslim villain putting one over on a gullible yet public-spirited press. Instead, this teacup-sized storm is a picture-perfect example of all the qualities of framing described in this book.

It is perfect because of the visual fit of Anjem Choudary—copiously bearded and clearly the self-fashioning bogeyman of secular, liberal Britain; the opportunity afforded the press to run, for the umpteenth wearisome time, an implicit questioning of Muslims' loyalty to Britain coupled with a contradictory avowal that mainstream Muslims were "not like that" (the *Daily Mail* website later featured an elderly Muslim couple who had turned out, on a freezing cold day in Wootton Bassett, for a vigil marking the return of yet another dead soldier); the lazy journalese in which Choudary was termed a "cleric" despite having, and claiming, no religious training; and encompassing all this the clearly demonstrated intense embrace in which the two opposing sides in the "War on Terror" discourse have necessarily become entangled. Just as politicians fell over themselves to countenance revoking the principle of free speech they were otherwise incessantly flaunting as something "we" had and "they" didn't by banning the march, so the extremists could be buoyed by the certainty that if the political establishment did not rise to their bait and the march actually went ahead, then the racist right—always up for a fight—most certainly would. Choudary and Islam4UK had cleverly contrived for themselves a win-win situation in which every eventuality served their purpose. Here, in the black and white of newsprint and the digital images of the broadcast media, is a living, breathing instance of the dialogic quality we have argued is at the heart of the framing of Muslims. Islamist fanatics rely on regular vilification to keep their rebel chic for the young and disaffected. Politicians and newspaper editors likewise depend on regular appearances from members of the lunatic fringe to remind "us" what "we" are fighting against (and to boost circulation figures).

In the depressing catalogue of Muslim framing since 9/11 and 7/7 with which we have been concerned, the Choudary/Islam4UK debacle offers a moment to stop and think about the incestuous dyad that blights representation and prevents things from ever moving on very far. Choudary is no foreign infiltrator—he was born in Welling and lives in Ilford, Essex—but is the kind of "traitor in our midst" whose very presence, it is said, justifies the regrettable but necessary extra measures in surveillance and the curtailment of civil liberties that have come with the "War on Terror." And all these debates play out in a context where both governments and extremists conduct themselves on the understanding that the mediascape now constitutes the terrain of battle.

Another example, this time foregrounding the role of new media forms as an airing space for unofficial opinions and as a conduit for rumor and paranoia, came with the curious case of Pastor Terry Jones and his ironically named Dove World Outreach Center in Florida. Pastor Jones grabbed the limelight with his plan to publically burn copies of the Koran, which he blamed for the 9/11 attacks. Previously Pastor Jones had written a largely ignored book entitled *Islam Is of the Devil,* which he nevertheless followed up with a (now defunct) website and a line of T-shirts. His plan to commemorate 9/11 with a bonfire rapidly gained notoriety via a Youtube video, a Facebook group, and his church's website. Bloggers responded, and soon the plan was receiving coverage on CNN, ABC, NPR, and Yahoo News and subsequently on international news agencies such as the Arab satellite broadcaster Al-Arabiya.[2] At this point the predictable backlash began in Muslim countries, with sometimes violent demonstrations in Afghanistan, Pakistan, Indonesia, India, and elsewhere. The presidents of Afghanistan and Indonesia warned of serious repercussions for American interests in their countries, while General David Petraeus, the commander of U.S. and Nato forces in Afghanistan, cautioned that the torching would lead to retaliation against U.S. troops on the front line. At this juncture the U.S. Secretary of State, Hillary Clinton, stepped in to express official outrage, and finally, in the face of Pastor Jones's intransigence, President Obama entered the fray, commenting: "This is a way of endangering our troops, our sons and daughters . . . you don't play games with that."[3] (Obama's own position in relation to Muslim framing has been made more difficult by right-wingers' persistent allegations that he is a closet Muslim who is determined to turn the country over to Islam, communism, or any other political bogey of the right. This kind of Islamophobic attack has gained currency and is particularly played on by those opposed to his policies on healthcare and social reform.)

The Jones case offers a textbook illustration of the dialogicality of framing this book has identified: an extreme right-wing Christian, previously only noted for making homophobic statements about local political candidates, asserts that it is time for America to "stand up to Islam," which he sees as irrational and satanically inspired; he does so in the most provocative way possible (but one that mimics the book- and effigy-burning antics of Muslim protesters in other parts of the world); and, in his turn, he provokes the kind of violent backlash that seems to prove his argument. Seen from the other "side," of course, the gesture of Koran burning acts as damning evidence of the godlessness and anti-Muslim attitude prevalent in the West and leads to the kind of frenzied, violent response that "proves" such societies' irrationality to Western onlookers . . . and so on and on.

Pastor Jones turned out to be skilled in public relations—albeit not of the intercultural variety. This was proved when, midway through the controversy, he suddenly hitched his Koran-burning bandwagon to the current controversy over plans for an Islamic Cultural Center near Ground Zero in Lower Manhattan. The proposed redevelopment quickly became known to the media and opponents as the "Ground Zero mosque," despite the fact that the proposed development was a few blocks away from the site where the World Trade Center's Twin Towers had once stood and included a swimming pool, tennis courts, and an auditorium for meetings (as well as a prayer area). Groups speaking on behalf of some relatives of the 9/11 victims opposed the redevelopment of the disused building at 45 Park Place, even though it had already been used for prayer by local Muslims for several years.[4] The debate became heated, as those claiming a personal stake in what they felt was an area sacred to the memory of their dead loved ones were joined by opportunistic politicians, and all the old arguments about Islam being an alien and hostile faith that had declared war on America with the 9/11 attacks came to the fore again. When Pastor Jones announced, midway through the Koran-burning furore, his willingness to cancel the event should the organizers of the New York cultural center agree to move to another site, he showed considerable media savvy. A story that had been initiated by a tiny fringe group, picked up in the new media, broadcast by mainstream agencies, and given a boost by high-level political interventions was suddenly brought into line with a simmering national controversy that triggered a raw emotional response in many. The coincidence of Pastor Jones's plans with the anniversary of 9/11, the festival of Eid-ul Fitr, and the runup to the midterm congressional elections made for a toxic brew. Again, from the perspective of the framing of Muslims, all the elements are in play: controversialists, a ravenous media, politicians who must appear to be doing something and, most important, the confluence of religious, national, and supposedly civilizational identities. No matter that Pastor Jones's followers only amount to a handful of reactionary Floridians, or that his views seem to have been informed by narrow reading and theological perspectives dating from the Middle Ages—his ability to link the two controversies catapulted him, albeit temporarily, from a marginal figure condemned by all other available spokespersons for his own religion to a national player and figurehead for a backlash against Islam that drew in right-wing media commentators and neo-conservative ideologues.[5]

In the cases of both Anjem Choudary and Terry Jones, onlookers may have been forgiven for feeling that neither publicity stunt was ever really likely to take place. Pastor Jones prayed hard and had a change of heart (as well as a visit from the FBI); Anjem Choudary decided that it was enough to have gained the attention of the media for his fringe group. However, what appears to unite these two very different fire-brands is an awareness of how easily the media can be persuaded to air their views with only the promise of some sensational images of con-frontation and conflagration at the end of it. With different kinds of media saturating our social relations and literally mediating between different groups more than ever before, it is essential that news agendas and reporting be held more to account and, where possible, that they question the political agendas passed on by repetition and convenience.

Numerous commentators quickly remarked that 9/11 was defini-tively and spectacularly a calculated media event. And we have seen how subsequent acts in the "War on Terror"—from insurgents' hostage beheadings to the U.S. army's torture at Abu Ghraib—have depended, for their power to terrify, on the mediation of experience through video footage, digital photography and the Internet. So at the end of a book on this very process—the framing of Muslims—we are entitled to ask whether postmodern society and its would-be enemies are both so lost in the desert of the real as to be unable to view the Muslim populations of the world in any way other than through the cripplingly limited range of options enumerated in the previous pages.[6]

Of course, it doesn't have to be this way. The positive self-fashioning of Muslims, both in their personal lives and in their utilizing of the very same new media often used by others to carry out framing, indicates the desire to find a space beyond the frame. Perhaps that space lies in the everyday, lived experience of low-level, peaceful, and communal (in the best sense) interaction that the mediated picture habitually ignores. This is not a call for a return to some pure premediated state of face-to-face relations. Rather it is a suggestion that such relationships already exist, "out there" in the space beyond the camera, and should be admitted back into the mediascape, into law, into political discourse: all areas that currently operate on the assumption that to be a Muslim is automatically to carry some kind of latent threat.

As we have seen, the media's responses to the altered landscape after 9/11 have been variable. Too often they have taken their cues, ideologies, and themes from the preoccupation of Western governments with the "War on Terror." In the immediate aftermath of 9/11 there was some interest in improving knowledge about Islam in both Britain and America. In particular, U.S. television, long starved of serious international news coverage as agencies preferred to focus instead on celebrity and domestic news, found itself trying to reconnect with a wider world that had suddenly forced its way to the top of the news agenda. Yet programs such as ABC's *Minefield: The United States and the Muslim World* and CNN's *An In-depth Look at Islam: The Realities and the Rhetoric*, for all their genuine attempts to explore the Muslim world, tended ultimately to be concerned with Islam primarily as a problem for U.S. strategic interests.[7] Although not all coverage was as naïve as this, it has taken some time for a true degree of self-consciousness to enter the media's consideration of its coverage of Islam. Notable for its perspicacity in this respect was Peter Oborne's Channel 4 documentary *It Shouldn't Happen to a Muslim* (2008), which directly considered the possibility that the reporting of Muslim stories since 9/11 and 7/7 had tangibly damaged the standing of Muslims in British society, resulting in prejudice and sometimes violence. (Predictably, Oborne's reflective piece was met with scorn in right-wing circles, where the vested interest in maintaining antipathy to Islamic values and practices is strongest.) Since then, a special issue of the *New Statesman*, entitled "Everything You Know about Islam Is Wrong," brought together a range of internationally respected commentators to explore the world beyond the stereotypes, without ever losing sight of the fact that those very stereotypes were likely to some extent to have colored its readership's understanding.[8]

Unfortunately, the number of knee-jerk news and magazine items on the "Islamic Peril" suggests that there is a long way to go before such self-consciousness is considered important enough to filter regularly into the practices of news editors, who seldom question their own commitment to a particular version of the truth. It is also the case that Muslim self-fashioning, in all its diversity, and the activities of the burgeoning Muslim media must play a central role in reshaping the nature of future representations. In the meantime, just as paranoia and aggression remain the default position in the United States when it comes to matters of Muslim political self-assertion, so, in the United Kingdom, the confluence of national security agendas and those of the mass media continue to create a climate where Muslims can be freely picked on and victimized. New groups—for example the English Defence League, a motley collective of hard right racists and soccer hooligans—now travel the country holding inflammatory "anti-Islamization" demonstrations, which draw out antifascist protesters and usually end in violence. At the same time, the British National Party can remodel itself as a party that is not expressly against nonwhite immigrants, just the supposed irrevocably alien Muslim. Certainly, increased radicalization in Muslim communities around the world, often in response to perceived Western aggression in their homelands, provides half the context for these tensions. However, it would be naïve in the extreme not to recognize that the incessant demonization of Muslims and their cultural practices by those with access to the major vehicles of public discourse in the West has indirectly given a green light to prejudice and vigilantism.

So there is no neat conclusion to the story of the framing of Muslims. From a mixture of convenience, familiarity, and genuinely felt, if perhaps misdirected, concern the same visual and narrative elements continue in circulation. They make us no wiser, but they will not go away. Until the day when politicians see advantage in seriously addressing all the aspects—social, political, economic, and international—that lead to alienation and injustice, Muslims are likely to remain in the frame. Both sides in the so-called clash of civilizations fetishize a "pure" (and entirely fanciful) idea of who they are and where they come from. At the same time, the media have a duty to deal seriously with the sometimes unappealing complexity of Muslim identity claims, not to dismiss them out of hand or make them the object of ridicule. We move forward by inches when we move forward at all. A greater diversity of voices must be brought to the table, allowed to speak *and be seriously listened to,* before any progress can be made to unpick stereotypes and allow Muslims as they are to walk out of the frame and into the political life of the twenty-first century.

**Notes**

**Acknowledgments**

**Index**

# Notes

## Introduction

1. Steven Vertovec, "Islamophobia and Muslim Recognition in Britain," in Yvonne Yazbeck Haddad (ed.), *Muslims in the West: From Sojourners to Citizens* (Oxford: Oxford University Press, 2002), 19–35.

2. See Iftikhar Malik, *Islam and Modernity: Muslims in Europe and the United States* (London: Pluto Press, 2004), 160–177; see also Geneive Abdo, *Mecca and Main Street: Muslim Life in America after 9/11* (Oxford: Oxford University Press, 2007), 1–10.

3. John Tolan, *Saracens: Islam and the Medieval European Imagination* (New York: Columbia University Press, 2002), 3–20.

4. Ibid., 41–50.

5. Ibid., 91.

6. Nabil Matar, *Islam in Britain, 1558–1685* (Cambridge: Cambridge University Press, 1998), 13.

7. Ibid., 50–73.

8. See Ziauddin Sardar and Merryl Wyn Davies, "Freeze Framing Muslims: Hollywood and the Slideshow of Western Imagination," *Interventions* 12:2 (2010): 239–250.

9. Mohja Kahf, *Western Representations of the Muslim Woman: From Termagant to Odalisque* (Austin: University of Texas Press, 1999).

10. Mahmood Mamdani, *Good Muslim, Bad Muslim: America, the Cold War and the Roots of Terror* (New York: Three Leaves Press, 2004), 33. As well as critiquing the historical notion of "the West," Mamdani also rejects the idea of "fundamentalism" as an adequate term for radical political Islam. Instead, he stresses the key distinction as being between more moderate, socially oriented political Islam and a radical Islam that seeks to act on the world stage and gain power over the state.

11. "Pope's Speech at University of Regensburg," www.catholicculture.org (accessed 8/30/10).

## 1. Muslims and the Nation-State

1. Edward W. Said, *Covering Islam: How the Media and the Experts Determine How We See the Rest of the World,* rev. ed. (London: Vintage 1997), li.

2. Ibid., 156–157.

3. Maxwell McCombs, *Setting the Agenda: The Mass Media and Public Opinion* (Cambridge: Polity, 2004), 87, 89.

4. Costas Douzinas, *Human Rights and Empire: The Political Philosophy of Cosmopolitanism* (New York: Routledge-Cavendish, 2007), 193.

5. Michael Pickering, *Stereotyping: The Politics of Representation* (London: Palgrave, 2001), 69.

6. Homi K. Bhabha, *The Location of Culture* (London: Routledge, 1994), 66–84.

7. Ibid., 77.

8. Sigmund Freud, *On Sexuality: Three Essays on the Theory of Sexuality and Other Works,* ed. Angela Richards (London: Penguin, 1977), 352–353.

9. Patrick French, "The Surprising Truth about Rage Boy, America's Hated Poster Boy of Islamic Radicalism," *Daily Mail,* 11 November 2007.

10. Ibid.

11. Ibid.

12. Christopher Hitchens, "Look Forward to Anger," www.slate.com (accessed 9/22/09).

13. Ibid. Steven Salaita has noted how the recent slew of books by celebrity atheists such as Hitchens, Richard Dawkins, and Sam Harris coincide with "a moment of pronounced Islamophobia in the West": "the new atheism, as presented by its public intellectuals, belongs to the realm of white male hauteur. The form of atheism that Harris, Dawkins and Hitchens promote is remarkably smug and Eurocentric." Salaita judiciously concludes: "There is absolutely no precedent to suggest that abandoning religion and adhering to science will make humans any less apt to commit injustice and act irrationally. The adamantly pro-war Hitchens, who continues to champion the disastrous invasion of Iraq, is clear evidence of this fact." See Steven Salaita, *The Uncultured Wars: Arabs, Muslims and the Poverty of Liberal Thought—New Essays* (London: Zed Books, 2008), 151, 152, 155.

14. Jacques Lacan, *Ecrits: A Selection,* trans. Alan Sheridan (London: Tavistock, 1977), 4.

15. Graham Allen, *Intertextuality* (London: Routledge, 2000), 11.

16. Jacques-Philippe Leyens, Vincent Yzerbyt, and Georges Schadron, *Stereotypes and Social Cognition* (London: Sage, 1994), 70–71.

17. Haideh Moghissi, Saeed Rahnema, and Mark J. Goodman (eds.), *Diaspora by Design: Muslim Immigrants in Canada and Beyond* (London: University of Toronto Press, 2009), 11.

18. Ian Buruma and Avishai Margalit, *Occidentalism: The West in the Eyes of Its Enemies* (New Delhi: Penguin, 2004).

19. Ewen MacAskill, "Fears of Backlash against US Muslims after Shooting Spree," *Guardian*, 7 November 2009.

20. Nancy Gibbs, "Terrified . . . or Terrorist?," *Time*, 23 November 2009, 22.

21. Susan D. Moeller, *Packaging Terrorism: Co-opting the News for Politics and Profit* (Chichester, England: Wiley-Blackwell, 2009), 18–19.

22. Salaita, *Uncultured Wars*, 75–76.

23. Mahmood Mamdani, *Good Muslim, Bad Muslim: America, the Cold War and the Roots of Terror* (New York: Three Leaves, 2004), 16–17.

24. Philip Schlesinger, *Media, State and Nation: Political Violence and Collective Identities* (London: Sage, 1991), 8–23.

25. Karim H. Karim, "Making sense of the 'Islamic Peril': Journalism as Cultural Practice," in Barbie Zelizer and Stuart Allen (eds.), *Journalism after September 11* (London: Routledge, 2002) 108–109.

26. Zygmunt Bauman, *Modernity and Ambivalence* (London: Polity, 1991), 59.

27. Antony Easthope, *Englishness and National Culture* (London: Routledge, 1999), 218–223.

28. Thijl Sunier and Mira van Kuijeren, "Islam in the Netherlands," in Yvonne Yazbeck Haddad (ed.), *Muslims in the West: From Sojourners to Citizens* (Oxford: Oxford University Press, 2002), 150–151.

29. Halleh Ghorashi, "Multiculturalism and Citizenship in the Netherlands," *ISIM Review* 15 (Spring 2005): 10.

30. Valérie Amiraux, "To Be Laic or Not to Be Laic? A French Dilemma," in Rosemary Bechler (ed.), *Faith and Secularism* (London: British Council, 2004), 12–30.

31. Gilles Kepel, *Beyond Terror and Martyrdom: The Future of the Middle East,* trans. Pascal Ghazaleh (Cambridge, Mass.: Harvard University Press, 2008), 182.

32. Tariq Modood, "Muslims and the Politics of Difference," *Political Quarterly* 74:1 (2003): 110.

33. Tariq Modood, " 'Difference,' Cultural Racism and Anti-Racism," in Pnina Werbner and Tariq Modood (eds.), *Debating Cultural Hybridity: Multicultural Identities and the Politics of Anti-Racism* (London: Zed Books) 1997, 155.

34. Matthew Tempest, "Blair Sees Iraq as 'Clash about **Civilization**,' " *Guardian*, 21 March 2006.

35. Matthew Beard and Robert Verkaik, "Mosque Defends Firearms Officer Stripped of His Post," *Independent,* 8 November 2006, and Robert Verkaik, "Sacked Muslim Officer Wants Police Protection," *Independent,* 10 November 2006.

36. Paul Gilroy, *After Empire: Melancholia or Convivial Culture* (Abingdon, England: Routledge, 2004), 67.

37. Johannes Fabian, *Time and the Other: How Anthropology Makes Its Object* (New York: Columbia University Press, 1983), 31.

38. Patrick Barkham, "Rushdie Calls for 'Muslim Reformation,'" *Guardian,* 12 August 2005.

## 2. Muslims, Multiculturalism, and the Media

1. Peter Fryer, *Staying Power: The History of Black People in Britain* (London: Pluto, 1984).

2. Tariq Modood, "'Difference,' Cultural Racism and Anti-Racism," in Pnina Werbner and Tariq Modood (eds.), *Debating Cultural Hybridity: Multicultural Identities and the Politics of Anti-Racism* (London: Zed Books, 1997), 156–157.

3. Ibid., 159.

4. Derek Rubin and Jaap Verheul (eds.), *American Multiculturalism after 9/11: Transatlantic Perspectives* (Amsterdam: Amsterdam University Press, 2009), 8 (emphasis added).

5. Tariq Modood, *Multiculturalism: A Civic Idea* (Cambridge: Polity, 2007), 2.

6. Charles Taylor, "The Politics of Recognition," in Amy Gutman (ed.), *Multiculturalism: Examining the Politics of Recognition* (Princeton, N.J.: Princeton University Press, 1994), 25–74; see also Seyla Benhabib, *The Claims of Culture* (Princeton, N.J.: Princeton University Press, 2002); Nancy Frazer and Axel Honneth, *Redistribution or Recognition: A Political-Philosophical Exchange* (London: Verso, 2003).

7. Runnymede Trust, *Islamophobia: A Challenge for Us All* (London: Runnymede, 1997).

8. Andrew Pilkington, "From Institutional Racism to Community Cohesion: the Changing Nature of Racial Discourse in Britain," *Sociological Research Online* 13:3 (2008): 1.1–1.3.

9. Ibid., 2.1–3.5.

10. Ibid., 4.9; See also Kenan Malik, *From Fatwa to Jihad: The Rushdie Affair and Its Legacy* (London: Atlantic, 2009).

11. Kenan Malik, *Islam, Mullahs and the Media*, BBC Radio 4, 2009.

12. Pilkington, "From Institutional Racism to Community Cohesion," 5.4.

13. Paul Gilroy, *After Empire: Melancholia or Convivial Culture* (Abingdon, England: Routledge, 2004).

14. Nicholas Watt and Julian Glover, "Multicultural Ideal 'Terrible' for UK—Tories," *Guardian*, 27 September 2008.

15. Liz Hazelton, "BNP Leader Nick Griffin in Fresh Storm after Claiming London Has Been Ethnically Cleansed as He Defends Question Time Debut," *Daily Mail*, 23 October 2009.

16. Melanie Phillips, *Londonistan: How Britain Is Creating a Terror State Within* (London: Gibson Square, 2006).

17. Ben Farmer, "BBC Favours Muslims," *Daily Telegraph*, 8 September 2008.

18. Vikram Dodd, "Universities Urged to Spy on Muslims," *Guardian*, 16 October 2006.

19. Simon Cottle, *Mediatized Conflict: Developments in Media and Conflict Studies* (Maidenhead, England: Open University Press, 2006), 9, 39.

20. Walter Pincus, "London Ricin Finding Called a False Positive," *Washington Post*, 14 April 2005.

21. Reda Hassaine and Sean O'Neill, "I Was Tortured, Says Ricin Plotter," *Times* (London), 9 May 2005; see also Sean O'Neill and Daniel McGrory, *The Suicide Factory: Abu Hamza and the Finsbury Park Mosque* (London: HarperPerennial, 2006).

22. See N. Craven and S. Wright, "Murdered Because We've Lost Control of Our Borders," *Daily Mail*, 14 April 2005.

23. Barbie Zelizer and Stuart Allan (eds.), *Journalism after September 11* (London: Routledge, 2002).

24. James Watson, *Media Communication: An Introduction to Theory and Process* (London: Palgrave, 1998).

25. Cottle, *Mediatized Conflict*, 191.

26. Elizabeth Poole, *Reporting Islam: Media Representations of British Muslims* (London: Tauris, 2002).

27. Ibid., 22.

28. Hugh Purcell, address to conference "Islam and the Media," One World Broadcasting Trust, London, 22 November 1993, quoted in Tariq Modood, "Beware of a Secular Intolerance," *Women against Fundamentalisms Journal* 6 (1995): 1–2.

29. David Smith and Vanessa Thorpe, "What Does It Mean to Be British?," *Observer,* 31 July 2005.

30. Tahira Sameera Ahmed, "Reading between the Lines—Muslims and the Media," in Tahir Abbas (ed.), *Muslim Britain: Communities under Pressure* (London: Zed Books, 2005), 109–126.

31. Michael Howard, "Talk about the British Dream," *Guardian,* 17 August 2005.

32. Matthew Tempest, "MacShane Speech Sparks Muslim Anger," *Guardian,* 21 November 2003.

33. Yasmin Alibhai-Brown, "Cultural Integration Is a Two-Way Street," *Independent,* 1 August 2005; Roger Hewitt, "Our Multiculturalism Has Strong Roots," *Independent,* 4 August 2005.

34. Alan Hamilton, "At Noon, Nation Keeps Two Minutes' Silence," *Times* (London), 7 July 2006.

35. Kim Sengupta and Arifa Akbar, "Born in Pakistan, Raised in Birmingham, Killed in Afghanistan," *Independent,* 4 July 2006.

36. Geraldine Bedell, "Death before Dishonour," *Observer,* 21 November 2004.

37. Emphasis added.

## 3. Representing the Representatives

1. Sanjay Seth, "Liberalism and the Politics of (Multi)culture: Or, Plurality Is Not Difference," *Postcolonial Studies* 4:1 (2001): 65–77.

2. Philip Schlesinger, *Media, State and Nation: Political Violence and Collective Identities* (London: Sage, 1991), 143.

3. See Immanuel Wallerstein, *European Universalism: The Rhetoric of Power* (New York: New Press, 2006).

4. Charles Taylor, "The Politics of Recognition," in Amy Gutman (ed.), *Multiculturalism: Examining the Politics of Recognition* (Princeton: Princeton University Press, 1994), 25.

5. Stuart Hall, "*New Ethnicities,*" in Kobena Mercer (ed.), *Black Film, British Cinema* (London: BFI/ICA Documents 7, 1989), 27–31.

6. Jonathan Birt, "Lobbying and Marching: British Muslims and the State," in Tahir Abbas (ed.), *Muslim Britain: Communities under Pressure* (London: Zed Books, 2005), 100.

7. Ibid., 92–96.

8. Pnina Werbner, "Revisiting the UK Muslim Diasporic Public Sphere at a

Time of Terror: From Local (Benign) Invisible Spaces to Seditious Conspiratorial Spaces and the 'Failure of Multiculturalism' Discourse," *South Asian Diaspora* 1:1 (2009): 33–34.

9. Jamie Doward, "British Muslim Leader Urged to Quit over Gaza," *Observer*, 8 March 2009; Vikram Dodd, "Government Suspends Links with Muslim Council of Britain over Gaza," *Guardian*, 23 March 2009.

10. Hazel Blears, "Letter to the MCB, 26 March 2009," , www.guardian.co.uk.

11. Nicholas Watt, "Government Restores Links with Biggest Muslim Group," *Guardian*, 15 January 2010.

12. Werbner, "Revisiting the UK Muslim Diasporic Public Sphere," 31.

13. Birt, "Lobbying and Marching," 105.

14. Olivier Roy, *Globalised Islam: The Search for a New Ummah* (London: Hurst, 2002), 208–209.

15. Birt, "Lobbying and Marching," 96.

16. Lucy Ward and Richard Norton-Taylor, "Muslim Peer Claims Phone Was Bugged," *Guardian*, 17 December 2001.

17. "An Unprecedented Letter," , www.yahyabirt.com (accessed 2/15/08).

18. Ned Temko, "Beckett Rejects Link between Foreign Policy and Terrorism," *Observer*, 13 August 2006.

19. Amir Saeed, "Media, Racism and Islamophobia: The Representation of Islam and Muslims in the Media," *Sociology Compass* 1:2 (2007): 459.

20. Paul Gilroy, *After Empire: Melancholia or Convivial Culture* (Abingdon, England: Routledge, 2004), 26.

21. Salma Yacoub quoted in Birt, "Lobbying and Marching," 103.

22. Tariq Ramadan, "Blair Can No Longer Deny a Link Exists between Terrorism and Foreign Policy," *Guardian*, 4 June 2007.

23. Rhys Blakely, "Calling It War on Terror Was Blunder, says Miliband," *Times* (London), 16 January 2009.

24. Robert Booth, "Minister for Terror: Gaza Will Fuel UK Extremism," *Guardian*, 28 January 2009.

25. Charles Guignon, *On Being Authentic* (Abingdon, England: Routledge, 2004), 66.

26. Ibid., 68–69.

27. Jean-Francois Bayart, *The Illusion of Cultural Identity*, trans. Steven Rendall, Janet Roitman, and Jonathan Derrick (London: Hurst, 2005), 78.

28. Simon Hattenstone, "I'm Cameron's Warm-up Act," *Guardian*, 28 March 2009.

29. Elizabeth Poole, *Reporting Islam: Media Representations of British Muslims* (London: Tauris, 2002), 23.

30. Guy Starkey and Andrew Crisell, *Radio Journalism* (London: Sage, 2009), 1.

31. "Dyke: BBC Is 'Hideously White,' " www.news.bbc.co.uk, 6 January 2001 (accessed 2/17/08).

32. Kevin Bakhurst, "Private Emotions," www.bbc.co.uk, 1 September 2006 (accessed 2/17/08).

33. Frank Gardner, "How Islam Got Political," in "Koran and Country" series, BBC Radio 4, 10 November 2005.

34. Mark Whitaker, "Radio Ramadan," in "Koran and Country" series, BBC Radio 4, 18 November 2005.

35. The Native Informant figured first in Kant's *Critique of Judgement* (1790) and has more recently been analyzed from a postcolonial perspective by Gayatri C. Spivak. Spivak critiques Kant's casually dismissive invocation of the inhabitants of New Holland and Tierra del Fuego as "unnecessary" and useless instances of humanity, arguing that it is through the expulsion of these natives "from the name of Man" that Western identity comes to be inscribed. The figure of the "Native," used in this way, remains a blank, despite giving shape to the self-perception of the colonial master. Spivak, *A Critique of Postcolonial Reason: Toward a History of the Vanishing Present* (Cambridge, Mass.: Harvard University Press, 1999), 9. Crucially, according to Spivak, the success of this project is dependent on the silence of the actual Native. The indigenous person is made into a kind of silent informant who is always mutely yielding to the colonizer what is necessary for the colonizer's self-constitution yet is never the speaking subject.

36. Spivak, *Critique of Postcolonial Reason,* 60.

37. Nasreen Suleaman, "Biography of a Bomber," in "Koran and Country" series, BBC Radio 4, 17 November 2005.

38. Jenny Cuffe, "Inside a Muslim School," in "Koran and Country" series, BBC Radio 4, 24 November 2005.

39. Shagufta Yaqub, "Inside the Harem," BBC Radio 4, program 1, "Polygamy: The Positives," 13 October 2004; program 2, "Polygamy: The Negatives," 20 October 2004.

40. An example of Manzoor's perspicacious views on the authenticity industry can be found in his journalism: see, for example, "Why Do Asian Writers Have to Be 'Authentic' to Succeed? ," *Observer,* 30 April 2006.

41. Sarah Ansari, "Polygamy, Purdah and Political Representation: Engendering Citizenship in 1950s Pakistan," *Modern Asian Studies* (2008), doi:10.1017/S0026749X08003776.

42. Bayart, *Illusion,* 33, 71.

43. Ibid., 98–99, 103.

44. Ibid., 92.

45. Amartya Sen, *Identity and Violence: The Illusion of Destiny* (New York: Norton, 2006), 165.

46. Kenan Malik, "Born in Bradford," *Prospect*, October 2005, 54–56.

47. Pragna Patel, "Faith in the State? Asian Women's Struggles for Human Rights in the UK," *Feminist Legal Studies* 16:1 (2008): 9–36.

48. Malik, "Born in Bradford," 55.

49. Ibid., 56.


## 4. Muslims in a Media Ghetto

1. Vikram Dodd, "Guantanamo Actors Quizzed under Terror Act after Film Festival," *Guardian*, 21 February 2006.

2. Edward Herman and Noam Chomsky, *Manufacturing Consent: The Political Economy of the Mass Media* (New York: Pantheon), 1988.

3. Steven Salaita, *The Uncultured Wars: Arabs, Muslims and the Poverty of Liberal Thought—New Essays* (London: Zed Books, 2008), 88, 140.

4. Samuel Huntington, *The Clash of Civilizations and the Remaking of World Order* (London: Touchstone, 1998), 58.

5. See Jack Shaheen, *Reel Bad Arabs: How Hollywood Vilifies a People* (Northampton, Mass.: Olive Branch Press, 2001), and *Guilty: Hollywood's Verdict on Arabs after 9/11* (Northampton, Mass.: Interlink, 2008). See also Paul Findley, *Silent No More: Confronting America's False Images of Islam* (Beltsville, Md.: Amana, 2001); and Fawzia Afzal Khan, *Shattering the Stereotype: Muslim Women Speak Out* (Northampton, Mass.: Olive Branch Press, 2005); Ziauddin Sardar and Merryl Wyn Davies, *American Terminator: Myths, Movies and Global Power* (New York: Disinformation, 2004); Amir Saeed, "Media, Racism and Islamophobia: The Representation of Islam and Muslims in the Media," *Sociology Compass* 1 and 2 (2007): 443–462.

6. See John Fiske and John Hartley, *Reading Television* (London: Routledge, 1989), 75.

7. Tzvetan Todorov, "The Origin of Genres," *New Literary History* 8:1 (Autumn 1976): 162–163. The mutual knowledge and existing expectation on which genres depend underline what Fiske and Hartley have called television's "bardic function." Written in the days before the proliferation of satellite channels and the advent of the Internet, their argument nevertheless still captures something of television's cultural centrality: "the classically conceived bard functions as a *mediator of language,* one who composes out of the available linguistic resources of the culture a

series of consciously structured messages which serve to communicate to the members of that culture a confirming, reinforcing version of themselves" See Fiske and Hartley, *Reading Television,* 85–86.

8. Steve Neale quoted in John Tulloch, *Television Drama: Agency, Audience and Myth* (London: Routledge, 1990), 249.

9. Fiske and Hartley, *Reading Television,* 18.

10. Interview with Kenny Glenaan by Jen Foley, www.bbc.co.uk, September 2004 (accessed 7/12/08).

11. Gayatri C. Spivak, *A Critique of Postcolonial Reason: Toward a History of the Vanishing Present* (Cambridge, Mass.: Harvard University Press, 1999), 98.

12. Ella Shohat and Robert Stam, *Unthinking Eurocentrism: Multiculturalism and the Media* (London: Routledge, 1994), 205.

13. Writing of the conventions governing the dramadoc genre, Derek Paget mentions two of the form's aims as being "to re-tell events from national or international histories" and "to portray issues of concern to national or international communities in order to provoke discussion about them." These aims are clearly written into both *Dirty War* and *The Hamburg Cell.* See Derek Paget, *No Other Way to Tell It: Dramadoc/Docudrama on Television* (Manchester: Manchester University Press, 1998), 61.

14. Another useful link might have been "What to do if you're asked to undress in a prime time drama," since this issue, rather than the disturbing central subject matter, exercised the censors when *Dirty War* was due to be aired on PBS channels in the United States. A scene in which a woman strips to enter a decontamination chamber was excised during the puritanical purge that gripped America in the wake of Janet Jackson's infamous "wardrobe malfunction" at the Superbowl in 2004. In a reflex response strangely reminiscent of the supposed "hang-ups" of those putative Muslim Others, television executives considered a glimpse of female flesh to be more disturbing than the idea of half a city laid waste by a chemical attack and made uninhabitable for thirty years! See "PBS Opts to Trim Nude Scene from Film *Dirty War,*" *Los Angeles Times,* 17 January 2005.

15. "Terror on TV," *Observer,* 12 September 2004.

16. Patrick Hennessey, "Blunkett Clashes with BBC over *Dirty War,*" *Daily Telegraph,* 3 October 2004.

17. Martin Amis, "The Last Days of Mohammad Atta," in *The Second Plane* (London: Cape, 2008).

18. T. W. Adorno, E. Frenkel-Brunswik, D. J. Levinson, and R. Nevitt Sanford, *The Authoritarian Personality* (1950; reprint, New York: W. W. Norton and Co., 1994).

## 5. Troubling Strangers

1. Vanessa Thorpe, "BBC under Fire for 'False Reality,'" *Observer,* 17 October 2004.

2. Tim Jon Semmerling, *"Evil" Arabs in American Popular Film: Orientalist Fear* (Austin: University of Texas Press, 2006), 2.

3. Quoted in John Tulloch, *Television Drama: Agency, Audience and Myth* (London: Routledge, 1990), 73.

4. See Karen Lury, *Interpreting Television* (London: Hodder Arnold, 2005), 170–174.

5. Quoted in Adam Sweeting, "Terror Vision," *Independent on Sunday,* 26 November 2006.

6. Ziauddin Sardar and Merryl Wyn Davies, "Freeze Framing Muslims: Hollywood and the Slideshow of Western Imagination," *Interventions* 12:2 (2010): 239–250.

7. In President Bush's address to a joint session of Congress on 20 September 2001, quoted in Sandra Silberstein, *War of Words: Language, Politics and 9/11* (London: Routledge, 2002), 26.

8. Simon Cottle, *Mediatized Conflict: Developments in Media and Conflict Studies* (Maidenhead, England: Open University Press, 2006), 160.

9. Hishaam Aidi, "From Harlem to Algiers: Black Internationalism and the Orient: Myth and Counter-Myth," paper presented at the third annual Muslim studies conference, Michigan State University, , 5 April 2008. See also Hishaam Aidi "Slavery, Genocide and the Politics of Outrage: Understanding the New Racial Olympics," *Middle East Report* 234 (Spring 2005): 40–56; Manning Marable and Hishaam Aidi (eds.), *Black Routes to Islam* (London: Palgrave 2009), *Souls* 8/4 (2006) and 9/2 (2007).

10. Moustafa Bayoumi, "The Race Is On: Muslims in the American Imagination," paper presented at the third annual Muslim studies conference, Michigan State University, , 5 April 2008.

11. Albert G. Mackey, *A Lexicon of Freemasonry* (London: Richard Griffin and Company, 1860), 180.

12. Peter Golding and Graham Murdock, "Culture, Communication and Political Economy," in James Curran and Michael Gurevitch (eds.), *Mass Media and Society,* 3rd ed. (London: Arnold, 2000), 85.

13. For similarly caustic responses to the presumed inherent "flaws" of a hyphenated identity, see Paul Gilroy's dissection of the news coverage of "shoebomber" Richard Reid's mixed parentage in *After Empire: Melancholia or Convivial Culture* (Abingdon, England: Routledge, 2004), 141–142.

14. Angelique Chrisafis, "BBC Suicide Bomb Drama Fuels Hatred, Say Muslims," *Guardian,* 11 June 2003.

15. "BBC Drama Program "Spooks"—Letter from Inayat Bunglawala and the Response," www.mcb.org.uk, , (accessed 25/08/08)

16. "BBC Drama "Spooks" Illustrates the Continuation of the Media Campaign to Demonise Islam," Website of Hizb ul-Tahrir, www.khilafah.com, (accessed 8/25/08)

17. Zygmunt Bauman, *Modernity and Ambivalence* (London: Polity Press, 1991), 55.

18. Ibid., 60.

19. Ibid., 1.

20. Faisal Abbas, "9/11 and the Birth of the Muslim Action Hero," Website of *Asharq Alawsar,* Arab Daily Newspaper, www.asharq-e.com, (accessed 9/02/08)

21. Steven Emerson, *American Jihad: the Terrorists Living among Us* (New York: Free Press, 2002).

22. Kathleen Pfeiffer, *Race Passing and American Individualism* (Amherst: University of Massachusetts Press, 2003), 4.

23. Ibid., 5. See also Werner Sollers, *Beyond Ethnicity: Consent and Descent in American Culture* (New York: Oxford University Press, 1986).

24. Semmerling, "*Evil" Arabs,* 24.

## 6. Performing beyond the Frame

1. Angelique Chrisafis, "Nicolas Sarkozy Says Islamic Veils Are Not Welcome in France," guardian.co.uk, 22 June 2009 (accessed 3/1/10).

2. See Leila Ahmed, "The Discourse of the Veil," in David A. Bailey and Gilane Tawadros (eds.), *Veil: Veiling, Representation and Contemporary Art* (London: Institute of International Visual Arts, 2003).

3. Dan Isaacs, "Pakistan Rape Victim's Blog Makes Waves," BBC News Islamabad, news.bbc.co.uk, updated 8 September 2006 (accessed 3/15/10).

4. See Rana Kabbani, *Europe's Myths of Orient* (Bloomington: Indiana University Press, 1986); Haideh Moghissi, *Feminism and Islamic Fundamentalism: The Limits of Postmodern Analysis* (London: Oxford University Press, 2000).

5. Ahmed, *Veil,* 43.

6. This is reminiscent of what Gayatri Spivak has theorized as the suppression of the subaltern voice in her analysis of sati (widow immolation) in colonial India. She argues that the position of the sati disappears in her appropriation by the

British, who banned the practice as barbaric, and the nationalists, who saw the "self-sacrificing woman" as an iconic expression of authenticity. See her essay "Can the Subaltern Speak?," in Patrick Williams and Laura Chrisman (eds.), *Colonial Discourse and Postcolonial Theory: A Reader* (Hemel Hempstead, England: Harvester Wheatsheaf, 1994).

7. Talal Asad, "Religion, Nation-State, Secularism," in Peter van der Veer and Hartmut Lehmann (eds.), *Nation and Religion: Perspectives on Europe and Asia* (Princeton, N.J.: Princeton University Press, 1999), 188–192.

8. Olivier Roy, *Globalised Islam: The Search for a New Ummah* (London: Hurst, 2004), 120.

9. See Roel Meijr, ed., *Cosmopolitanism, Identity and Authenticity in the Middle East* (London: Curzon, 1999).

10. Bruce B. Lawrence, "Islamicate Civilization: The View from Asia," in Brannon M. Wheeler (ed.), *Teaching Islam* (New York: Oxford University Press, 2003), 61.

11. Miriam Cooke and Bruce B. Lawrence, editor's introduction to *Muslim Networks: From Hajj to Hip Hop* (Chapel Hill: University of North Carolina Press, 2005), 11.

12. Jan Nederveen Pieterse, *Ethnicities and Global Multiculture: Pants for an Octopus* (Lanham, Md.: Rowman and Littlefield, 2007), 186. There are of course countless Islamic cybernetworks that have emerged post-9/11, ranging from jihadi websites to those selling the hijab, and it is not in the scope of this book to present an overview. See Gary Bunt, "Defining Islamic Interconnectivity," in Cooke and Lawrence, *Muslim Networks,* 235–251.

13. In the words of Timothy Brennan, "the cosmopolitan fantasy" in its contemporary form perpetuates a "national idea based on America as a universal nation—hegemonized through popular culture, fashion and the Internet"; Brennan,*Wars of Position: The Cultural Politics of Left and Right* (New York: Columbia University Press, 2006), 231.

14. Sally Howell, "Cultural Interventions: Arab American Aesthetics between the Transnational and the Ethnic," *Diaspora* 9:1 (2000): 59–82.

15. Andrew Stern, "US Muslims Seek Alternatives to American Products," www.noorart.com, (accessed 3/4/06).

16. "Muslim Dolls Tackle 'Wanton' Barbie," www.news.bbc.co.uk, 5 March 2002 (accessed 3/4/06).

17. "Iran Calls for Ban on Barbie Doll," news.bbc.co.uk, 28 April 2008 (accessed 3/25/10).

18. Frances Harrison, "Iran Police Move into Fashion Business," BBC News Tehran, news.bbc.co.uk, 2 January 2007 (accessed 3/25/10).

19. www.theglobeandmail.com/servlet/story/LAC.20051027 (accessed 31/10/2005).

20. See Christian Joppke, "The Extreme Headscarf in Multicultural Britain," in his *Veil: Mirror of Identity* (Cambridge: Polity, 2009), 81–106.

21. For an engaged analysis of the sartorial agenda of Hizb ut-Tahrir and its connection to the Shabina Begum case see Emma Tarlo, "Reconsidering Stereotypes: Anthropological Reflections on the Jilbab Controversy," *Anthropology Today* 21:6 (2005): 13–17.

22. "Saudi Religious Police Say Barbie Is a Moral Threat," 10 September 2003, www.foxnews.com (accessed 2/6/06).

23. , *Daily Star,* 15 November 2005.

24. Jo Tatchell, "Meet the Islamic Barbie," *Guardian,* 30 September 2004.

25. Quoted in "Muslim Doll Offers Modest Alternative to Barbie," Associated Press, www.cnn.com., 8 October 2003 (accessed 3/4/05).

26. Inderpal Grewal, "Traveling Barbie: Indian Transnationality and New Consumer Subjects," *Positions* 7:3 (1999): 800.

27. Radha S. Hegde, "Global Makeovers and Maneuvers: Barbie's Presence in India," *Feminist Media Studies* 1:1 (2001): 129–133.

28. Ann Ducille, "Dyes and Dolls: Multicultural Barbie and the Merchandising of Difference," *Differences* 6:1 (1994): 47–68.

29. Mary F. Rogers, *Barbie Culture* (London: Sage, 1999).

30. Ibid., 136.

31. Judith Butler, *Gender Trouble: Feminism and the Subversion of Identity,* 2nd ed. (New York: Routledge, 1999).

32. "Muslim Doll."

33. Valerie Moghadam (ed.), *Gender and National Identity: Women and Politics in Muslim Societies* (London: Zed Books, 1994).

34. See Kari Huus, "Quest for the Muslim Niche Market: Entrepreneurs and Artists Offer Up Fresh Fare for Long-Neglected Minority," 3 October 2003, www .msnbc.msn.com (accessed 03/4/06).

35. This fashioning of a gendered dress code is not done in isolation, for children also engage in a dialogic pattern of familiarization through storytelling. For instance, Noorart's website offers heroic tales such as "The Swirling Hijab," in which the hijab ranges from a flying carpet to a sword, building on themes from *The Thousand and One Nights.* There is also the "Meat-Eating Vegetarian," a story focusing on the dilemmas faced by young children who adhere to a halal meat diet in a predominantly non-Muslim environment. Finally, we also find reappropriations of familiar nursery rhymes such as "Twinkle Twinkle Little Star," which include

references to God up above, in the effort to shape a culturally aware new Muslim identity.

36. Aisha Mirza, "All Dolled Up," *Emel,* March, 2010, 27.

37. Emma Tarlo, "Islamic Cosmopolitanism: The Sartorial Biographies of Three Muslim Women of London," *Fashion Theory* 11:2/3 (2007) 158–159.

38. Butler, *Gender Trouble,* 204.

39. We borrow the phrase "undecidability" from Paul Gilroy's reading of (other people's readings of) Ali G, in *After Empire: Melancholia or Convivial Culture* (Abingdon, England: Routledge, 2004), 149.

40. Tarlo, "Islamic Cosmopolitanism," 161.

41. Bakirathi Mani, "Undressing the Diaspora," in Nirmal Puwar and Parvati Raghuram (eds.), *South Asian Women in the Diaspora* (Oxford: Berg, 2003), 125.

42. Yasmeen Khan, "Does Islam Have a Sense of Humour?," news.bbc.co.uk., 20 November 2007 (accessed 3/25/10).

43. Pnina Werbner, "Introduction: The Dialectics of Cultural Hybridity," in Pnina Werbner and Tariq Modood (eds.), *Debating Culturally Hybridity: Multicultural Identities and the Politics of Anti-Racism* (London: Zed Books, 1997), 12.

44. See Nabil Matar, *Islam in Britain 1558–1685* (Cambridge: Cambridge University Press, 1998); *Turks, Moors and Englishmen in the Age of Discovery* (New York: Columbia University Press, 1999); *In the Lands of the Christians: Arab Travel Writing in the Seventeenth Century* (London: Routledge, 2003).

## Conclusion

1. Tom Sutcliffe: "Outrage Would Suit This Panto Villain Nicely," *Independent,* 5 January 2010.

2. For an account of how the story spread, see Matthew Weaver, "Cautionary Tale of the Marginal Extremist Who Became a Threat to World Peace," *Guardian,* 11 September 2010.

3. Ewan MacAskill and Aunohita Mojumdar, "Obama Appeal Halts Pastor's Plan to Burn Qur'ans—For Now," *Guardian,* 11 September 2010.

4. The debate over how to commemorate 9/11 has been politicized and, arguably, racialized. Mention is seldom made of the estimated sixty Muslim victims of 9/11.

5. Pastor Jones admitted his actual ignorance of the **Koran**: "I have no experience with it whatsoever. I only know what the Bible says." Damien Cave, "Far from

Ground Zero, Obscure Pastor Is Ignored No Longer," *New York Times,* 25 August 2010.

6. I use the term "desert of the real" in the sense used by Slavoj Zizek in *Welcome to the Desert of the Real: Five Essays on September 11 and Related Dates* (London: Verso, 2002).

7. See Sandra Silberstein, *War of Words: Language, Politics and 9/11* (London: Routledge, 2002), 149–160.

8. *New Statesman,* 15 February 2010.

# Acknowledgments

The origins of this book can be traced back to conversations had and ideas sketched before the attacks of 11 September 2001, although, of course, they gained an unanticipated urgency after that epochal event. Latterly, impetus was added by the international research network, also called *Framing Muslims,* that we were able to set up thanks to generous funding provided by the Arts and Humanities Research Council between 2007 and 2010. Not only were our thoughts refined and arguments developed during this period but, in the workshops and seminars that took place, we were able to benefit from the experience and sharp insights of numerous scholars of world renown. We would like to thank them here, albeit with the usual caveat that many of them may disagree with the conclusions we have drawn. Nonetheless, we were inspired by the generosity and intellectual rigor of Hishaam Aidi, Nabil Matar, Haideh Moghissi, Kamran Pasha, Sherene Razack, Amena Saiyid, Steven Salaita, Tim Jon Semmerling, Pnina Werbner, Maruta Herding, Humayun Ansari, Aamer Hussein, Siobhan Lambert-Hurley, Salman Sayyid, Sara Wajid, Rehana Ahmed, Florian Stadtler, Ali Zaidi, Ziad AbuZayyad, Ivan Kalmar, Adi Kuntsman, Sarah Lambert, Fiyaz Mughal, Tudor Parfitt, Hagai van der Horst, Nadje Al-Ali, Sohail Daulatzai, Moustafa Bayoumi, Bob Cannon, Anita Fabos, Usama Hasan, Gabeba Baderoon, Schirin Amir-Moazami, Humera Khan, Andrew Pilkington, Katherine Brown, Tahir Abbas, Eric Mace, Dibyesh Anand, Anshuman Mondal, Sarfraz Manzoor, Mohsin Hamid, Tariq Ramadan, Inderpal Grewal, Carla Jones, Reina Lewis, Maleiha Malik, Tariq Modood, Annelies Moors, Elizabeth Poole, Christoph Ramm, Ziauddin Sardar,

Emma Tarlo, Susheila Nasta, Dennis Walder, Bart Moore-Gilbert, and Jeevan Deol.

The network's smooth running was guaranteed by the efforts of our dedicated administrators, who were on hand with problem-solving ideas as well as clerical and organizational know-how. Jane Savory, Rahima Begum, and Jo Sherman should take a bow for keeping the *Framing Muslims* show on the road. We would like to also acknowledge the dedication of Ed Spick, who provided invaluable technical support of all kinds; Madeline Clements, for her bibliographical and reporting skills, and Maciej Hrybowicz, for designing a fine and user-friendly project website. Please see the fruits of their respective labors at www .framingmuslims.org.

As authors we would also like to acknowledge the support of our respective institutions, the School of Humanities and Social Sciences at the University of East London and the School of Oriental and African Studies, University of London. Assistance was rendered by the research support structures of both universities and also by individuals who gave their support in various ways and at various times. These include Paul Webley, Tom Tomlinson, Phil Jagar, Gavin Poynter, and Steve Trevillion. Annabelle Sreberny has been an inspiration to us, selfless in her support and generous with advice. The colleagues with whom we teach also deserve mention for their forbearance as we changed reading lists and rewrote lectures in light of our new discoveries.

Finally, we would like to thank the team at Harvard University Press for their faith in the ideas behind this book and practical assistance in making it a reality. Ian Stevenson and Heather Hughes dealt with procedures and kept us up to speed. We would also like to thank Tonnya Norwood for her patience and hard work throughout the copyediting, proofing, and indexing stages. But most of all we would like to acknowledge the unfailing support and sage advice of Sharmila Sen, without whom this book would never have seen the light of day.

Earlier versions of parts of the Introduction and Chapter 5 first appeared in the special issue of *Interventions: International Journal of Postcolonial Studies* (2010, vol. 12, no. 2) that we edited. An earlier version of the first part of the argument in Chapter 6 appeared in *Fashion Theory* 11:2/3 (2007).

# Index